PUNISHMENT AND PENANCE

Two Phases in the History of the Bishop's Tribunal of Novara

THOMAS B. DEUTSCHER

Punishment and Penance

Two Phases in the History of the Bishop's Tribunal of Novara

UNIVERSITY OF TORONTO PRESS
Toronto Buffalo London

Toronto Buffalo London
www.utppublishing.com

ISBN 978-1-4426-4442-7

Toronto Italian Studies

Library and Archives Canada Cataloguing in Publication

Deutscher, Thomas Brian, 1949–
Punishment and penance : two phases in the history of the bishop's tribunal of Novara / Thomas B. Deutscher.

Includes bibliographical references and index.
ISBN 978-1-4426-4442-7

1. Ecclesiastical courts – Italy – Novara – History. 2. Trials (Blasphemy) – Italy – Novara – History. 3. Punishment – Italy – Novara – History. 4. Penance – Italy – Novara – History. 5. Catholic Church. Diocese of Novara (Italy) – Discipline – History. 6. Catholic Church. Diocese of Novara (Italy) – Bishops – Biography. 7. Novara (Italy) – Church history. I. Title.

KKH285.E22D49 2013 345.45⊠0288 C2012-904483-0

University of Toronto Press acknowledges the financial assistance to its publishing program of the Canada Council for the Arts and the Ontario Arts Council.

Canada Council for the Arts Conseil des Arts du Canada

This book has been published with the help of a grant from the Canadian Federation for the Humanities and Social Sciences, through the Awards to Scholarly Publications Program, using funds provided by the Social Sciences and Humanities Research Council of Canada.

University of Toronto Press acknowledges the financial support of the Government of Canada through the Canada Book Fund for our publishing activities.

To Marci

For making everything possible

Contents

Acknowledgments

I wish to express my profound gratitude to the Novarese archivists and scholars who did much to facilitate my research. This began with Don Angelo Stoppa (1915–98) and Pier Giorgio Longo who introduced me to the archive and who raised the history of Novara to new standards. Their proud tradition has been ably upheld by Don Mario Perotti and his colleague Dr Paolo Monticelli.

I am also deeply indebted to the three anonymous readers for the University of Toronto Press, whose comments and suggestions enriched my work by helping me place it within the context of recent Italian studies on the parish clergy, the Roman Inquisition, and the ecclesiastical tribunals of the early modern period. My argument has been greatly enhanced and deepened as a result of their patient review of my first drafts. The enthusiasm with which they greeted my topic has buoyed my spirits and spurred me to complete the final phases of my research.

I also wish to thank Michael Hayden, professor emeritus of history at the University of Saskatchewan, for critiquing a number of my chapters and offering insights into the theory of confessionalization from the perspective of French and German history. Professor Michael Cichon of the Department of English at St Thomas More College also read parts of the work and provided valuable stylistic insights.

I wish to thank Ron Schoeffel and the staff of the University of Toronto Press for facilitating the publication of this book by enthusiastically embracing it from the beginning and by responding so promptly to my queries.

This book has been published with the help of a grant from the Canadian Federation for the Humanities and Social Sciences, through the Aid to Scholarly Publications Program, using funds provided by the Social Sciences and Humanities Research Council of Canada. I would also like to thank the SSHRCC for a general research grant awarded some years ago, which helped lay the groundwork for this study. As well, St Thomas More College has generously contributed funds for my research in Italy and for the final preparation of the manuscript.

I also wish to express my deepest gratitude to Professors Peter Bietenholz, Paul Grendler, and James McConica whose enthusiasm for sixteenth-century history has been a constant inspiration to me and to many others.

Finally, I wish to thank my wife Marci, without whose love and patience this book would not have been possible.

Note on Currency

In the sixteenth and seventeenth centuries the most commonly used currencies in the diocese of Novara were the *scudo* and the *lira*, with one scudo being worth between six and seven lire. Each lira was worth twenty *soldi*, and each soldo was further divided into twelve *denarii*. Exchange rates, however, varied with time and place. For example, in the early 1600s when Benedetto Salina, a merchant from Croveo in the northern Antigorio valley, contracted with the shepherd Domenico Pignolo to work for him for three months for five scudi, each scudo was valued at only five lire and eight soldi.[1]

Another currency frequently mentioned in the Novarese records was the *ducatone* or *ducatone argento*. The ducatone, also valued between six and seven lire, was in use in the duchy of Parma as well as at Florence. The Dukes of Parma held Novara in feud from the Spanish crown in the last half of the sixteenth century. Ducats (*ducati*) were in a slightly lower range, valued at between four and five lire, although in 1594 Carlo Bascapè, bishop of Novara from 1593 to 1615, stated that the exchange rate for a ducat was six lire and twelve soldi.[2]

For the sake of comparison, in the period 1563–1615, the minimum income expected for a parish priest was in the range of fifty scudi a year, in addition to the advantage of having housing in a rectory. While parish priests of the larger towns of the plains, such as Trecate and Cerano, enjoyed incomes in the range of one hundred scudi, many of the mountain parishes had difficulty providing the basic fifty. In 1616 clerics at the seminary of Novara were assessed three and a half scudi a month for expenses, a sum which was deemed insufficient to cover the true costs of the institution.[3]

By the eighteenth century the lira had, to a great extent, supplanted the scudo and the ducatone as the basic unit of exchange. In the middle decades of the century, over half of the diocese's parish priests enjoyed incomes over 1000 lire a year, and a handful enjoyed incomes over 2000 lire. Chaplancies, on the other hand, provided their incumbents with only between 100 and 500 lire a year. Professors of speculative and moral theology received the sum of 240 lire for eight months of teaching at the seminary of Novara in 1764; instructors in rhetoric and philosophy received only 180 lire, the same as the seminary cook. These were small sums when it is considered that board at the seminary of Novara was valued at fifty lire a month at that time.[4] While the instructors also received their meals as part of their contract, it is easy to see how many of them would have wanted to supplement their incomes by celebrating masses for legacies.

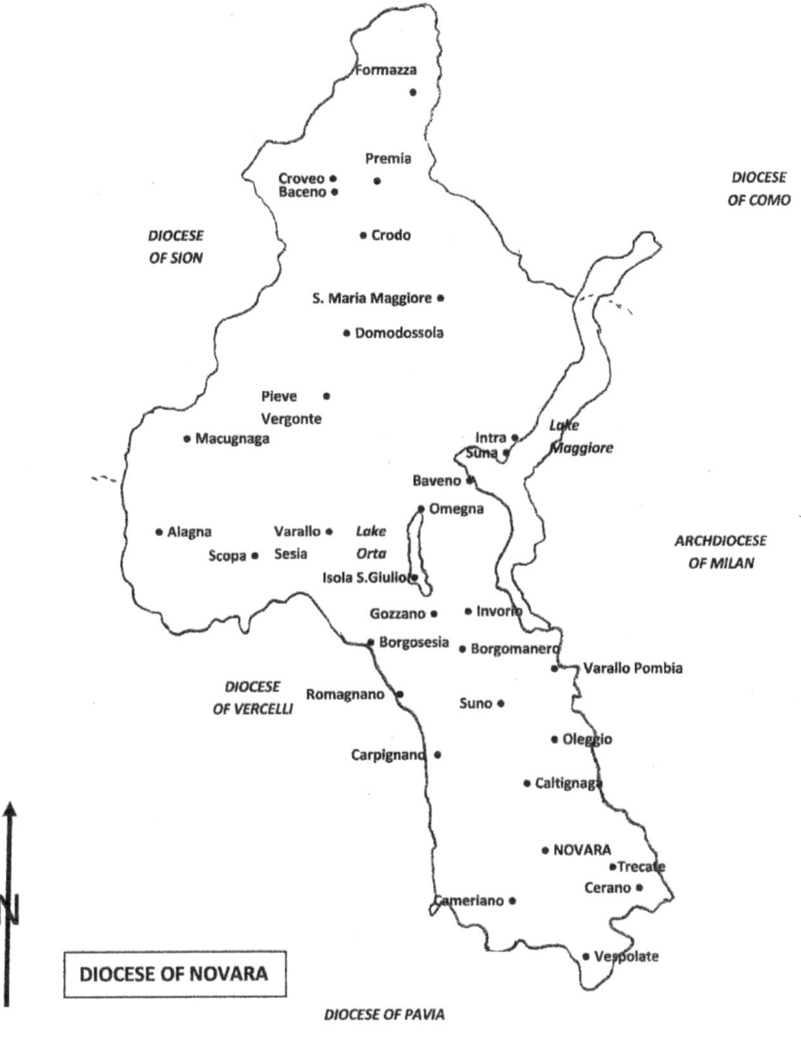
Formazza
Premia
Croveo
Baceno
Crodo
S. Maria Maggiore
Domodossola
Pieve
Vergonte
Macugnaga
Intra
Suna
Lake
Maggiore
Baveno
Omegna
Alagna
Varallo
Sesia
Lake
Orta
Scopa
Isola S.Giulio
Gozzano
Invorio
Borgosesia
Borgomanero
Varallo Pombia
Romagnano
Suno
Oleggio
Carpignano
Caltignaga
NOVARA
Trecate
Cerano
Cameriano
Vespolate
DIOCESE
OF COMO
DIOCESE
OF SION
ARCHDIOCESE
OF MILAN
DIOCESE
OF VERCELLI
DIOCESE OF PAVIA
DIOCESE OF VIGEVANO
N
DIOCESE OF NOVARA

PUNISHMENT AND PENANCE

Two Phases in the History of the Bishop's Tribunal of Novara

Introduction

In August 1593 Pier Paolo Burro, curate of Beura in the northern vicariate of Pieve Vergonte, diocese of Novara, appeared before the bishop's tribunal to respond to a wide range of charges, including failure to say the masses required of him on weekdays, not teaching Christian doctrine on Sundays and feast days, and failure to say vespers on Sunday evenings. He was also alleged to have mocked a pastoral letter of the bishop and to have told parishioners who complained about empty holy water fonts to go and wash their hands in the gutter. He had refused to let the Confraternity of Santa Marta say prayers on their feast day, calling the confraternity a 'synagogue.' A woman with whom he was at odds was refused the sacrament of confession. Burro's interrogation also revealed that in recent years he had confessed to keeping a widow named Margherita in his house as a concubine. Unbowed, the curate excused his negligence in celebrating Mass, teaching catechism, and holding vespers by arguing that his parishioners did not come to these functions despite his frequent admonitions because they lived in a number of far-flung communities. On 3 April 1594, Ludovico Boido, the vicar general of newly appointed Bishop Carlo Bascapè (r. 1593–1615), pronounced a sentence absolving Burro from further prosecution but ordering him to teach catechism and sing vespers regardless of attendance, under penalty of two scudi for each failure.[1] On 16 January 1597, Burro was arraigned again, this time to answer questions about suspicious dealings with his laundress Antonia, wife of Anselmo del Furno, a woodworker. Other charges were that he gambled, stole trees from the banks of the River Toce, and had an arrangement with a merchant named Pietro del Orso that he would absolve him from transporting wine on feast days and not report this offence to the episcopal curia in return for a payment of two ducatoni.[2] Again Burro denied all charges. Although the result of this case is not known, he appeared before the tribunal again in 1602, 1603, and 1606, when he was in his fifties. He was accused of further shortcomings in the care of souls and fathering a child by a woman named Domenica di Pianezza, the wife of a former servant of his, who was said to have died after childbirth. This he denied, saying that he had not had sexual contact with a woman for the past ten years. He was accused of doing manual work around his house and in the fields while wearing secular clothing and refusing to leave this work when called to minister to the sick. He replied that if he was seen chopping wood it was because the boy who lived with him was not skilled enough to do it, and that if he worked in the fields it was to help the workers and to encourage them to do more because they were inclined to work only when it was convenient. When told by the vicar general that he would make a better fieldworker than a priest and that he gave the laity 'not a little to marvel at and causing scandal with his anxiousness to work not for exercise and the justifiable use of time in work but out of excessive anxiety and avarice,' he replied defiantly that his detractors could say what they would, he was fifty-four years of age and did not have the physical stamina to do all that was attributed to him. He dismissed the charges as the fabrications of one of his brothers and his cronies. Other accusations followed, including committing a series of assaults, verbal and physical, on people of the parish and blaspheming by saying '*sangue di Dio*' (blood of God). His avarice was said to be such that he had stripped a mill owned by the parish in order to equip a second mill which he controlled with a business associate named Bernardino Venturina. Burro was again accused of negligence in teaching catechism. Unflappable, he returned to his old excuse, namely that attendance was low, and added that he could not be expected to carry people to the church.[3] This time the penalty was harsher but not devastating: suspension as parish priest and the loss of revenue from the parish and other benefices for one year.[4]

The trials of Pier Paolo Burro can be viewed in two ways. On the one hand, they might serve to illustrate the tenacity of the episcopal curia of Novara when pursuing an insubordinate priest, especially a priest exercising the care of souls. At Novara, as elsewhere in Italy following the Council of Trent, reform-minded bishops and their agents sought to mould the clergy into a strong cadre for advancing the Catholic Church. With varying degrees of success, they established seminaries, issued decrees governing the proper clothing, conduct, and morals of priests, and enforced these regulations through frequent scrutiny and through judicial action. The bishop's tribunal was the ultimate weapon for ensuring observance of the rules.

On the other hand, one wonders why Burro was able to endure so many prosecutions and survive for so long in the role of curate of Beura, and why his sentences seemed to be so light. His case was extreme in terms of his insubordinate ways, his defiant attitude, and the number of times he was prosecuted, but it was by no means unique. Other parish priests appeared before the tribunal on multiple occasions on a wide range of charges, sometimes demonstrating a degree of moral lassitude and even violence that surpassed Burro. They serve as reminders not only of human frailties but also of how much parish priests were tied to the land and the communities from which they came. They were intermediaries between the upper levels of culture represented by their ecclesiastical superiors and the lower levels represented by their parishioners, and in many ways were closer to the cares, wants, and even superstitions of the people they served than to the reforming ideals of their bishops and vicars general.[5]

The fact that Burro and others could survive for so long in the role of curate points to several important shortcomings of episcopal justice at Novara in the post-Tridentine period. One was the difficulty faced by the bishops and curia in finding suitable candidates for the care of souls and in removing those who proved unsuitable. A second was systemic weaknesses in the tribunal itself, including inadequate forms of punishment and overburdened vicars general. A third – not so obvious perhaps in the particular case of Burro but hinted at in his early confession of concubinage with the widow Margherita – was the willingness of the hierarchy to hear and respond compassionately to admissions of guilt, petitions for clemency, and promises to amend behaviour. There was a fine line between the tribunal as a judicial instrument and the penitential process, even in the church marked by the lofty aspirations of Tridentine reform.

Bishops' tribunals of the early modern era were concerned with more than just the transgressions of the clergy. Laypersons were also of concern to the ecclesiastical courts in a number of areas, among which two stand out. One was the use of the courts to enforce the rules of the church for the sacraments and in particular matrimony. Petitions for annulments and the legal separation of incompatible spouses were taken to the ecclesiastical courts, although questions pertaining to the disposition of property and support of children were often left in the hands of secular courts. The second use of the tribunals was to prosecute laypersons for certain crimes and moral transgressions, paralleling their activity with the clergy. These involved lay assaults on members of the clergy, adultery, bigamy, usury, neglect of the annual obligation of confession and communion, and matters of faith such as heresy, illicit magic, and blasphemy. This was part of an ambitious attempt to refashion not just the clergy but society as a whole along the lines demanded by religious reform. Many of the matters under the purview of the bishops' tribunals fell into the category of what some Protestant reformers and twenty-first century historians would call not crime but sin. Following canon law the episcopal tribunal of Novara did not make such a distinction. As Carlo Bascapè, bishop of Novara from 1593 to 1615, argued, the ecclesiastical court had full power to deal with adulterers and other criminals.[6] But if adulterers and other sinners were to be called before the ecclesiastical justice system with its allegedly rigorous approach, they at least benefited from the fact that the bishop's tribunal saw itself as an extension of the pastoral and penitential system of the church and tempered its decisions with the desire to correct and reform the individual.[7]

That religion was the cement holding society together was a maxim shared by both church and state in the sixteenth and early seventeenth centuries. In 1589 Giovanni Botero (1544–1617), a former Jesuit, wrote that religion was the foundation of any state and a powerful instrument in the hands of the prince, and that of all religions, Christianity was the most advantageous for rulers because it gave them control not only over the bodies and possessions of their subjects but also over their souls and consciences.[8] Since the 1970s a number of historians have referred to the epoch as a time of 'confessionalization' in which church and state interacted with and supported one another in the fashioning of a new and dynamic Christian society, a society in which Christianity would no longer be limited to the elite but penetrate to the uneducated masses of not only the cities but also the countryside. The church provided the rising state with the ideology and disciplinary mechanisms essential for its development. The theory of confessionalization first gained popularity among German historians, with Heinz Schilling, Wolfgang Reinhard, and others detailing how the spiritual and secular spheres cooperated in the imposition of clear formulas of belief and codes of conduct leading, in Schilling's words, to 'the formation of an early modern society of disciplined subjects.'[9] The process of confessionalization began with the adoption of a distinctive creed or confession, whether it was one of the Lutheran or Calvinist statements of belief in Protestant lands or the Tridentine profession of faith in states which remained loyal to Rome. Other steps included the development of schools, colleges, and seminaries to instil the proper codes of belief in children, adolescents, and the professional cadres of society, both lay and clerical. Efforts to raise standards of private and public morality and to promote the development of lay confraternities and organizations for assisting the poor also played roles in the refashioning of Christian societies.[10]

A number of Italian historians have also taken up the concept of confessionalization. Oscar Di Simplicio has studied patterns of social development at Siena, arguing that special emphasis was placed on the control and reform of the nobility and the parish clergy as the sectors of society expected to provide leadership to the rest. In a rather sweeping comment on confessionalization he argues that the population of Europe was under a constant pressure to maintain high moral standards and that people were expected to obey not only the laws of the state but also those of the Decalogue.[11]

In his multifaceted study *Tribunali della coscienza*, Adriano Prosperi has explored the common ground and linkages between Tridentine bishops and the Roman Inquisition. Both the bishops and the Inquisition focused on the creation of a truly Christian society and developed parallel and often overlapping networks of officials not only to combat heresies but also to impose moral reform on the people. If the bishop's powers appeared to be broader than those of the inquisitor, the Inquisition benefited from having a more consistent period of activity. Further, Prosperi underlined how the secret, internal nature of the sacrament of penance was undermined by such practices as delaying absolution for serious and repeat offenders, imposing public penances on public sinners, and reserving absolution for certain serious sins to the judgment of the bishop. Mechanisms for enforcing the obligation of annual confession and communion allowed the church to infringe on the secrecy of the penitential rite with a form of external policing.[12]

In a further elaboration of the theme, Wietse de Boer, in his study of the activities of Carlo Borromeo, the cardinal-archbishop of Milan (r. 1564–84), has referred to Borromeo's work of moral reform as an attempt to establish social control, reaching into the consciences of the people in a way that would transform the social order.[13] The preferred instrument of social control was the sacrament of penance administered by what Borromeo hoped would be a cohort of highly trained diocesan priests. De Boer argues that under Borromeo the healing role of the sacrament was overshadowed by a new emphasis on the confessional as a legal tribunal where sins were weighed and penalties assigned. To enforce the rigour of the sacrament, the absolution of serious offences such as incest was taken from the normal confessors and reserved to the discretion of the archbishop. Further, a number of strategies were adopted to support the power of the confessional including the imposition of public penances on public sinners, sumptuary legislation, and attacks on what Borromeo referred to as 'occasions of sin.' Confessors were to treat frequenting taverns, playing card games, and dancing as reprehensible practices, and were to recognize that certain occupations such as that of the merchant and those within the legal profession and the military – though licit – were dangerous because they presented frequent opportunities for sinful behaviour.[14] Behind these strategies, de Boer implies, was the threat of prosecution of serious and persistent offenders by the courts of the archbishop and of the Roman Inquisition. Borromeo insisted that confessors refuse or at least defer absolution for grave, habitual sinners. If not resolved, failure to obtain absolution would mean failure to perform the Easter duty of communion, which could lead to ecclesiastical censure and ultimately prosecution by the ecclesiastical courts.[15] Thus, offences which were initially hidden by the seal of confession could find their way to the external forum of the bishop's tribunal, the *foro ecclesiastico*.

The theory of confessionalization has been questioned in a number of ways.[16] Wietse de Boer concludes his own study of the use of the sacrament of confession at Milan with a series of observations on the limitations of Borromeo's work and its inherent contradictions: there is little evidence that the practice of frequent confession which Borromeo favoured took hold among more than a small minority of devout followers, and during the Lenten season the sheer numbers of penitents led to cursory confessions and absolutions granted in haste. As well, lay resistance to the archbishop's rigorous morality was considerable. Enforcing more than minimum standards of good conduct would have alienated the secular authorities of Milan who were, after all, essential partners in the process of confessionalization.[17] On another front, Marc Forster has argued that in southwest Germany the development of a Catholic identity had more to do with popular devotional practices than with religious policies imposed from above.[18] Giovanni Romeo, while observing that the regular functioning of diocesan tribunals was an innovation of the post-Tridentine era, has underscored the reluctance of parish priests in Italy to act as moral agents in the extreme manner demanded by Borromeo.[19] In the meantime, Danilo Zardin suggested that too much emphasis has been placed on the repressive and juridical aspects of the Catholic reform, pointing out that the work of Carlo Borromeo and his associates had a more positive side that involved the promotion of the spiritual life of family, parish, and confraternity. Their method was not to set unattainable goals, uniform for all and enforced by a harsh system of 'judicial coercion,' but to promote ideal types which took into account the peculiarities of individual conditions of life.[20]

Nevertheless the power of the ecclesiastical courts over laypersons, the right of the archbishop to retain his own armed agents (*famiglia armata*), and efforts to limit carnivals and to stop tournaments on feast days were hotly contested points in controversies that flared between Borromeo and the Spanish governors of Milan in the 1570s and 1580s. Like Borromeo, the secular authorities of Milan saw religion as protecting the social order, but they wanted a lower common denominator for behaviour than did Borromeo, whom they regarded as an extremist and a threat to good order and to their own power.[21] Late in his life Borromeo succeeded, with some difficulty, in deflecting the complaints made about himself by the senate of Milan to Pope Gregory XIII (r. 1572–85) and to King Philip II of Spain (r. 1555–98), Milan's overlord. Although the archbishop won support for his policies, the question of the extent of ecclesiastical power was never satisfactorily resolved. After the brief and some would say ineffective episcopate of Gaspare Visconti (r. 1584–95), controversies raged again under

Cardinal Federico Borromeo, Carlo's second successor as archbishop of Milan (r. 1595–1631), over the right of the ecclesiastical courts to hear civil cases involving the laity. The issue was especially heated in 1597–1600 when the cardinal abandoned Milan during a period of self-imposed exile at Rome. It was only settled in 1615 when a fragile concordat was signed.

Despite the energy which Carlo Borromeo and his successors and imitators devoted to establishing and maintaining the freedom of the ecclesiastical courts, it remains to be seen how large a role they played in the fashioning of a new society in early modern Italy. Although the opening of the central archives of the Roman Inquisition to scholarly investigation in 1998 has resulted in a flurry of activity concerning this feared institution,[22] studies of the records of the episcopal tribunals have been hampered by the disorganized and incomplete nature of the diocesan archives and are only now beginning to gather momentum, with much of the attention focused on matrimonial issues such as annulments, requests for the legal separation of spouses, and bigamy.[23] In his study of clerical and noble crime in seventeenth- and eighteenth-century Siena, Di Simplicio has employed the records of the state and archiepiscopal archives. From the vantage point of Milan, de Boer has noted that the records of the episcopal courts are too scattered to permit a systematic study,[24] although Danilo Zardin has published an in-depth analysis of a noble assault on the curate of a Milanese parish, interpreted by Zardin as indicative of a widespread resistance to the innovations demanded by Borromean reform in the late sixteenth century.[25] Others, most notably Adriano Prosperi and Paolo Prodi, while lamenting the lack of studies of diocesan tribunals, have offered the opinion that by the early seventeenth century, episcopal tribunals lost momentum and assumed a secondary place in the ecclesiastical judicial system behind the tribunals of the Roman Inquisition.[26]

The lack of information on the activities of the Italian ecclesiastical courts can be remedied in part by records of the bishop's tribunal of the northern diocese of Novara in the two and one-half centuries following the Council of Trent (1545–63). Novara was the western neighbour of the archdiocese of Milan and a member of its ecclesiastical province. Although its 280 parishes were dwarfed in number by the 750 parishes of the archdiocese, it was nevertheless a large diocese by Italian standards. As well, its topography was similar to that of Milan, extending from the fertile Lombard plain, through the woodland regions of lakes Maggiore and Orta, and branching out into the Sesia, Ossola, and Vigezzo valleys in the Italian Alps. The bishops of Novara were to a great extent influenced by Carlo Borromeo, both as an inspirational leader and through the six provincial councils that he conducted.

The surviving records of the bishop's tribunal of Novara concern cases that were in their day considered criminal, including assaults by and against members of the clergy, inappropriate sexual activity by members of the clergy and the laity, neglect of parish responsibilities, and cases of faith such as heresy, blasphemy, and illicit magic. They do include some matrimonial issues like bigamy, incest, and concubinage, which in the eyes of the curia fell into the category of criminal behaviour. However other matrimonial matters such as requests for annulments and for separations are not included in the volumes of criminal cases.[27]

The Novarese records provide a unique opportunity to study the inner workings of an Italian diocesan court. Their potential is enhanced by the fact that the extant documents cover two important periods or phases of tribunal activity: the pivotal years following the closure of the Council of Trent, 1563 to 1615 (with gaps between 1565–75 and 1599–1600), and the closing decades of the Old Regime, 1745 to 1799. The files include names and cases of hundreds of priests and laypersons who for one reason or another caught the negative attention of the bishops and their officials. The records do not provide a statistical basis for measuring the incidence of clerical misbehaviour or lay sin in the diocese. The episcopal curia did not have the resources or the time to investigate all cases. However, the tribunal records do provide insight into what matters occupied the time and attention of the hierarchy. They reveal the methods used and the types of punishment employed. They enable a quantitative and comparative analysis, albeit limited, of the number of priests and laypersons appearing before the court. And they enable the historian to test the limits of the theory of confessionalization when applied to northern Italy.

Separated as they are by almost 150 years, the two sets of documents are dissimilar in a number of ways. The earlier collection consists of the records of formal trials conducted at Novara before the vicars general and prosecutors (*avvocati fiscali*) of the diocese and recorded by the chancellors in folio volumes. These include the *Libri informationum* (information taken from plaintiffs and witnesses) from roughly 1563 to 1590, the *Libri constitutorum* (interrogations of the accused) from 1593 to 1614, and the *Libri sententiarum* (sentences) for the years 1591–8. The documents of the eighteenth century fill thirty file boxes and cover the years 1745 to 1799 without gaps. However, they are more diversified than the post-Tridentine documents. Loosely arranged and without pagination, they include complaints, citations to appear, injunctions to avoid suspicious contacts, and the testimony of witnesses, interspersed with summaries of completed processes including sentences and statements of expenses. The files of the eighteenth-century tribunal are not as complete as those of the post-Tridentine period, and several dozen additional complaints, summons to appear, and investigative reports may be gleaned from the voluminous files of the eighteenth-century bishops and curia. Though diverse and incomplete, the two sets of records provide the basis for an assessment and comparison of tribunal activity in the two periods.

A variety of other sources supplement the tribunal records. Chief among these are the acts of visitation conducted at intervals of from ten to thirty years from the late sixteenth through the seventeenth century, with others held in the eighteenth century, albeit less frequently.[28] These include a personal report (*status personalis*) for most of the secular priests who lived and served in the parishes of the diocese and thus enable the historian to track the progress of many of those who appear in the records of the bishop's court. The acts of visitation also provide the basis for two surveys of the total population of the diocese and numbers of secular priests, one in the early seventeenth century and the other in the mid-eighteenth century.[29] As well, there are the published decrees of synods conducted in the time under study, the earliest in 1568 and the latest in 1778, and the published decrees and writings of Carlo Bascapè, who in his twenty-three years as bishop embodied the spirit of Tridentine reform at Novara. These are valuable in underlining the demands which the diocesan hierarchy placed on the clergy. The archival sources also include the twenty-six-volume register of letters written by Bascapè as bishop, which provides an added window for studying events of his lengthy episcopate.[30] While there is no parallel to Bascapè's register for the eighteenth-century bishops, there is nevertheless a substantial collection of miscellaneous records from their period including letters, instructions, edicts, and as noted above, legal documents.

This book will examine the role of the episcopal tribunal of Novara in dealing with moral transgressions and criminal behaviour in the post-Tridentine period and in the last half-century before the fall of the Old Regime. To establish the physical and historical background to the activity of the tribunal, the book will begin with a broad outline of conditions in the diocese and the pastoral activity and administrative structures employed by its bishops, with a special focus on the office of the vicar general and his assistants. The second chapter will comment briefly on the challenges which the Novarese hierarchy faced in dealing with appeals to other ecclesiastical courts in Lombardy and at Rome and on its at times strained relationship with the Roman Inquisition. But in response to modern theories of church-state cooperation and confessionalization, the chapter will mainly focus on the jurisdictional battles which raged between the Lombard bishops and the secular officials of Milan, regarded by the bishops as the greatest threat to the freedom of action of their tribunals. Chapter 3 will consider the role of the bishop's tribunal in the disciplining of the clergy in the post-Tridentine era. It will demonstrate that the tribunal acted vigorously and independently of state authorities to correct and even intimidate members of the clergy, especially parish priests. Its reach extended not just to the spiritual and moral failings of members of the clergy, but also to acts of violence including homicides and banditry as the episcopal curia successfully asserted the *privilegium fori*, the right of ecclesiastics to be judged by their own courts. And yet there were limitations to the power of the tribunal and to what it could accomplish. Its activity depended on the energy of a small, overworked group of officers of the curia, led by the vicar general of the diocese. Its decisions were often appealed to Rome and to the tribunals of neighbouring dioceses. A shortage of suitable candidates for the care of souls made it difficult to impose more than the lightest penalties on those found guilty. As well, even reforming bishops and their vicars were prepared to temper severity with clemency, to hear appeals, and to grant second chances. The fourth chapter will consider the laity in the sixteenth and early seventeenth century and will argue that the tribunal had neither the time nor the resources to be an effective means of controlling lay conduct. By the early seventeenth century, after it made a number of incursions into the area of lay morals, the episcopal curia for the most part abandoned efforts to deal with adultery and other sins of the laity as criminal matters and focused increasingly on matters of faith where its powers overlapped with that of the Inquisition: regulating contacts with heretical regions to the north of Italy and responding to the perceived threats of magic and witchcraft. The last chapter will consider the work of the tribunal in the second half of the eighteenth century, when the diocese of Novara had been transferred to the control of the Kingdom of Piedmont-Sardinia. In the closing decades of the Old Regime, lay cases disappeared almost completely from the tribunal's files and cases regarding matters of faith, though still present, were found in small numbers. The tribunal played a diminished role even in the disciplining of the clergy. Although the evidence is fragmentary, the principle of clerical immunity from secular prosecution was waning in the last days of the Old Regime. As well, the episcopal curia had adopted a milder, less formal approach centred on fraternal admonition, penances, and remedial activity more than intimidation, fines, and imprisonment.

1 The Diocese of Novara and Its Bishops

The bishops of Novara and their officials faced a challenging set of geographic, economic, and political conditions in the late sixteenth and early seventeenth centuries, conditions which would affect their ability to use judicial procedures and remedies to refashion the clergy and laity of the diocese. Although the size and geographical location of the diocese presented many problems similar to those facing Carlo Borromeo at Milan, and although Novara was under the influence of the archdiocese in many ways, its bishops lacked the human and economic resources available to Borromeo and his curia.

In the sixteenth century the diocese of Novara was in the westernmost territory of the duchy of Milan, from the 1530s under the control of the kings of Spain. The city itself, fifty kilometres from Milan, had a population of approximately 7300 souls, less than a tenth the size of its neighbour.[1] Although garrisoned by Spanish troops and ultimately under the Spanish governor and senate of Milan, the city was held in feud by the Farnese dukes of Parma, who purchased the 'marquisate' from Emperor Charles V in 1538 and administered it through a *podestà* and a vice-marquis. The city seems to have enjoyed having the Farnese dukes as intermediaries between itself and the Spanish authorities at Milan, but the arrangement ended in the early 1600s when the Farnese surrendered control, again for a monetary payment.[2]

As the western neighbour of the archdiocese of Milan, the diocese of Novara was a member of its ecclesiastical province. Its bishops participated in the six provincial councils held by Carlo Borromeo and were in many ways under his influence. In the early seventeenth century the diocese encompassed over 280 parishes and its total population, including the city, was approximately 186,000 souls.[3] Although the number of parishes was dwarfed by the over 750 parishes of the archdiocese of Milan, the largest see in the peninsula, Novara was a large diocese by Italian standards.[4] As Carlo Bascapè, bishop from 1593 to 1615, observed, it was tree-shaped, with a narrow southern trunk rooted in the fertile Lombard plain, rising gradually to the woodland regions of lakes Orta and Maggiore, and branching out into the Sesia, Ossola, and Vigezzo valleys.[5] In latitude it extended from Novara in the south approximately 130 kilometres north to Switzerland where it bordered on territories of the Swiss cantons, the modern-day Canton Ticino on the northeast and the Valais on the northwest.[6] Its width varied from 25 kilometres in the southern trunk to over 60 kilometres in the northern areas.

Size and location presented its bishops with a number of challenges. The diocese was largely rural. In the late sixteenth century, the city contained only seventeen parishes including those of the two cathedral churches of Santa Maria and San Gaudenzio, the former with a collegiate body of twenty-five canons, the latter with seventeen canons.[7] The large number of rural parishes, the great distances between Novara and northern regions, and the rugged topography of Alpine areas presented problems for communication and for pastoral visitation. From the early years of the Tridentine reform, the bishops, in imitation of Carlo Borromeo, grouped the parishes of their diocese into vicariates for pastoral and administrative purposes. The first configuration was of five vicariates with a number of prefectures under them. Carlo Bascapè made a more lasting rearrangement into thirty vicariates, which can be divided into four regions: the Lombard plain, the centre, the territory of lakes Maggiore and Orta, and the mountain valleys.

Slightly over a third of the parishes of the diocese were located in the mountainous north where rugged terrain, poor fields, and dispersed parish communities presented obstacles to the development of a vibrant parish life. There were several larger towns with sizeable ecclesiastical establishments. One was Domodossola, the gateway to the Ossola valley, with a population of six hundred and a collegiate church with five canons in 1617.[8] Another was Varallo in the Sesia valley with a population of over 2500 souls in 1617, shared among eight hamlets. The parish had two curates and seven chaplains, a number of which were attached to the Sacred Mountain of Varallo, a popular pilgrimage site founded in the late fifteenth century to recreate the Holy Land through shrines and chapels which depicted the life and Passion of Christ.[9] The order of the Franciscan Observance was prominent in the life of this shrine.

On the other end of the spectrum were mountain parishes which could barely support a curate. In 1594 Bascapè named twenty-seven parishes in a list prepared for the Congregation of Bishops and Regulars, including eight Alpine parishes which bordered on lands of Swiss Protestants and which included sizeable German-speaking populations. Among the eight were Rimasco, Fobello, and Rimella in the Sesia valley, each with populations between 700 and 1400 souls, Macugnaga in the Ossola valley with 700 souls, and Formazza in the Antigorio valley, the northernmost parish of the diocese, also with 700 souls. Another nineteen mountain parishes which did not border Swiss lands lacked sufficient income to attract a parish priest. These included Balmuccia and Alagna in the vicariate of Scopa; Sabbia and Camasco in the Sesia valley; Vognoga, Caddo, and Premia in the Ossola valley; and Genesio and Fosseno in the Pieve Vergonte.[10]

The Novarese hierarchy viewed proximity to Swiss Protestantism as a major problem. The greatest perceived dangers were presented by the Protestant canton of Bern, which lay several kilometres from the northernmost tip of the diocese, and the Valais, which was penetrated by Calvinist preachers in the last half of the sixteenth century.[11] The bishops had to cope with the northward emigration of Catholics, the commercial relations of their flock with Protestant towns, and the threat of the infiltration of suspect books and ideas.

Although topography and geographical location meant that the bishops of Novara faced problems similar to those found in the neighbouring archdiocese, they lacked the financial resources available to the archbishops of Milan. In 1593 the nominal income of the bishopric was, by Bascapè's estimate, five thousand scudi a year, a sum which compared quite favourably to the seven thousand scudi generated by the archdiocese in 1563.[12] However, while Carlo Borromeo enjoyed additional revenues from abbacies and other sources, Bascapè paid approximately three thousand scudi to former bishops as pensioners.[13] During the early years of his episcopate he had to rely on the good will of relatives and bankers to pay for the expenses of his installation. It was only in the closing years of his twenty-three-year episcopate that he could state that the last of the pensions had been discharged and that he could afford to invest money in expensive projects.[14] The bishop of Novara did have one advantage in terms of influence and power. A central region of the diocese known as the Riviera d'Orta, which included twenty-six parishes in the vicariates of Gozzano, Riviera East, and Riviera West, was held by him as a feudal possession, giving him temporal as well as spiritual power in the region.

The Novarese hierarchy benefited in many ways from the leadership shown by Milan, but lacked the educational resources available in the in larger archdiocese. Novara possessed a number of grammar schools in the sixteenth century, but no colleges and other institutions of higher learning comparable to those found in the archdiocese of Milan. Part of the problem was a lack of religious orders, in particular religious orders of recent vintage. Novara possessed only ten religious houses of men.[15] All but one of these were houses of the older orders: Franciscans, Augustinians, Hieronymites, and Dominicans. Members of these orders often served the diocese as Lenten preachers and founded numerous lay confraternities, but were not employed in the work of pastoral visitation and reform. They were often viewed with suspicion by the bishops, most notably Bascapè who had been a member of one of the new orders of the Catholic reformation, the Congregation of Clerics Regular of St Paul (Barnabites). With the exception of the Capuchins, who established a hospice at Novara, the newer orders of the Catholic reformation established no houses at Novara until relatively late in the post-Tridentine era. Thus while Carlo Borromeo and his successors were able to draw on the membership of Jesuit, Barnabite, Theatine, and other communities within the archdiocese to aid as teachers, preachers, confessors, and visitors, the bishops of Novara had to borrow members of these orders from houses outside the confines of the diocese.

Also problematic was the existence of a number of minor houses or hospices of religious orders, which were scattered through the diocese. Their original purpose had been to provide masses, grammar schools, and other services to the people, but with time the hierarchy came to regard a number of them as a threat to good order. In 1601 Bascapè sent a list of six of these to the Congregation of Bishops and Regulars in the hope that they would be dissolved and their revenues attached to local parishes or to the seminary. This included a house of Augustinian Hermits at Gravelona, established in 1573 to celebrate Mass and teach boys to read and write. Two or three monks lived there, but because they lacked a suitable house and income, they rarely celebrated Mass at Gravelona, going elsewhere to find income for their support. What was worse, according to Bascapè, they had adopted a worldly lifestyle and gave scandal by their secular pursuits. Another house, this time of the Hermits of the Lombard province, located twenty-seven kilometres from Novara, had revenues of twenty scudi a year and was only occupied by one monk at a time, if at all. The house had become a haven for bandits and other criminals.[16]

Communities of women were better documented because the Council of Trent had placed their overall supervision under the bishops or ordinaries, and the Novarese bishops were firm in asserting their right to visit them and regulate their observance of the monastic life. However, monasteries of women were relatively few in the diocese. In 1590 approximately three hundred nuns lived in its confines with seven houses in the city itself: Sant'Agnese and Santa Chiara under the Franciscan rule, Santa Barbara and Santa Maria of the Annunciation under Humiliati rule, Sant'Agostino and Santa Maria Maddalena under the Augustinian Hermits, and Sant'Agata under the Canons Regular of St Augustine. Each house had between ten and forty-four members. There were also two small houses in the diocese, Sant'Antonio at Intra and San Bartolemeo at Momo, and a number of Ursuline communities, the largest at Novara with seventeen members in 1606.[17] By comparison, the archdiocese of Milan had over three thousand nuns in 1599, and Cremona, another wealthy diocese, had approximately one thousand.[18] All of the Novarese convents were extremely poor and, what alarmed Bascapè the most, several had obtained permission to send members out in search of alms.[19]

The problems presented by economic, social, and geographic conditions in the diocese and by the shortage of episcopal revenues were not insurmountable obstacles to the development of the life of the church or to reform efforts. Religion was an internal matter. The zeal of parish priests did not vary in proportion to their income, nor could piety be equated with proximity to the parish church. The people of the diocese, even of mountain areas, would give signs of their devotion and loyalty to the Catholic faith throughout the episcopate of Bascapè. Nevertheless, factors such as poor finances and the size of the diocese impeded episcopal activity, and variations in the size, economies, and terrain of parishes would at times hinder the development of the spiritual life of the people.

The history of Novara in the sixteenth century can be divided into two stages. From 1494 to 1559 the diocese shared in the miseries of foreign invasion and war that afflicted the duchy of Milan. Like Milan, it endured a series of absentee bishops. In the second phase, from 1559 to the 1620s, the diocese enjoyed a period of almost uninterrupted peace under the control of Spain – the *pax Hispanica* – while the final sessions of the Council of Trent in 1562 and 1563 spurred a revival of pastoral activity on the part of its bishops.[20] The reform culminated in the work of Carlo Bascapè.

During the first half of the sixteenth century a series of powerful cardinals administered the diocese. They achieved prominence as officials of the Roman curia, papal legates, and protagonists in the struggles among France, Spain, and the papacy. Among them were Federico Sanseverino (r. 1507–11 and 1513–16), who was a partisan of France and a participant in the schismatic council of Pisa (1511–12), Matthias Schiner (r. 1511–13 and 1521–2), the famous Swiss diplomat and supplier of mercenary troops to Pope Julius II (r. 1503–13), Antonio del Monte (r. 1516–25), who was the uncle of Pope Julius III (r. 1550–5), and Ippolito d'Este (r. 1550–3), who was the archbishop of Milan from 1520 to 1550. Only one of the bishops of this era had a reputation in matters of religion and reform: Giovanni Cardinal Morone (r. 1553–60), who was a figure of importance in the history of the Catholic reform and presided over the closing sessions of the Council of Trent (1562–3). But even Morone was absent for most of his episcopate, both in the service of Rome and, from 1557 to 1559, a prisoner of Pope Paul IV (r. 1555–9) and of the Roman Inquisition.

During this time of absentee bishops and military incursions, Novara endured the religious and moral turmoil that Federico Chabod described in his magisterial study of the duchy of Milan under the Emperor Charles V.[21] Throughout Lombardy, members of the secular clergy were frequently accused of ignorance, negligence in the care of souls, sexual offences, and other vices. Plurality of benefices and absenteeism were other symptoms of the religious decay. In 1568 canons of the cathedral of Novara still possessed many of the wealthier parishes of the plains region of Trecate, administering them through vice-curates.[22] Wandering friars and wayward nuns scandalized the people. In 1563 three lay sisters, who were called servants (*serve*), fled the convent of Sant'Agata of Novara and established themselves in the suburbs. They were accused of leading 'evil lives in the manner of prostitutes,' to the scandal of their house and the prejudice of their souls.[23] In the eyes of the hierarchy, heresy, magic, and witchcraft were also serious threats. Although few cases of heresy appeared in the records of the Novarese tribunal, the episcopal curia was deeply concerned by the threats posed by trade and migration over the frontier with Switzerland, which was crucial to the economic survival of communities in the northern parts of the diocese. Both bishops and inquisitors were ever watchful for Protestant books in transit from Switzerland.[24] Military garrisons also posed a threat within the diocese, both because of the morals of the soldiers and their lack of observance of the regulations governing the sacraments and because of the potential for mercenaries of a Protestant background to appear in the diocese.[25] Trials for witchcraft had been common in the diocese since the 1400s and continued unabated through the post-Tridentine period.[26]

However, there were positive signs in the diocese, even in the period before the Council of Trent. At the time of the fifth Lateran Council (1512–17) the vicars general drafted a series of edicts for the reform of clergy and laity. Cardinal Morone did the same in 1553.[27] Although the absenteeism of the cardinal bishops probably meant that little was done to enforce the decrees, their existence marked a growing awareness in the episcopal curia of the need for reform. The laity for its part also demanded improved clerical morals and improvements in the administration of the sacraments. In the mountainous regions, as in other northern dioceses, they requested and endowed the establishment of new parishes so that they could have pastors close at hand.[28] As well, the first half of the century witnessed the foundation in Lombardy of new religious orders and institutions that would one day become part of the religious fabric of Novara: the Barnabite congregation at Milan, Schools of Christian Doctrine for the catechization of the young at Como, and the Ursulines of St Angela Merici (1474–1540) at Brescia.[29]

The Council of Trent synthesized the projects for reform into a united movement and reasserted the episcopal obligations of residence and pastoral activity. However, in the first thirty years following the council's closure, Rome entrusted

Novara to a series of seven bishops who were unable to devote their undivided attention to their see because of factors such as poor health and willingness to undertake missions in the papal service.

The first was Giovanni Antonio Cardinal Serbelloni, a cousin of Carlo Borromeo and nephew of Pope Pius IV (r. 1560–5), who held the diocese from 1560 to 1574. Unlike his cousin who resided at Milan despite pressures to remain in Rome, Serbelloni chose to serve papal diplomacy and the Roman curia. He visited Novara briefly in the late 1560s but resigned the see in 1574, keeping a pension of one thousand scudi.

Between 1574 and 1593, none of the bishops of Novara served longer than six years. The cardinal was succeeded by Romulo Archinto, who was an energetic pastor but died less than two years after his arrival in the city. Francesco Bossi governed the diocese from 1579 to 1584. He was esteemed by Borromeo but agreed to conduct apostolic visitations of Genoa and Lodi with the result, wryly noted by Bascapè, that he could not visit the better part of his own diocese. Cesare Speciano, formerly Borromeo's agent in Rome and secretary of the Congregation of Bishops and Regulars, became bishop of Novara in 1585 but spent four years of his episcopate as papal legate to Spain. In 1591 he was transferred to the bishopric of Cremona. Pietro Martire Ponzone, his successor, was an old man when he came to the diocese and died in November 1592.[30]

Despite their absences, the bishops who served Novara between 1563 and 1593 set the legal, institutional, and organizational basis of the reform according to the guidelines established by Carlo Borromeo. They held five diocesan synods: Serbelloni in 1568, Archinto in 1576, Bossi in 1580 and 1584, and Speciano in 1590.[31] Through them they promulgated and elaborated the decrees of the Council of Trent and of the provincial councils of Milan on the most important aspects of the reform. They outlined the obligations of the clergy in the care of souls, passed regulations on clerical clothing, and outlawed concubinage and association with bandits. They regulated travel to Protestant lands. They ordered the foundation of Schools of Christian Doctrine and regulated lay confraternities. They adopted Milanese rules for the cloister of nuns and their observance of vows. They set specifications for the administration of the sacraments and the construction of churches, baptismal fonts, and confessionals.

Legislation was only the first step in the work of reform. The bishops also established institutions modelled on those of Borromeo. In 1564 the vicar general of Serbelloni founded the first seminary in the city, and in later years smaller seminaries were established at Varallo and at the Island of San Giulio on Lake Orta.[32] Parish priests of the regions of the diocese were expected to convene each month to discuss cases of conscience or questions concerning the sacrament of penance. For the laity, the bishops and their vicars general promoted the foundation of Schools of Christian Doctrine and lay confraternities.

The bishops also developed a pastoral organization designed to cope with problems presented by the size of the diocese and the distance between Novara and the Alpine valleys. At the centre of their system they employed canons of the city to aid in pastoral visitation.[33] On the local level they created a network of officials to aid the reform. In 1581 Francesco Bossi divided the mountain and hill areas of the diocese into five large vicariates, each under a rural vicar (*vicario foraneo*), and subdivided the vicariates into a total of twenty-one prefectures, each under a prefect. He also created nine prefectures for the parishes of the plains. The rural vicars performed a number of important functions. They conducted annual visitations of the parishes under their supervision and kept the episcopal office informed of local conditions. They also had limited jurisdictional powers in civil and criminal cases. The prefects did not enjoy jurisdictional powers but kept the bishop informed of local needs and abuses, and supervised monthly meetings or congregations of parish priests.[34]

The legislative and organizational efforts of the bishops provided the foundation for a more thorough reform to come. By 1593 they and their assistants had visited the diocese several times,[35] while the bishop's tribunal had prosecuted a number of parish priests, canons, chaplains, and clerics for moral offences and lapses in the care of souls. When he came to the diocese in 1593, Bascapè found a number of areas for improvement but did not have to introduce Tridentine reform to the diocese, and he capitalized on the pastoral activity of his predecessors. With single-minded devotion to the affairs of his church, and with the advantage of a long episcopate, Bascapè gave Novara its strongest pastoral government in over a century. His adminisration, however, was not a new departure for the diocese but the culmination of years of pastoral activity.

Although the basic structures of ecclesiastical governance were in place before Bascapè, it is worth examining them as they existed during his episcopate. The system was hierarchical, with the bishop and his closest assistants at the top and a number of rural vicars at the local level. Next to the bishop, the vicar general was the most powerful person in the curia. A doctor in canon and civil law with the added honour of being a 'protonotary apostolic,' the vicar general presided over the episcopal tribunal in both civil and criminal matters and in cases pertaining to the defence of the faith. But the tribunal was only one of his many concerns. His office was also administrative and pastoral. He functioned as a confessor, with power to absolve persons from sins reserved to the judgment of the bishop. Under the bishop's supervision, he played a role in appointing priests to benefice and in establishing new parishes. He had power to visit churches, convents, and religious foundations (*luoghi pii*). When the bishop was absent or conducting pastoral visitations, he was expected to maintain a steady correspondence with him. As well, during the absence of the bishop he served as governor of the temporal dominion of the Riviera d'Orta.[36]

The vicar general was assisted in his judicial functions by the *avvocato fiscale* or *fiscale* who acted as prosecutor, preparing cases for the tribunal and from time to time presiding in the absence of the vicar general. Through much of Bascapè's episcopate the office of *avvocato fiscale* was filled by a layman named Curzio Gattico, *dottore novarese*, who was accepted by Bascapè because of his experience and good references, although the bishop hoped he would one day become an ecclesiastic.[37] The third major official of the episcopal tribunal was the diocesan chancellor who recorded the trials, using Latin for court procedures and questions and Italian for the testimony of witnesses and accused. In addition to preserving the documents of the tribunal, the episcopal chancellor was also responsible for publishing edicts and instructions, supervising notaries employed by the curia, and maintaining the diocesan archive.[38] The bishop's curia also employed a jailer (*bargello*) who supervised the bishop's jail and administered the strappado when people were questioned under torture. He also helped police the observance of cloister and regulations against working on Sundays and feast days, serving as an informant for the curia. The Novarese bishops do not appear to have developed a full *famiglia armata* to apprehend the accused, although Bascapè defended the practice in his *Commentarii canonici* of 1615. For this the bishops appear to have relied on the cooperation of secular officials (*podestà* and *sbirri*), a practice which Bascapè also defended in the *Commentarii canonici*, noting that calling on the support of the secular arm should in no way be prejudicial to the bishop's power: the secular authorities must never claim to review or judge a case before committing resources to the bishop's tribunal.[39]

In addition to an indeterminate number of notaries who served the curia from time to time, there were also visitors and visitors general who travelled to parts of the diocese each year.[40] A vicar for nuns assisted in the regulation of convents, enforced the rules of cloister and of the monastic life, and appointed confessors and chaplains.[41]

Although the Novarese curia had well-defined offices, it was nevertheless dwarfed by that of Milan, which had been reorganized under Carlo Borromeo and had a wide variety of chancellors, visitors, notaries, and others, who were under the direction of a vicar general assisted by two vicars, one for civil and the other for criminal cases.[42] To focus on the vicar general of Novara, it is easy to see that, in terms of work schedule alone, his tasks would have been daunting and that his administrative and pastoral duties would have infringed on his work as a judge. The roles of pastor, confessor, and judge no doubt shaded into one another, the judge acting as confessor and the confessor as judge.

On the regional level, Bascapè continued the system of rural vicars developed by Borromeo and imitated by the bishops of Novara. As noted above, he divided the five northern vicariates into a number of smaller jurisdictions and elevated the prefectures of the plains to the status of vicariates. In this way he raised the number of rural vicars to thirty. Bascapè did not substantially change the duties of the rural vicars, which were detailed and onerous, especially in light of the fact that they were parish priests with other pastoral and administrative duties to fulfil. Vicars were also asked to convey episcopal instructions to parish priests, to conduct annual visitations of the parishes under their supervision, and to inform the curia immediately should a benefice in their jurisdiction fall vacant. They presided over monthly meetings or congregations in which parish priests discussed cases of conscience. Each year they assembled at Novara to discuss their activities with the bishop.[43]

Rural vicars also played a role in the work of the bishop's tribunal, providing the bishop and curia with a network of officials on the grassroots level and sometimes, no doubt, finding themselves in positions of personal danger. They were to inform the bishop about conditions within their regions and from time to time were called on to gather information about the conduct of specific priests and parishioners. For example, in 1593 Bascapè instructed the vicar of Baveno on Lake Maggiore to order the curate of Montrigiasco to appear before the curia and to search his house for forbidden weapons. Beginning with the consuls and syndics of the land, he was to inquire whether the same priest had vomited in the presence of his people at Christmas, if he worked on feast days, and if he left a deceased infant without burial for three days. In the same letter he asked whether the vicar had destroyed the license of the curate of Fosseno to have a female servant in his house and advised him to ensure that other curates of the vicariate said their required weekday masses and taught catechism on feast days, this under penalty of one scudo per violation.[44] In addition to gathering evidence on the conduct and offences of priests and clerics, rural vicars had the power to detain those who were suspected of violating laws that fell under the purview of the episcopal tribunal, but not the power to interrogate them or to release them. They also had limited powers in civil cases.[45] In the work of uncovering the crimes and sins of clergy and laity of the diocese, the episcopal curia and the rural vicars also without doubt relied on the information provided by the parish priests of the diocese, as well as numerous lay informants who ranged from syndics of communal councils and churches to jilted spouses, outraged parents, and victims of clerical violence.

In choosing his assistants, Bascapè relied principally on the secular clergy of the diocese. His visitors and chancellors were usually the more trustworthy canons of the urban cathedrals of Santa Maria and San Gaudenzio.[46] The same held true for vicars of nuns. Bascapè once commented that he favoured secular priests over friars as confessors and visitors of nuns despite the fact that they could not personally set a good example of life according to a rule. It was better, he said, not to have something than to have it in a corrupt form. A secular priest could teach the regular life from a book more effectively than a corrupt friar by example.[47] Rural vicars, meanwhile, were selected from the most trustworthy parish priests of the diocese. In keeping with a principle established by Borromeo, archpriests and archdeacons, who in the past performed functions similar to those of the rural vicars, were chosen only when found worthy and were removed if found wanting. Thus in 1598 Bascapè dismissed the provost of Intra from the position of rural vicar because of the charges pending against him before the tribunal.[48] The power of rural vicars rested on episcopal approval and letters patent and not on the titles of their benefices.

Bascapè made an exception to the general rule when selecting his vicars general, preferring to employ priests from outside his diocese. In Bascapè's opinion, a Novarese vicar general, especially a canon of the city, would be open to accusations of personal interest in the administration of justice.[49]

Bascapè's decision to involve the Novarese clergy in the administration and reform of the diocese was, in his own words, based on the example of Milan. Not only would this encourage and honour the clergy of the diocese and prepare a solid foundation for the future, it would also enable him to govern them with greater ease.[50] There may also have been a financial reason. While Borromeo could afford to maintain advisors from outside Milan during his first years as archbishop,[51] the loss of income to pensions impeded Bascapè's activity through much of his episcopate. He could afford more expensive projects only late in his life. By then the principle of ruling the diocese using local talent was too firmly established to warrant change.

The religious orders, as noted above, played a modest role in the pastoral activity of the diocese, not surprisingly given Bascapè's often expressed antipathy towards the older orders. Members of the Franciscan and Dominican orders served as Lenten preachers and confessors but did not assist with pastoral visitation or seminary instruction. In the early years of his episcopate, Bascapè obtained some assistance from the new orders of the sixteenth century – most notably Jesuits and members of his own order, the Barnabites – who served temporarily as visitors, preachers, and confessors.[52] In 1594 he asked the Barnabites to found a college at Novara, but a number of citizens objected that the city could not support a new religious establishment. and the project was shelved. In 1599 the bishop found funds for a Barnabite college at the Church of San Marco near the cathedral. Although the community remained small, with no more than four or five Barnabites, it provided excellent teachers for the seminary of Novara. In 1624 the Barnabites were supplanted by the Jesuits who assumed control over the Cannobian School, originally established in 1603 from a legacy left by the Abbate Amico Cannobbio. Another important development of the early seventeenth century was Bascapè's foundation of the oblates of San Gaudenzio and San Carlo in imitation of the oblates of Sant'Ambrogio at Milan. The oblates were a congregation of secular priests who took a special vow of obedience to the bishop and served the diocese as confessors, instructors in cases of conscience, and retreat masters. They also maintained the college of Santa Cristina at Borgomanero.[53]

Thus, the personnel whom Bascapè employed in the governance of the diocese remained similar to that under his immediate predecessors with some important modifications. However, the most important new element was the presence of the bishop, for Bascapè made the care of souls his constant concern. He set the tone of the reform at Novara, determining which aspects of Tridentine and provincial decrees were to be emphasized through his edicts and when.[54] He saw to the growth and financial stability of seminaries and of convents of nuns, took steps to increase the revenues of poor parishes, and supervised the examination of candidates for the priesthood. When appointment to a benefice fell to Rome or to one of the cathedral chapters, he used his influence in favour of the candidate he felt to be most suitable.[55]

Bascapè kept his collaborators under tight control. His vicars general felt his presence most directly. He watched over, but did not attend, sessions of the bishop's tribunal and insisted on reviewing all criminal cases before sentence was passed. This was certainly his intent on 23 March 1594 when he received a list of decisions rendered in criminal cases (*speditioni criminali*) made in January and wrote to Ludovico Boido, his first vicar general: 'in the future you will inform [me] before you expedite [the cases] and not after.'[56] In June 1605 Bascapè had occasion to comment more fully on the office and qualities of a good vicar general when seeking a replacement for Orazio Besozzo who had served him in that capacity since 1598. In a letter to Don Aurelio, a Barnabite at Bologna, he said that a vicar general must have good knowledge of the law, experience in ecclesiastical matters, zeal, and integrity. Personal qualities were also important: whether candidates were reserved or lively, patient or impatient, and above all, whether they were apt to conform to the will of the bishop. Attention to ecclesiastical discipline and to detail were also of paramount importance. The pay, Bascapè continued, was in the range of two hundred scudi a year, roughly twice what one of the better remunerated parish priests could hope to receive. This sum was to come largely from fees paid to the ecclesiastical court, something prohibited by the provincial councils but permitted at Novara by papal brief, possibly because of the bishop's lack of income. Finally, he preferred not to use canons of the diocese because they would desire benefices as a reward.[57]

Despite his authoritarian temperament, Bascapè enjoyed good relations with most of his vicars general. Girolamo Settala of Milan, who served as vicar general from 1594 to 1598, left when he was appointed Archpriest of Monza. He returned briefly in 1609 when Bascapè could not find a suitable vicar general and again in 1615 to help conduct Bascapè's last synod.[58] Orazio Besozzo, also of Milan, served as Bascapè's vicar general for the longest period of time, from 1598 to 1605. He had formerly been the bishop's agent in Rome and left Novara to become a Capuchin friar.[59] The Abbate Melchior Aimo, a canon of Cremona, served from 1607 to 1609. He was a capable vicar but was forced to return to Cremona because he possessed a benefice requiring residence in that diocese.[60] In the last years of his life Bascapè broke with his long-standing policy of not employing a local canon as vicar general. Niccolò Leonardi, the head of the chapter of San Gaudenzio filled the post. Bascapè was pleased with his work and delayed seeking a replacement even after a number of canons of the cathedral of Santa Maria complained about the presence of a Novarese vicar general.[61]

The exceptions – the vicars general who were dismissed from service on short notice – underscored the importance of episcopal supervision. In 1594 Bascapè released his first vicar general, Ludovico Boido of Pavia, because Boido was too rigorous and outspoken in reprimanding the clergy and because he transferred money from the tribunal to his servant.[62] Boido left the diocese on good terms, however, going on to serve as vicar general to the bishop of Tortona.[63] In 1612 Bascapè dismissed Angelo de Caia, nephew of no less a figure than Robert Bellarmine (1542–1621), the Jesuit cardinal and theologian, for committing a number of irregularities in the administration of justice. Most significant of these was the unauthorized execution of two bandits from the episcopal dominion of the Riviera d'Orta, who were wanted for questioning by the senate of Milan.[64]

Bascapè's concern about the activities of his vicars general bears witness to the importance of the office even when a diocese was under the strong guiding hand of a bishop. In addition to the pressures of their many pastoral and administrative duties, it was the vicars general who presided over the bishop's tribunal and were expected to give teeth to the decrees and edicts set out by the Council of Trent, the provincial councils, diocesan synods, and the bishops. Their workload would be a problem for the administration of ecclesiastical justice in the diocese, and one wonders whether Bascapè's strong guiding hand might have been a discouragement to some of them and partly account for the frequent turnover in the office. But before the tribunal's activity can be examined in detail, it is appropriate to examine the difficulties created for the Novarese tribunal by ecclesiastical entities outside the diocese and by the jurisdictional controversies which overshadowed relations with the state in the post-Tridentine years.

2 Episcopal Jurisdiction Put to the Test: Rival Ecclesiastical Courts and Confrontation with the State of Milan, 1563–1615

In the post-Tridentine era, the episcopal tribunal of Novara did not operate in isolation but in a complex environment of overlapping and competing claims for jurisdictional control. There were conflicts between the Novarese court and other ecclesiastical bodies including the tribunals of the archdiocese of Milan, the Sacred Congregation of Bishops and Regulars at Rome, and the Dominican inquisitor of Novara.[1] There were tensions and a number of debilitating controversies between the secular government of Milan, then under the crown of Spain, and the dioceses of Lombardy, including Novara. All of these undermined or at least weakened the ability of the tribunal to resolve problems in the diocese. This chapter will briefly describe several of the conflicts with diocesan courts and the inquisitor of Novara, before taking a more in-depth look at the controversies between church and state.

In his correspondence Bascapè frequently complained that ecclesiastical courts outside his diocese meddled in the proceedings and rulings of his tribunal. In 1595 he wrote in protest to Antonio Seneca, vicar general of Milan, because a tribunal of the archdiocese had interfered with a ruling against Vittore Beniolo, canon of Intra, judged by the tribunal of Novara to have been under the canonical age when he obtained a benefice involving the care of souls. The challenges, Bascapè wrote, posed by the world and the devil to his diocese were great enough without the added inconvenience of the metropolitan authority meddling on its own behalf. Nor could he afford to retain a lawyer at Milan to defend the steps he had taken. The service of God would go poorly if the proper respect was not shown to the churches of the province. He begged Seneca not to let such intrusions occur in the future.[2]

Bascapè's complaint appears to have had little impact. His letters and the records of the tribunal speak to a number of cases where the accused appealed beyond the Novarese tribunal to Rome, Milan, and other dioceses. One notorious example was the case of Bernardino Aloysio, curate of the northern village of Zuccaro. In 1602–3 Aloysio, aged in his early forties, was arraigned on a number of occasions by the Novarese tribunal and accused of involvement in over twenty crimes, including extorting money from a number of his parishioners, assaults leading to wounds, and the seduction of women of the region. He escaped from Novara after bribing his jailer, but was apprehended again in the diocese of Vercelli in 1604. In January 1605 he appeared before the bishop's tribunal under sentence of excommunication and was charged with murdering a man when he was in the company of two known bandits.[3] He was sentenced to be deprived of his parish and to ten years in the galleys. The sentence was remarkably light when one considers the gravity of the charges, but Aloysio appealed to the archdiocesan tribunal of Milan, which overturned the sentence on the grounds that he had suffered a long trial, torture, and imprisonment lasting seven years. Although Aloysio kept title to his parish, the Milanese court ordered him to stand in exile from the diocese of Novara for as long as Bascapè desired, to maintain a vice-curate in his parish, and to restore sums of money extorted from his parishioners. In 1612 he wrote to the Congregation of Bishops and Regulars at Rome to have them order Bascapè to grant him formal dismissal from Novara so that he could earn a living by celebrating Mass. He had exhausted his money paying for his defence, and his parish now provided only a pittance towards his upkeep.[4] The response of the Congregation is not known, but Bascapè was no doubt displeased with the process.[5]

Any feelings of resentment which Bascapè might have had over the interventions of the neighbouring tribunals were, however, equalled and surpassed by his early animosity towards the representative of the Roman Inquisition at Novara. Like Carlo Borromeo, Bascapè took special interest in matters of faith, regarding bishops to be 'the old and ordinary inquisitors in their dioceses.'[6] Although the records of the Inquisition of Novara have for the most part been lost, it is known that a resident inquisitor, a member of the Dominican order, had functioned in the diocese since the middle of the fourteenth century, and in the fifteenth century the Inquisition had been aggressively hunting witches in the diocese and throughout northern Italy.[7] It was in those years that the prosecution and execution of witches in Italy were at their height, in advance of the hunt in the rest of Europe.[8] The Inquisition received new life in 1542 when it was reorganized to combat new threats of heresy from northern Europe and from within Italy. Centralized under a congregation of cardinals at Rome, it developed a network of local inquisitors, largely of the Dominican and Franciscan orders, in the cities of northern Italy, Tuscany, and the Papal States. Each of these were assisted in turn by rural vicars, secretaries, supporters called familiars, and in many cities a lay confraternity known as the Crocesignati ('those signed with the cross').[9]

The areas of interest of the Roman Inquisition were many, expanding to include not just heresy and the dissemination of heretical books, but also illicit magic, witchcraft, blasphemy, bigamy, sodomy, and solicitation in the confessional. The scope of the Inquistion overlapped with those of the episcopal courts and the secular legal system, and tensions were bound to follow.[10]

In the 1570s and 1580s Domenico Buelli, the incumbent inquisitor at Novara, was prominent in pursuing alleged witches in the Ossola valley.[11] In 1593 Buelli complained that Bascapè was slow to publish an edict in defence of the Inquisition and that his vicar general, Ludovico Boido, had been meddling in the business of the Holy Office. In Bascapè's view, the real reason for Buelli's displeasure was that the bishop's curia had denied the inquisitor the right to proceed to torture and sentence without the bishop's representative in attendance. Elaborating on this point in a private letter to Orazio Besozzo, his agent in Rome, Bascapè complained that the inquisitor and his vicar had abused their power for financial gain by making the Ossola valley their 'Indies' (that is, their gold mine), on one occasion taking forty-five pounds of silver and a fine horse from one of the towns. The comment underscored a deep-seated antagonism between inquisitor and bishop.[12]

A new issue arose in 1597 when Giulio Santorio, the cardinal of Santa Severina and head of the Congregation of the Holy Office, complained about Bascapè's decision to give his rural vicars authority to form processes in matters of faith and demanded that he withdraw this faculty from them. He was probably acting on Buelli's prompting. Bascapè replied that the powers he had granted were only to gather information and to detain or incarcerate the accused, but not to interrogate or release them without permission from the episcopal curia. He felt it was necessary for them to have this authority because of the close commercial ties of the diocese with Protestant areas. He agreed to remove the authority to deal with matters of faith when he next issued patents for the rural vicars if the cardinal so wished, but pointed out that the inquisitor of Novara had also deputized priests of the diocese to serve as his own vicars, alleging that he gave them perpetual powers and the right to proceed in all aspects of cases short of employing torture and passing sentence.[13]

Although there were later squabbles over who held responsibility to enforce the Index of Prohibited Books and to police travel to northern lands, over time Bascapè and the episcopal tribunal worked with the inquisitor in the matters where cooperation was clearly mandated by papal policy.[14] For example, as required by papal constitutions, the bishop's vicar general and the inquisitor both participated when those accused in matters of faith were interrogated under torture and when sentences were pronounced.[15] That the old rancour was set aside can be attributed to a number of factors. First, it is possible that

Buelli's death in 1603 and the appointment of a new inquisitor, the Dominican Gregorio Manino of Gozzano, may have slowed the work of the Inquisition at Novara and cleared the way for a more aggressive approach on the part of the episcopal curia.[16] Second, the Novarese inquisitors may have sensed Bascapè's determination to deal with matters of faith and decided it would be easiest to work with him. The Inquisition would benefit from the resources and work of the episcopal curia. Although it is known that the inquisitor of Novara had a network of rural vicars, the number of his familiars is not known, and there is no record that a Confraternity of Crocesignati existed in the city and diocese to advance the Inquisition's work by denouncing those suspected of heresy.[17] In short, it seems possible that the Inquisition at Novara, like the bishop's tribunal, lacked resources and would accept assistance wherever it could be found.

At any rate, in the long run the most prominent jurisdictional rivalry in Lombardy was that between the ecclesiastical courts and those of the duchy of Milan, which had over decades developed statutory law in areas that the church had perceived as its own. Italian historians have characterized this situation as one of 'dualism,' with the claims of secular and ecclesiastical courts, civil and canon law, standing in opposition to one another. The rivalry led at times to jurisdictional controversies as church and state sought to defend their prerogatives and independence of action from one another. The controversies have tended to attract a great amount of interest from historians, perhaps disproportionately great. As a result, the state is often seen as undermining the objectives of the church, a view reinforced by the claims made by the church that public morality and the well-being and safety of the Christian community were undermined by lay attacks on ecclesiastical jurisdiction. However, it would be more accurate to note that, in the era of the Council of Trent, cooperation between church and state was stronger than the periodic conflicts between the two might suggest. The government of Milan, which was under the Spanish crown since the time of the Emperor Charles V, did not question the existence of ecclesiastical jurisdiction. The secular authorities from King Philip II down saw the reform of Catholic society as essential to the maintenance of their own power over their dominions. What was at issue was the extent of ecclesiastical jurisdiction, whether of the bishop's court or of the Roman Inquisition.[18] Neither the Spanish authorities nor the senate of Milan, the body charged with the maintenance of the statute law of the duchy, wanted the church to increase its jurisdictional power if it meant weakening their own. Italian governments of the period did not attempt to shrink the sphere of church action but to resolve the conflicts which inevitably arose between civil and ecclesiastical jurisdictions.[19]

The activity of the episcopal tribunal of Novara was part of a greater trend in the period 1563 to 1615 of the church to reassert its authority over clergy and laity alike. The trend was already in evidence during the fifth Lateran Council of 1512–17, but attained full force only with the closing sessions (1562–3) of the Council of Trent and the coming of the zealous Carlo Borromeo to Milan in 1565. The church's areas of concern were broad. They involved questions of the *privilegium fori* (the right of the clergy to be tried only by ecclesiastical courts), even for crimes such as assault, murder, and theft. They included questions of ecclesiastical property. A major issue in the post-Tridentine period was whether laypersons could be cited before the ecclesiastical courts to resolve property conflicts with the church, contrary to the principle that cases were to be pursued in the tribunal of the accused. Another issue was the degree to which laypersons could be cited on moral matters, especially cases of sexual morality. Usury was also especially contentious because it involved trade and property. The claims of the church to jurisdictional independence led to a series of struggles with the secular government of Milan under Carlo Borromeo and his immediate successors. These were partially resolved when church and state agreed to a concordat governing jurisdictional issues in 1615.

The powers of ecclesiastical courts had long been an issue in the medieval church, waxing and waning with time and circumstance. Ecclesiastical courts, particularly those of Rome, enjoyed their greatest power in the thirteenth century as the papacy claimed unprecedented rights to fill ecclesiastical benefices. Papal claims continued to mount during the Avignon period (1305–77), but the ensuing Great Schism, conciliar movement, and Renaissance papacy led to a decline in the viability of the church's claims to enforce its own laws over both clergy and laity. From the fourteenth century it was the annual practice at Rome to publish a bull asserting papal and ecclesiastical immunities from secular taxation and rights of jurisdiction. The bull, called *In Coena Domini* because it was proclaimed on Holy Thursday, the feast of the Lord's Supper, came to include a series of provisions in defence of the ecclesiastical courts, both papal and episcopal. It condemned the transfer of cases from ecclesiastical to lay courts, the trial of clerics before secular courts, attacks on ecclesiastical judges, attacks on those who took cases before the Roman courts, and the usurpation of church property by laypersons and authorities.[20] Although resisted by secular states, Rome expected bishops to regularly publish *In Coena Domini* in their dioceses .[21] Such was the case at Novara, where in 1576 Romulo Archinto included cases drawn from *In Coena Domini* among a list of cases reserved to episcopal absolution[22] and where Carlo Bascapè circulated copies of the bull to all parish priests, including an Italian summary with the Latin text.[23]

The Great Schism of 1378 to 1414 and its aftermath seriously undermined the jurisdictional power of the church, but claims to ecclesiastical liberty remained.

In the early sixteenth century the church reasserted its right to jurisdiction in civil and criminal matters. The decrees of the fifth Lateran Council of 1512–17 included statements in defence of ecclesiastical jurisdiction. A bull issued by Pope Leo X and included in the documents of the tenth session of 4 May 1515 condemned secular rulers and nobles who usurped ecclesiastical property and who ignored the principle of clerical immunity from secular jurisdiction. Asserting the principle that laypersons enjoyed no power over clerics or over church property, Leo X went on not to draft new legislation but to renew the old canons and decrees in support of ecclesiastical liberty.[24]

The pronouncements of the fifth Lateran Council were soon taken up by vicars general of Novara, beginning on 15 March 1516 with a series of decrees issued by Lorenzo Casazza, vicar general of Cardinal Federico Sanseverino. Included among regulations governing the Easter duty, proper clothing for clerics, and the denunciation of sins such as concubinage and usury, Casazza defended ecclesiastical jurisdiction against secular judges, saying that if the judges impeded ecclesiastical jurisdiction in any way it would be against the liberty of the church and cause for excommunication.[25] Excommunication was to be backed by heavy fines against the violators of this and the other decrees. The decree in defence of episcopal jurisdiction was repeated with variations in ensuing pronouncements by the vicars general of Novara, but it is not known to what effect. The fact that most bishops ruled the diocese from afar in the first half of the sixteenth century suggests that the episcopal tribunal probably had a limited impact on the implementation of reform in the diocese. The trend in Lombardy in the first half of the sixteenth century and until the closing phases of the Council of Trent ran counter to the claims of the fifth Lateran Council and of Leo X on clerical immunity and ecclesiastical liberty. The secular magistrates of the last Sforza dukes and of the Emperor Charles V not only maintained a strict control over the nomination of bishops, exercising the ducal placet in this regard, but also intruded in the apprehension and trial of religious dissenters and from time to time violated clerical immunity by prosecuting ecclesiastics in criminal and civil cases. Interventions of the secular power in religious matters were common throughout Italy, and the church struggled to reassert its powers after the closure of the Council of Trent in other areas of Italy as well as in the duchy of Milan.[26]

Given the widespread and entrenched influence of the princes over ecclesiastical matters, it is little wonder that the Council of Trent adopted a conciliatory tone when it turned to safeguarding ecclesiastical jurisdiction in its twenty-fifth and final session, held under Pius IV in December 1563.[27] Secular princes were not ordered but admonished to do their duty in defence of ecclesiastical immunity from secular laws. They were further admonished to punish their ministers and magistrates if they ever obstructed the liberty, immunity, and jurisdiction of the church. The result, according to the Council fathers, would be peace in the church.[28]

Focused though they were on the good will of secular rulers, the Tridentine decrees marked a turning point in the history of episcopal tribunals in the sixteenth century and most notably in Lombardy. Here the animating force, as in so many aspects of Tridentine reform, was the tenacious work of Carlo Borromeo, who left his favoured position as cardinal-nephew at Rome in 1565 to assume direct control over the archdiocese of Milan, Italy's largest see. The city's first resident archbishop in eighty years, Borromeo aimed at the complete and radical transformation of the Milanese church into a community dedicated to the honour and service of God. This involved the restoration of episcopal functions to their fullest possible extent.[29] Borromeo's instruments for reform included the seminary, the School of Christian Doctrine, the confessional, the pulpit, and a network of approximately four hundred vicars, visitors, and other officials.[30] In short, he employed all available means for the attainment of his goals, and the most powerful of these were the punitive measures sanctioned by canon law and enforced by the episcopal tribunal. The archbishop's curia was thoroughly reorganized by Borromeo and his chief agents, his vicars general. The vicars general stood at the top of the judicial machinery of the curia, assisted by two lesser vicars, one for criminal and the other for civil cases. These were joined by a procurator (*procuratore del fisco*) who acted as defender of ecclesiastical interests, an auditor who provided assistance, and the chancellors who notarized documents and oversaw proceedings. One of the more contentious elements was the creation of the archbishop's *famiglia armata*, a body of eight constables (*sbirri*) and their head (*bargello*), who assisted in security and in the apprehension and imprisonment of those accused of violating canon law.[31]

The episcopal tribunal gave teeth to Borromeo's project for Tridentine reform. Borromeo's use of canon law and the ecclesiastical courts was especially focused on the clergy. He was intent on enforcing the *privilegium fori* which required that ecclesiastics could be tried only before the ecclesiastical tribunals. He was convinced that the restoration of ecclesiastical discipline was contingent upon a total dependency of the clergy on the authority of the bishop, and that this dependency would not be achieved if the civil power could interfere in the actions of the church. Further, Borromeo claimed sweeping powers for the ecclesiastical tribunal to cite laypersons for judgment. This included not only heresy, matrimonial issues, and questions of morality, but also civil cases regardless of whether the church was acting as plaintiff or as defendant. Thus, he claimed that the ecclesiastical courts could arraign laypersons in civil cases as defendants because there was a Milanese custom of calling laity before the ecclesiastical tribunal (*consuetudo trahendi laicos ad forum ecclesiasticum*), although this went against the general canonical principle that the plaintiff proceed in the court of the defendant (*actor sequitur forum rei*).[32] Borromeo's convictions soon led to a number of conflicts with the Spanish governors and the senate of Milan.

Borromeo's work at Milan began on a positive note. Reports to the court at Madrid indicated that the cardinal was a man of 'intense spirituality and exemplary life' who appeared to favour Spanish interests and who would help the common cause of promoting Catholic reform. King Philip II favoured the religious regeneration of his dominions and on numerous occasions supported the implementation of Tridentine reform and the pastoral activity of his bishops. However, despite Philip's support for Borromeo's goals, the crown was not prepared to allow the archbishop to extend ecclesiastical jurisdiction at the expense of its own rights.[33] As a result, Borromeo's twenty years at Milan were marked by almost constant tensions between ecclesiastical and secular authorities. Two months after Borromeo's arrival, an argument occurred when the governor, Gabriel de la Cueva, duke of Alburquerque, claimed precedence over the archbishop even in religious ceremonies. This was followed by an attempt by the Milanese senate to modify the decrees of the first provincial council, for example, questioning the requirement that all physicians and schoolteachers make a profession of Catholic faith before being able to practice. This intervention was made even after the decrees of the provincial council had been approved by Rome. The crux of the division between Borromeo and the secular government was that Borromeo wanted to revive to the fullest the ecclesiastical courts and the *famiglia armata*. This seemed to signify that the ecclesiastical jurisdiction could function without calling on the help of the secular arm and indeed without having to inform the secular authorities of its activities. Although the Spanish government was also dedicated to furthering the process of Catholic reform, it tended to see Borromeo's claims to independent jurisdiction as an infringement on royal prerogative and as innovations which lacked firm legal or historical precedents.[34] The government held that the cardinal's reforms were too severe and challenged Borromeo's right to maintain an armed police force and the power of the episcopal tribunal to cite and pass sentence against laypersons in civil cases.[35]

Relations between Borromeo and the government were especially tense during the brief period of Luis de Requeséns, who became governor of Milan in 1572 after serving as ambassador at Rome. Requeséns was excommunicated by Borromeo in 1573 after the governor issued an edict limiting the size of the archbishop's *famiglia armata* and restricting the weapons it could employ. Stung by the excommunication, Requeséns questioned Borromeo's loyalty to the Spanish monarchy and expressed suspicion of Milanese lay confraternities, saying that their 20,000 members could become a seditious element in the state. With Philip II's permission, Requeséns issued orders that royal representatives must attend the meetings of confraternities and that confraternity members could not participate in processions with their faces covered.[36] Requeséns soon moved on to assume the governorship of the Spanish Netherlands, absolved from excommunication by Pope Gregory XIII. However, his regulations for confraternities remained in effect.[37] The controversies continued under his successor, Antonio de Guzmán, the marquis of Ayamonte, who served from 1573 to 1580. The old points of contention – the archbishop's *famiglia armata* and the scope of episcopal jurisdiction – continued with new ones added: the right of ecclesiastical authorities to visit pious foundations governed by the laity, whether ecclesiastical immunity covered clergy and their tenants when they ignored secular regulations governing the cultivation of rice, and Borromeo's attempts to prohibit tournaments and dramas on feast days and to remove the governor's seat of honour from the chancel of the cathedral. At Madrid and at Rome Borromeo was accused of excessive rigidity, introducing novelties, and disturbing the public peace.[38]

The year 1579 was critical for Borromeo. At Rome, Pope Gregory XIII renewed negotiations with Spain for a concordat which would encompass all Spanish possessions in Italy. Gregory ordered Borromeo not to attempt any innovations which might jeopardize the negotiations, but the cardinal, goaded by the belligerent actions of the governor and other civic officials of Milan, precipitated a crisis by issuing an edict banning tournaments and other celebrations on Sundays and feast days.[39] The papal court disapproved of Borromeo's action and rumours soon reached Milan that all of his edicts would be suspended. In the spring and summer of 1579 Borromeo's work appeared to be crumbling, and in the fall the cardinal departed for Rome. The results of this trip were the opposite of what his enemies might have hoped. Gregory was won over by the personality and arguments of Borromeo, who returned to Milan in January 1580 with a vote of confidence.[40]

Borromeo, however, remained dissatisfied with the slow pace of negotiations for a concordat. In April the governor, Ayamonte, died, and Borromeo decided to use this occasion to send a personal emissary to Philip II to correct the misrepresentations he believed were being made by royal ministers and to appeal to the conscience of the king, calling for a united effort against the forces undermining morality in the archdiocese. Hence, he was determined to send a member of a religious order, and in April 1580 he selected Carlo Bascapè, then a member of the new Congregation of Clerics Regular of St Paul and known for his exemplary religious life, knowledge of canon law, and familiarity with events in Milan.[41] Cesare Speciano, who was Borromeo's agent in Rome and ironically went on to become one of Bascapè's predecessors as bishop of Novara, questioned the choice, suggesting that any secular priest in the cardinal's entourage might accomplish as much as Bascapè because the Clerics Regular of St Paul were not known in Spain. Speciano thought that, in a spiritual affair such as this, a Capuchin monk would fare better because the order was internationally renowned and because Philip II employed Capuchins on his own secret missions.[42] Borromeo, however, held to his original selection, and in May 1580 Bascapè set out for Spain in the train of the papal legate, Cardinal Alessandro Riario. Bascapè's mission was of utmost secrecy, and Riario especially was not to be informed of its purpose.

Bascapè carried letters from Borromeo and precise instructions on what he was to say to Philip II. Appealing to the 'piety and God-fearing conscience' of the king, he was to inform him that the cardinal wanted only to promote the glory of God and the salvation of souls and did not wish to threaten royal jurisdiction. He was to point out that the majority of the people of Milan sided with Borromeo but that royal ministers, led by Ayamonte, had blocked attempts to prohibit public dancing and games on feast days and had created secular officials to oversee lay confraternities. He was to seek Philip's support against gambling, prostitution, frequenting taverns, and other abuses.[43]

Bascapè had his first interview with the king on 6 August 1580 at Badajoz, where Philip had established the headquarters for his occupation of the kingdom of Portugal, which fell under his rule in that year. Philip received him with courtesy and expressed his good intentions towards the archbishop. Bascapè presented his letters and in a second audience gave his verbal report from the cardinal. Philip then authorized him to continue discussions with the royal confessor, Diego de Chaves. After delays caused by Philip's poor health and the death of his queen, Bascapè received letters to carry to his patron. The contents disappointed Bascapè. Although the king and his confessor expressed a desire to cooperate with the archbishop, they did so in general terms and with the advice that Borromeo adopt a more conciliatory approach, speaking of the need for honest recreation and pointing out that few were called to spiritual perfection.[44]

Borromeo, for his part, was satisfied with the royal letters and awaited proof of the king's good intentions. Bascapè's mission led to a truce in church-state relations at Milan, partly because the new governor was more sympathetic to the cause of religious reform. The last years of Borromeo's life saw what has been called a complete collaboration between secular and spiritual powers in which the influence of the cardinal reached its height.[45] However, the negotiations in Rome for a concordat were abandoned in July 1581, partly because both the Spanish authorities and Borromeo were satisfied with their improved relationship. In effect, the jurisdictional questions remained unresolved.

The truce continued through the episcopate of Gaspare Visconti (r.1585–95), in part because the new archbishop did not press the rights of his tribunal and in part due to the good will of the government. However, the jurisdictional issue raised its head again at the turn of the seventeenth century with the renewal of controversies at Milan, Naples, and Venice. In Lombardy Cardinal Federico Borromeo, archbishop of Milan from 1595 to 1631, engaged in a protracted struggle with the secular government of the duchy. In the process he alienated not only many state officials but also a number of bishops of the province. One of his most prominent critics was Carlo Bascapè, who accused the cardinal of intransigence, lack of leadership, and allowing the jurisdictional struggle to interfere with pastoral care.

When he succeeded Visconti in 1595, Federico Borromeo attempted to reassert ecclesiastical prerogatives. The first issue concerned a point of ceremony already raised by his cousin: Borromeo ordered the governor of Milan, Juan Fernández de Velasco, to remove his throne from its favoured position near the main altar of the cathedral. In 1596 the question of who should pass and enforce legislation against the cultivation of rice in the vicinity of Milan led to a more serious confrontation. When Borromeo excommunicated a magistrate for prosecuting a lay tenant of church property on a charge of illegally sowing rice, Velasco responded with an edict that prescribed the penalties of high treason for anyone guilty of impeding or harming royal jurisdiction. According to Bascapè, who commented on the struggle in his *ad limina* reports to Rome, fear of the edict led notaries, advocates, and even members of the clergy to avoid using ecclesiastical tribunals and instead take their grievances before the secular magistrates.[46] The ensuing controversy lasted for twenty years, but can be divided into two stages. From 1596 to 1600 negotiations failed to remove Velasco's edict, and a series of incidents – among them the invasion of Borromeo's palace by Spanish troops in 1599 – caused church-state relations to deteriorate even more. Federico Borromeo had abandoned Milan in 1597 and for five years remained in self-imposed exile at Rome in an attempt to defend the rights of the church while the papacy negotiated to resolve the matter. In 1600 Velasco suspended his edict and a new governor came to Milan. Don Pedro Enríquez de Acevedo, count of Fuentes, was much more conciliatory and was prepared to collaborate with Borromeo. However, the basic question of whether the ecclesiastical tribunals could prosecute laypersons remained unresolved, and the intransigence of the two parties caused negotiations for a concordat to drag on until 1615.[47] The concordat was a pyrrhic victory for the church. The state recognized ecclesiastical rights to prosecute and sentence laypersons, but abandoned none of its own claims to jurisdiction over church property and tenants, thus leaving the door open for future disagreements.[48]

In the early stages of the controversy Bascapè played a leading role in attempts to attain a settlement. In October 1596 when Borromeo called the bishops of his province to Milan to discuss a common policy, Bascapè was one of two bishops selected to present the church's case to Velasco. His first meetings with the governor, which ended in threats to the bishops, convinced Bascapè of the seriousness of the situation and the threat to ecclesiastical jurisdiction.[49] Among his fears was the belief that public sinners would use the weakness of the episcopal tribunals to return to their old ways.[50] Bascapè decided to pursue a moderate, cautious policy which contrasted sharply with Borromeo's impetuosity. Between 1596 and 1600 Bascapè engaged in a series of skirmishes over the prerogatives of the episcopal tribunal with the magistrates of Novara and the countryside, but he resorted to excommunication on only one occasion. The incident involved the *podestà* (chief magistrate) of the city who was excommunicated after he interfered in a case involving the property of a deceased canon. Even then Bascapè delayed acting as long as possible and managed to settle the matter without outside arbitration. He later stated that the secular authorities asked him to help settle the controversies in Milan, but unfortunately he could not comply.[51]

After 1600 there were signs of a growing rift between Bascapè and Borromeo over the strategy to be followed in negotiations with the state. In his report to Rome (*ad limina apostolorum*) of 1606, Bascapè noted that the rights of the church of Milan were being restored but that fear of a renewal of Velasco's edict still caused lawyers and plaintiffs to avoid using the ecclesiastical tribunals at Novara and other dioceses of the Lombard province.[52] He was convinced that the church must obtain a concordat at all costs to stop the erosion of its power.[53] In 1609, when Federico Borromeo called the seventh provincial council to petition for the canonization of his cousin, Bascapè was part of the party calling for renewing negotiations for a concordat. The provincial council, following the lead of Borromeo and Antonio Seneca, bishop of Anagni and a former vicar general of Milan, opted for presenting a list of ecclesiastical grievances to Pope Paul V (r. 1605–21) and recommended no further action. In the meantime, Bascapè and Giulio Careta, the bishop of Casale (r. 1594–1615), were chosen to travel to Rome to request the canonization of Carlo Borromeo and the implementation of the decrees of the council. Both bishops used the opportunity to lobby for the renewal of negotiations for a concordat.[54] On 14 November 1609 Careta wrote to Borromeo that he had spoken to the Spanish ambassador about the desirability of opening negotiations and that he had received a favourable response. In Careta's opinion, more was being lost to the secular authorities every day 'in such a way that within a few years we will have no other jurisdiction concerning laypersons than to celebrate the Mass for them and administer the Holy Sacraments to them, it being the characteristic of evil to always grow with time if remedy is not provided.'[55] Bascapè for his part tried to persuade Paul V to send letters to Madrid requesting a reopening of negotiations. Writing to Paolo Emilio Sfondrati, the cardinal-bishop of Cremona, in late February 1610, he stated that the recent incidents and troubles were like weeds which must be pulled even if they could not be completely eradicated. And to the argument that royal ministers would not honour a concordat, he replied that they would leave much less to the church if agreements were lacking. He concluded that negotiations would only become more difficult because the lay officials went from day to day enjoying the powers that they claimed and establishing precedents against the rights of the church.[56]

Antonio Seneca, when he heard of the proposed overture, advised Borromeo that such a step would be a 'mortal blow' (*una botta mortale*) to the bishops' aspirations because asking the king of Spain to send personnel for negotiations would oblige the bishops to grant concessions when the time was not ripe for negotiations. It would be better to let the king take the first step.[57] When Bascapè asked Borromeo to resume negotiations, the cardinal did nothing. Bascapè left Rome not knowing whether the Pope had written to Madrid, with the bitter feeling that Borromeo had done nothing to defend ecclesiastical jurisdiction.[58]

Shortly after his belated initiative of 1609–10, Bascapè began his commentary on the first eighteen years of the episcopate of Federico Borromeo. In it he presented a partisan account of the jurisdictional struggles. The main targets of his attack were the royal ministers, led by Velasco, who were contemptuous of the church's jurisdictional powers and censures and who ignored signs of divine disfavour towards Milan. However, Bascapè also criticized the archbishop of Milan, suggesting that Federico had engaged in the controversy too quickly but then allowed it to drag on by refusing to deal with Velasco, being suspicious of papal negotiators, and failing to act in 1609–10.[59] Federico's actions, Bascapè continued, were contrary to the example of Carlo Borromeo, who settled such controversies quickly: when the now-sainted archbishop faced an edict similar to Velasco's in 1569 he obtained its removal in three months.[60] According to Bascapè, the prolonged controversy of 1596 to 1615 weakened the ecclesiastical tribunals and led to moral decline at Milan. Gambling, drunkenness, luxury, assaults, and thefts – always alien to Milanese decorum – became frequent and serious problems. Borromeo's self-imposed exile at Rome from 1597–1601 did little to settle the controversy and led to a steady decline of clerical discipline. The Milanese church – which had flourished under Carlo Borromeo – was reduced to a miserable state.[61]

Historians of the episcopate of Federico Borromeo have placed considerable weight on Bascapè's commentary and have accused the cardinal not only of intransigence and a lack of leadership but also of failing to subordinate the question of ecclesiastical jurisdiction to the more important end of pastoral care.[62] However, Bascapè's argument that Borromeo failed to act in 1609 and 1610 was not completely accurate. The cardinal, like Bascapè, was hoping for a concordat, disagreeing with him mainly on matters of timing and strategy. While Bascapè may have been correct in suggesting that Borromeo was intransigent, he might also have been more understanding of Federico's problems as the successor of Carlo Borromeo, whose force of personality and reputation for saintliness helped achieve the truce of 1580 and were difficult for any successor to match. Finally, the younger Borromeo appears to have learned from his experiences of the late 1590s and developed a more tactful and successful approach in dealing with the Spanish authorities. In 1606–7 tensions with a Spanish visitor to Milan, Felipe de Haro, were resolved through moderation and compromise rather than confrontation.[63]

Bascapè's comments that the jurisdictional controversy led to a decline in discipline and morals must be taken with even greater care. Members of the hierarchy frequently resorted to this line of argument during such struggles. The closest supporters of Federico Borromeo took up the theme in 1599 when they presented a polemic at Madrid that described the deterioration of religion in Milan following the opening of the controversy. The city council of Milan reacted immediately by asking Borromeo to explain the accusations, and the cardinal meekly replied that the polemic referred not to the citizens in general but to a few malcontents who threatened to undermine the morals of the entire society. Not satisfied, the city sent a special ambassador to Pope Clement VIII to protest its good faith and conduct.[64]

The activity of the bishop's tribunal of Novara in the period 1563 to 1615 was part of a greater trend for the church to reassert its authority over clergy and laity alike. This trend was in evidence at least since the fifth Lateran Council of 1512–17, and achieved its full force with the closing sessions (1562–3) of the Council of Trent and with the coming of the zealous, some would say fanatical, Carlo Borromeo to Milan in 1565. It led to a number of clashes with the government of Milan, which were resolved by the concordat of 1615. The jurisdictional controversy posed a threat to the independent action of the church and revealed the difficulties involved in maintaining the prerogatives established by Borromeo. How it affected questions such as clerical immunity and the power of the ecclesiastical courts over laypersons would be reflected in the activities of the bishop's tribunal of Novara.

3 The Bishop's Tribunal and the Disciplining of the Clergy, 1563–1615

Tribunal Objectives, Procedures, and Punishments

In the late sixteenth and early seventeenth centuries the reform of the clergy was one of the principle goals set by the Council of Trent and the provincial councils of Milan. The bishops of Novara approached this objective in a number of ways: by holding diocesan synods, by issuing edicts governing clerical behaviour, and by founding and developing seminaries. The objective was to set the clergy apart from the rest of society as exemplars of a good and holy life. The final weapon in the arsenal of the bishops was the episcopal tribunal, deployed to keep the clergy on the straight path through correction and, if necessary, intimidation. A surprising percentage of Novarese priests came before the tribunal at one time or another in this period, charged with a wide variety of violations of the code of clerical conduct. The records of the bishop's tribunal say more about the objectives and priorities of the hierarchy than they do about the views and practices of the rank and file of the clergy, the majority of whom were native to the diocese and similar to their families and parishioners in interests and lifestyle. The tribunal devoted a considerable amount of time and effort to curbing the sexual lapses of members of the clergy, but was focused on other issues as well. Most notable were crimes of violence, which the church claimed to prosecute on its own because of the *privilegium fori*, the principle that the clergy were to be tried only before the ecclesiastical courts. After these were infractions such as negligence in the care of souls, conduct deemed detrimental to the clerical estate, thefts, suspicion of heresy, and the practice of magic, none of which occupied as much of the tribunal's time as matters of sex and violence. The penalties ranged from penances and fines to suspension from the celebration of Mass and deprivation of benefice. In the majority of cases the punishments were lenient and many sentences simply absolved ecclesiastics as a way of bringing closure to a trial. Whether acting through the confessional or the tribunal, Christianity places a premium on clemency and forgiveness. As a result, many priests managed to avoid the worst of the punishments and to continue in the care of souls for decades despite repeated, persistent offences.

In the half-century following the closure of the Council of Trent in 1563, improving the calibre of the clergy and especially of parish priests was the primary concern of the ecclesiastical hierarchy. At Novara, as elsewhere in Italy, efforts were made to mould the secular clergy into a strong cadre for advancing the Catholic Church. The Council of Trent, in underlining the centrality of clerical reform, emphasized the role played by the clergy as examples to the Christian laity: by their speech, attire, and mannerisms, they were to demonstrate only what was serious, moderate, and devout.[1] The clergy were to be professionals dedicated to the care of souls and set apart from other people not only by their education, orders, and the rule of celibacy, but also by their clothing, devout lifestyle, and avoidance of secular pursuits and occupations.[2]

In the period 1563 to 1615 the spirit of reform was at its height at Novara. Bishops Giovanni Antonio Cardinal Serbelloni (r. 1560–74), Romulo Archinto (r. 1574–6), Francesco Bossi (r. 1579–84), Cesare Speciano (r. 1584–91), and especially Carlo Bascapè (r. 1593–1615) were dedicated to implementing the decrees of the Council of Trent and of the provincial councils of Milan, to which Novara was tied as the western neighbour of the Lombard archdiocese. The reform of the Novarese clergy was fostered in a variety of ways. The bishops held six synods between 1568 and 1615 to inspect and direct the clergy, issued edicts devoted to the theme of the dignity of the priesthood, and conducted visitations of the parishes of the diocese.[3] The tenor of their demands on the life of the clergy can be grasped from the decree 'On the Life and Honour of Clerics' (*De vita et honestate clericorum*), which Cardinal Serbelloni issued in his synod of 1568. The decree began by exhorting the clergy not to follow the way of life of the rank and file of the faithful but to seek a more elevated life, separated from the community, 'never seeking their own things but the things of Jesus Christ, since they themselves should be the light of the world, the salt of the earth, and the city set on a mountain.' They were to flee the vices of the flesh and cultivate the virtues of piety, diligence, charity, gentleness, humility, justice, and detachment from the riches of the world. They were to recite the canonical hours each day diligently and prayerfully and to avoid occasions of sin and scandal: banquets, drunken singing, public spectacles, hunting, taverns, dances, and familiarity with women. They were always to keep their hair properly tonsured so that they could be easily distinguished from laypersons, and wear the biretta and clerical dress, 'an outer robe which is closed at the neck and descends down at least to the shin or what is more decent down to the ankles.' Finally, all priests and clerics were required to attend the main Mass and vespers at the cathedral or at the rural parish churches under threat of penalty if they missed Mass and vespers on three consecutive occasions.[4] The synod also prescribed the books for the clergy to keep close at hand: Old and New Testaments, the decrees of Trent, the *Manipulus curatorum*, the summas for confessors of St Antoninus of Florence, Angelo Carletti da Chiavasso, Silvestro Mazzolini da Prierio, and Bartolomeo Fumi, as well as short works by saints Augustine, Leo, Cyprian, John Chrysostom, and Bernard.[5] Similar injunctions were repeated by Romulo Archinto in his synod of 1576, with additions that reflected new decrees of the provincial councils of Milan. New, for example, was a requirement that all priests attend monthly congregations held in their regions to discuss cases of conscience or points of moral theology to be employed by confessors. This was to be supervised by the rural vicars who were to send reports to the city. Another section prohibited clerical involvement in secular professions and specified that no priest was to serve as a notary or as an agent for the defence in a court of law, or to enter the service of a layperson no matter what the layperson's estate.[6]

Clearly, the vision set out by the bishops was to have the clergy set apart from the laity and serving as examples for them. Their prescriptions for the clergy were no different from those adopted by dioceses throughout Italy. Whether the clergy would accept the orders from above remained open to some question. The reformed lifestyle envisaged for them was austere at times, especially some of the more restrictive rules governing clothing, visiting taverns, engaging in the more common pastimes enjoyed by their friends and families, and avoiding familiarity with women, who were, after all, half of their parishioners. The records of the Novarese episcopal tribunal provide evidence of the resistance of individual priests to orders from above, and at least one event during the episcopate of Carlo Bascapè suggests the possibility of a more organized opposition. In 1600 the canons and parish priests of the city appealed to Rome against an order of the bishop that all priests hire a cleric in minor orders to assist at Mass. Although Bascapè dramatized the appeal as an attack on the entire reform, the majority of parish priests simply could not afford to hire clerics, and the edict remained unenforceable in most parishes.[7] Bascapè, who enjoyed neither the power base nor the self-confidence of Carlo Borromeo when it came to dealing with Rome, was constantly on guard against complaints concerning his governance of the diocese. It was also telling that one of his reasons for not calling a diocesan synod between 1598 and 1615, the year of his death, was concern that seditious members of the clergy might use this as an occasion to protest against his programs. This opinion, however, was expressed in his last published work, the *Commentarii canonici*, and may have been more a theoretical reflection than a deep-seated fear on his part.[8] He also seemed to have doubted the need for more synods to inspect the clergy and to draft new decrees. For him the decrees of Trent and of the provincial councils provided perfect guidelines for the diocesan reform.

The bishops also laid the foundation for the systematic training of priests establishing a seminary at Novara in 1565 and minor seminaries at Varallo Sesia and the Island of San Giulio on Lake Orta. The three small institutions had little impact on the clergy of the diocese before the end of the sixteenth century. Initial progress was painfully slow because the clergy resisted efforts to impose a tax on their benefices. When Carlo Bascapè came to the diocese in 1593 there were only thirty-three students in the three inadequately funded institutions. Expanding the system of seminaries and securing stable revenues was a major objective during his twenty-three-year episcopate. By giving the main seminary of Novara the revenues of 'simple benefices' – smaller endowments originally intended for the maintenance of clerics in minor orders – he provided an income of 1200 scudi per year by the time of his death, meeting the target prescribed for the diocese by the provincial councils. He also added a fourth seminary at Santa Cristina in Borgomanero for older clerics to study cases of conscience, placing this institution under the control of the oblates of San Gaudenzio and San Carlo, a newly founded association of priests dedicated to serving bishop and diocese, created in imitation of the oblates of Sant'Ambrogio at Milan. By 1615 the majority of candidates for the priesthood received at least part of their instructions while attending one of the diocesan institutions.[9] Here boys and young men lived under the surveillance of their rectors and prefects and received training in grammar and letters, the Roman catechism, singing, the rites of the church, and the study of cases of conscience. Emphasis was placed on practical training in the areas most useful for the care of souls.[10] The Novarese seminaries of this time, like those of other Italian dioceses, did not include sufficient spaces for all the clerics of the diocese. The main seminary in the city typically housed around thirty students, most of whom were required to pay three and a half scudi a month for their expenses to supplement seminary revenues. The seminaries of San Giulio and Santa Cristina each boarded eighteen students in 1617, with the former focusing on younger clerics and the study of grammar and the latter on older clerics and cases of conscience.[11] The seminaries were not the only pathway to ordination to the priesthood. They existed beside a variety of other more or less formal possibilities for instruction: colleges of the religious orders inside and outside the diocese, grammar schools, and study at the side of parish priests, who employed a variety of books for training in grammar, ceremonies, cases of conscience, and other aspects of the priestly profession. Nevertheless, by the end of Bascapè's episcopate the seminaries of the diocese were, by the standards of sixteenth- and early seventeenth-century Italy, relatively advanced and stable, surpassed by the seminaries of few dioceses, most notably, those of the archdiocese of Milan.[12]

After the seminary, clerics could expect a further screening process before appointment to the care of souls. Candidates for parishes in episcopal control were examined on a competitive basis, in a process referred to as the *concursus*, which involved testimonials of good behaviour from parish priests and seminary rectors and examination of knowledge of Catholic doctrine and cases of conscience. Candidates for parishes in the control of the cathedral chapters or of lay patrons were also subject to examination by the bishop. Once he obtained a parish, a priest was expected to shepherd his parishioners by celebrating Mass on Sundays, feast days, and weekdays, preaching and holding vespers on Sundays and feast days, hearing confessions, ministering to the sick, supervising catechism lessons for children, monitoring the conduct of lay confraternities, and keeping registers of baptisms, marriages, and the performance of the annual obligations of confession and communion. If their parishes were in the countryside, as the vast majority were, priests were required to gather each month at a designated parish to be inspected by the rural vicar and to study cases of conscience with their confrères. They were to maintain the decorum and morals now demanded of members of their estate: wearing proper clerical garb, refraining from bearing arms and from acts of violence, avoiding taverns and gambling, and above all avoiding any suspicious contact with women. Those who fell short of the standards for personal conduct or for the care of souls were to be admonished to mend their ways by the rural vicars, the diocesan vicars general, and ultimately the bishop.

Failing correction, the ultimate instrument of discipline and control was the episcopal tribunal. In the period of Tridentine reform, the bishops of Novara used the bishop's tribunal to control and intimidate wayward and at times rebellious members of the clergy. In his correspondence, Bascapè frequently spoke of the need to make examples of clergy guilty of public sins. For example, on 17 September 1594 he wrote to Hieronimo Gritti, an advocate who assisted the tribunal, about the need to set an example in the case of Canon Ludovico Tornielli of the cathedral of San Gaudenzio because his case was public and also for 'other circumstances,' which might have had to do with the power of the noble Tornielli family at Novara. Tornielli had been prosecuted in the early 1580s for his liaison with a married woman, and despite Bascapè's comment to Gritti, avoided prosecution in 1594, possibly because he convinced the bishop and vicar general that his sin had been kept secret.[13] If so, he probably escaped with a penance or small fine.

How well the episcopal tribunal fared in achieving its goals is one thing that may be studied in its files. Although the records of the tribunal cover most of the years between 1563 and 1614, they are incomplete and uneven. The first volume to survive is a register of accusations (*denuncie*) from 1563 to 1564, the early years of Cardinal Serbelloni's episcopate and the time of the closure of the Council of Trent. In these early years it is not certain that the vicar general had the opportunity to follow up on the accusations by questioning all of the witnesses and arraigning the accused. The volumes from the period 1576 to 1591 (*informationum, criminalia*) include accusations, the testimony of witnesses, and some interrogations of the accused. Again, it is not known whether all of those accused were arraigned and prosecuted by the court. It is only from 1593 to 1614 that the interrogations of those actually arraigned (the *libri constitutorum*) have survived in a consistent fashion in an almost complete series (1593–8 and 1601–14). These are supplemented by interrogations of the accused in matters of faith (*in causis fidei*) from 1596 to 1603 and from 1609 to 1614, and a book of sentences from 1591 to 1598. Despite the gaps, most notably 1565 to 1575 and 1599 to 1600, and the existence of sentences for only eight years, the volumes provide a solid basis for observations about the tribunal's interventions in the life of the clergy of the diocese.

A number of observations can be made about the work of the episcopal tribunal of Novara. First, its activities are more indicative of the priorities and goals of the bishops than they are of the incidence of clerical crime and lay sin in the diocese. That is, while the tribunal's activity to some degree reflected problems among the clergy and laity of the diocese, it was a clearer index of where the hierarchy felt it must act given the limitations of time and resources. Second, the records of the tribunal give some indication of the effectiveness of judicial intervention on the part of the episcopal curia. In public, certainly, the hierarchy adopted a tough stance in dealing with clerical, and for that matter lay, misbehaviour. As many cases demonstrated, it could be both expensive and painful to be caught up in the mesh of the early modern legal system. On the other hand, there are also many examples of priests and clerics who sought and obtained forgiveness and clemency from the bishop and his curia, allowing them to survive for decades as parish priests. Third, in the light of the jurisdictional controversies which occupied so much of the energy of church and state in this period, the records help answer other questions, such as whether the Milanese state respected the principle of clerical immunity from prosecution by the secular courts and the degree to which the ecclesiastical hierarchy used their courts to correct what they perceived to be instances of lay misconduct. Fourth, although the perspective of the tribunal records was still very much a view of the diocese from the top down, they do include the words and reactions of plaintiffs, witnesses, and the accused, and in this way provide a window to view the attitudes, desires, and fears of both clergy and laity.

The great majority of the clergy, as high as 90 per cent, were from the diocese and more specifically from the regions and even the villages that they served. Although there were exceptions, they tended to be the sons of neither the nobility nor the very poor, but of the middling ranks of the rural society from which they came. They were the sons of merchants, shopkeepers, advocates, notaries, artisans, and farmers.[14] In other words, they came from sectors of society that had the desire and the means to provide an education and a patrimony for their sons. Many of their families had sufficient funds to endow either a lifelong chaplaincy or at least a number of masses for the dead. As an alternative, many of their family members belonged to confraternities which were eager to establish masses and chaplaincies for their group. The priests had close ties with their communities and intense involvement with their families. Most had a hand in administering family properties, their patrimony. A good number, including many chaplains and priests not involved in the care of souls, continued to live in family homes. Although some of them shared, to an extent at least, in the reforming zeal of the hierarchy, for many the legislation of Trent and the provincial councils must have seemed an alien law, imposed by bishops and officials whose origins were outside their diocese. Their acts of resistance and petty rebellion were chronicled in the files of the episcopal tribunal.

In all, over 550 cases came before the tribunal, approximately 350 of which dealt with the members of the secular or diocesan clergy and 200 with laypersons. Nine cases concerned members of the regular clergy, friars, and nuns. Because of their small numbers, cases involving friars and nuns have been included with those involving the secular clergy in the following charts. The cases included four nuns in all and an undetermined number of friars, the majority accused of violating rules of cloister when visiting nuns.

Chart 3.1 records the cases brought before the bishop's tribunal of Novara by the lowest common denominator of persons accused. As noted, there is a divide in the statistics in the sense that in the first half of the chart, 1563 to 1590, the numbers are based on denunciations made and testimony taken. In all but a few cases, interrogations of the accused are lacking. The second half of the chart, from 1593 to 1614, consists exclusively of cases where the accused was arraigned and interrogated.

Despite the irregularities, several observations can be made. There were, for example, several notable spikes in tribunal activity. The first occurred in 1563–4 when Cesare Andena, vicar general of Cardinal Serbelloni, heard numerous complaints concerning clergy and laity of the diocese. There were twenty accusations made against priests and clerics and nine against laypersons in 1563, and eleven made against clergymen and four against laypersons in the partial year January to August 1564.[15] Among the denunciations, thirty-two of the forty-four persons

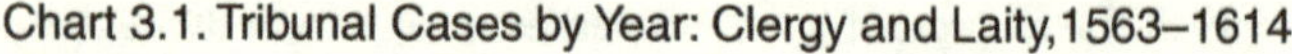
Chart 3.1. Tribunal Cases by Year: Clergy and Laity, 1563–1614

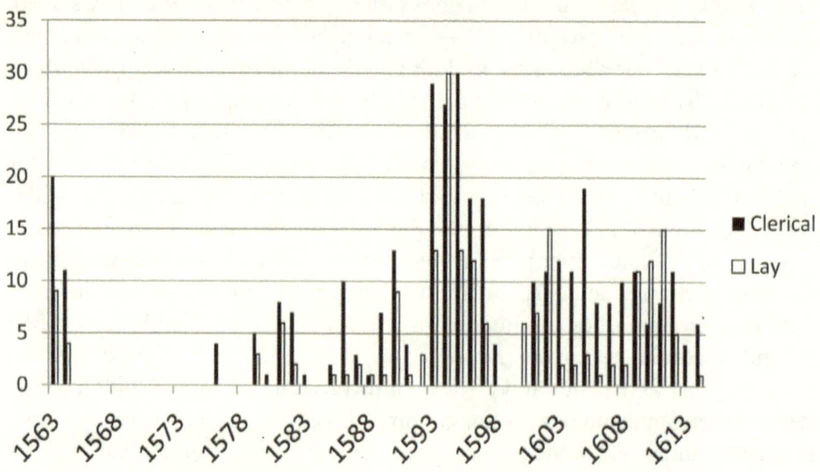

were from the city of Novara and towns in the Lombard plain such as Cerano and Sillavengo, suggesting that at this stage in its history the reach of the bishop's tribunal, which was not yet supported by a network of rural vicars, did not extend far beyond the city itself. Seven cases came from the central towns of the diocese such as Invorio and Oleggio and only three from mountain areas such as the Pieve Vergonte and the Vigezzo valley, with none from the region of lakes Orta and Maggiore. The same trend continued in the period 1576 to 1590 (see table 3.1).

Two reasons, not mutually exclusive, can be offered for the high number of accusations made in 1563–4. First, Serbelloni and Andena were eager to begin implementing disciplinary measures during the months when the Council of Trent was in its closing sessions. In August 1562 Andena issued a series of edicts for the reform of the clery and of the liturgy.[16] This was followed by measures to enforce such matters as the observance of the cloister of nuns. Second, the level of activity may have reflected a degree of pent-up frustration in the people of the city and its hinterland, possibly due to a lack of effectiveness on the part of the episcopal curia in earlier years. At least one of the complainants, Giovanni Maria de Ploto of Novara, alleged in March 1563 that Paolo de Barengo, curate of San Paolo at Novara, had maintained an adulterous relationship with his estranged wife for four years despite frequent complaints to Serbelloni's predecessor.[17] How effective Andena was in responding to the denunciations and complaints remains open to question given the fact that Serbelloni himself did not reside in the diocese for extended periods of time but was occupied on missions for the

Chart 3.2. Clergy Accused by Year

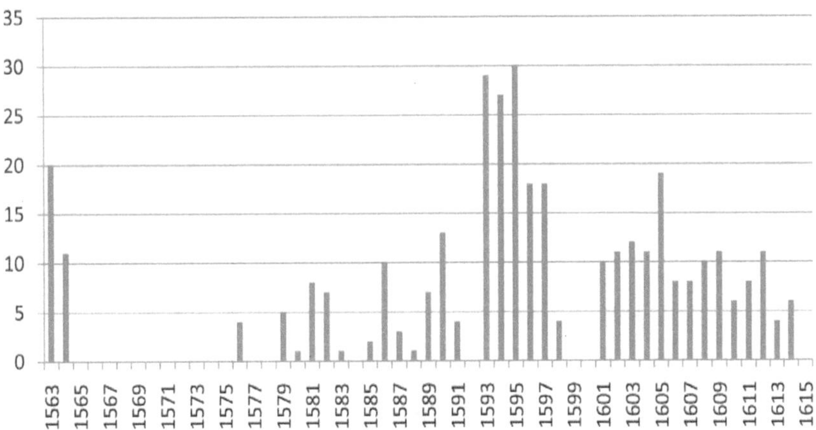

Holy See. A number of incidents demonstrate that Andena and his agents had difficulty establishing their authority. In April 1563, when Giovanni Antonio de Vigno, from the household of the episcopal jailer, confronted several Franciscan friars from the monastery of San Quirico who were visiting the nuns of Santa Barbara in violation of an episcopal edict, the friars responded with obscene gestures and refused to leave. When their prior and sub-prior arrived on the scene they only added to Vigno's misery by allegedly saying: 'The vicar does not command friars and we would prefer to renounce the faith sooner than obey him.'[18] The friars continued to visit Santa Barbara, resulting in a new denunciation in July.[19] Laypersons could be equally obstinate. In November 1563, when Giovanni Ambrogio de Scolari, the episcopal jailer, was sent to question Margarita, the wife of Giovanni Battista Ballosi of Caltignaca who was estranged from her spouse and living with another man, he returned with the message that Margarita absolutely refused to return to her husband.[20]

The second spike in tribunal activity occurred in the years 1593 to 1595 when Carlo Bascapè became bishop. A collaborator of Carlo Borromeo, archbishop of Milan, Bascapè burned with a desire to reform the diocese as demonstrated by his efforts to improve the system of seminaries. In the early years of his episcopate, the total number of processes initiated against clergy and laity peaked at forty-two in 1593, fifty-seven in 1594, and forty-three in 1595, before declining to thirty in 1596 and twenty-four in 1597. In the first five years of Bascapè's episcopate, an average of twenty-four ecclesiastics were arraigned and interrogated each year, as demonstrated by chart 3.2.

Charts 3.1 and 3.2 also demonstrate a notable decline in cases during the period 1601–14, when the average annual number of ecclesiastics and laypersons arraigned fell to approximately fifteen, with slightly fewer than ten prosecutions of ecclesiastics each year. The reasons for the decline are not clear, but one factor might have been the distractions created for the bishop and his curia by the jurisdictional struggles with the secular government and by the frequent trips Bascapè was forced to make to Milan and to Rome after 1600. More probable, perhaps, is that after the initial rush to prosecute offending ecclesiastics, a time consuming process which did not always enjoy immediate success, the curia's zeal for judicial action may have flagged. Limitations in the number of personnel, both in the curia and on the ground level of the parishes, and the possibility of appeal to tribunals outside the diocese would have contributed to this. The vicars general and their assistants were aggressive in prosecuting the wayward in the first years of Bascapè's episcopate, to the point that Bascapè himself seems to have felt that his first vicar general, Ludovico Boido of Pavia, had been harsh in dealing with the clergy, an issue he raised when dismissing Boido in 1594.[21] The level of tribunal activity was maintained by Girolamo Settala in the first year of his tenure as vicar general, but declined in 1596 and 1597, as noted above. A further decline followed under Orazio Besozzo, vicar general from 1598 to 1605, and the series of vicars general who replaced him.

During Bascapè's episcopate the reach of the tribunal extended to every corner of the diocese as the curia benefited from the newly elaborated network of rural vicars. As table 3.1 demonstrates, in the five-year intervals beginning in 1590 and ending in 1614, there was a greater balance among cases arising from the plains area of the diocese and the outlying areas of centre, lakes, and mountains.

During Bascapè's episcopate cases before the tribunal reflected the spread of the clergy through the diocese. Although statistics for the total number of secular priests are not available for the 1590s and early 1600s, they are available for the years 1616–18, as indicated in table 3.2.[22] The 'census' of 1616–18 does not include tonsured clerics or clerics up to and including the order of deacon because they are not always included in the acts of visitation.

The 350 cases in which the bishop's tribunal dealt with the clergy included only approximately 275 individuals because the number of repeat offenders was relatively high. Some priests and clerics appeared before the tribunal on as many as four or five occasions as the curia tracked their activity over a long period of time. Of the approximately 275 clergy accused before the tribunal at one time or another, 134 (almost a half) were directly involved in the care of souls (118 curates or parish priests, 14 vice-curates or temporary replacements, and 2 coadjutors or assistants). Over one-third of the 134 parish priests and vice-curates were prosecuted on two or more occasions.[23] Almost one-quarter, 61 of

Table 3.1. Cases of clergy and religious by region

Years	Plains	Centre	Lakes	Mountains
1560–4	25	4	0	2
1575–9	5	2	1	1
1580–4	9	3	2	1
1585–9	16	5	1	1
1590–4	22	16	18	13
1595–9	18	12	21	18
1600–4	10	4	11	17
1605–9	16	9	9	22
1610–14	10	5	9	11

Table 3.2. Novarese priests by region, 1616–18

Region	Curates	Other Priests	Total
Lombard Plain	72	81	153
Centre Region	57	36	93
Lakes	75	43	118
Mountains	104	17	121
Total	308	177	485

the 275 accused, were described as chaplains or simply as priests. Among this group, 16 were prosecuted on more than one occasion.[24] Among the remaining accused, 32 were canons of Novara and of the collegiate churches at Isola, Gozzano, and other towns of the diocese, and 41 were clerics who had received ecclesiastical tonsure or one of the orders up to and including that of deacon.[25]

The high incidence of repeat prosecutions may be interpreted in a number of ways. First, they are indicative of the efforts of the bishops and their vicars general to use the tribunal as a method of disciplining the clergy. Their attention focused especially on the parish clergy who were at the heart of the religious life of the diocese and the intermediaries between the hierarchy and the people. Second, despite threats of punishment, the bishops were prepared to temper the severity of the tribunal by responding to appeals for clemency and by mitigating punishments. While it was rare for one of the accused to confess to the more serious charges – it was so much better, it seemed, to plead innocence or at least ignorance – there was always the possibility of a private, off-the-record confession to the vicar general or the bishop, an early modern, ecclesiastical version of the plea bargain. The bishop, as loving pastor, often extended clemency, especially when heartfelt promises of good behaviour were given. In the case of parish priests, the willingness of the ecclesiastical superiors to forgive also reflected the shortage of suitable candidates for the care of souls, especially in the mountainous regions of the diocese, a matter long bemoaned by Bascapè and his successors.[26] This shortage allowed priests who were chronic offenders, at least in the eyes of the hierarchy, to continue in parish work despite repeat offences. As well, it was difficult in the late sixteenth and early seventeenth centuries to remove a parish priest from office. A parish benefice was not, strictly speaking, a piece of property owned by a curate, but it did involve the lifelong right to parish revenues arising from lands, buildings, tithes, and donations arising from the administration of the sacraments. A priest could be deprived of benefice only for reasons clearly defined by canon law.[27] The possibility of appeal to Rome, to Milan, or to the tribunals of other neighbouring dioceses could cause delays in the legal process and added expense for the Novarese curia. Finally, the high incidence of trials and repeat offenders underscored the degree to which the clergy were part of the parish communities which they served. Although parish priests and chaplains might perform their basic duties and from time to time demonstrate feelings of intense devotion, many did not share the concern of the reforming hierarchy that visiting taverns, playing cards, and mingling with women were vices which must be eradicated. Nor were they as avid as their superiors in calling to task the laity of their parishes for sins such as concubinage and usury, especially when the accused were the more powerful or belligerent members of their parishes.[28] As secular priests they were allowed to possess property and required to monitor the flow of parish revenues. It was hardly surprising that they shared the same desires and emotions as their flocks when it came to possessions and concern for their future from a worldly perspective.

It is possible to form a rough estimate of the proportion of Novarese clergy drawn into the net of the ecclesiastical tribunal. The processes conducted during Bascapè's episcopate, the period when the tribunal was at its most active and its records the most complete, resulted in the arraignment of approximately 150 priests and clerics on at least one occasion each. Approximately one hundred of the priests arraigned during Bascapè's years were directly involved in the care of souls as curates, vice-curates, and coadjutors. The total number of priests in the diocese was approximately 450 at any one time, with 485 appearing in the 'census' data of 1616–18. Priests engaged in the care of souls numbered approximately 300 in any one year, with 308 appearing in the 1616–18 visitations. However, the figures 300 and 450 cannot be used as baselines for numbers of parish priests and total priests because the turnover of priests during the twenty-three-year episcopate of Bascapè added substantially to the numbers of priests serving in the diocese. Advanced age and mortality meant that relatively few priests lived in the diocese through the entire period 1593 to 1615. For example, there were eight parish priests and twelve other priests in the plains vicariate of Trecate when Bascapè visited in 1594. Of these, one was aged seventy-five and eight were between forty-one and fifty-seven years of age. When Cardinal Taverna visited the vicariate in 1617, only six of the original twenty remained. In the vicariate of Oleggio, five parish priests and seven chaplains were named in 1595, two of them in their sixties. Only two remained in 1618, although it is possible that some of the chaplains moved on to other regions. In the Antigorio valley, there were seven parish priests, one vice-curate, and one chaplain in 1596, the majority in their mid to late twenties. Six were still in the vicariate during the visit of 1616. If the mortality or attrition rate was as high as this sampling suggests, with forty-one total priests reduced to fourteen, or by roughly two-thirds, it can be argued that there were approximately 750 priests in the diocese during the course of Bascapè's episcopate, with approximately 500 serving as curates. Therefore the 100 parish priests and 50 other priests arraigned during this period was roughly one-fifth of the total number serving in the diocese. Priests who were accused of serious breaches of the regulations were a minority among the Novarese clergy, but a sizeable minority.

By the 1580s, and certainly during the episcopate of Bascapè, priests and clerics denounced to the bishop's tribunal were at least potentially subject to a full legal process, up to and including the passing of sentence. Accusations were received, witnesses interrogated, and the accused were cited to appear at Novara before the vicar general and the prosecutor of the diocese, accompanied by the bishop's chancellor who recorded the proceedings. The accused (*constitutus*) appeared either of his or her volition (*sponte*) or under guard from the episcopal jail (*eductus e carceribus*). During his tenure, Bascapè frequently called upon local secular officials to assist his rural vicars in the gathering of evidence and with the loan of soldiers to apprehend the accused.[29] In all cases the accused was interrogated without the benefit of having legal counsel in attendance, and often without seeing the specific charges against himself or herself. These were only revealed during the opening rounds of questioning. In serious cases involving crimes such as homicide or entrenched sexual activity by a priest or cleric, the interrogation of the accused often included torture. The same was true in cases of faith such as heresy, magic, or witchcraft, in which cases the inquisitor of Novara was also as a rule in attendance. Torture was employed to obtain confessions when there was strong evidence against the accused. From time to time it was also used to verify the testimony of the person making an accusation. At Novara it was administered in the episcopal jail in the form of the strappado (*la corda*), in which the victim's hands were tied behind his or her back and he or she was elevated by a rope attached to the hands and arms.[30] In the period from 1563 to 1614, torture was employed in at least thirty-six cases, twenty-one involving members of the clergy: sixteen different priests and one cleric. All but three of those on record were from the time of Bascapè, which is not surprising since it was in his years that the interrogations of the accused are consistently available.

In all cases but one, torture lasted approximately fifteen minutes, the length of time needed to recite the *Miserere* (Psalm 50), and the accused maintained their innocence. The exception occurred in April and June 1609 when Giovanni Anselmo, curate of Balmuccia, and Magdalena de Marinero were forced to confess that they had sexual relations. What may have increased the ardour of the tribunal in this case was the fact that the bishop's jailer, acting as agent of the court, had surprised the two together in the priest's house at five in the morning. Magdalena, who claimed that she was a virgin and ignorant of sexual matters, was tortured for three-quarters of an hour with her interrogators raising her several times to increase the pain. She suffered the added humiliation of having her hair shorn by her male captors because of fear that witches held in the jail at that time might have given her a charm or spell to help her resist the pain. In the end she confessed only to sleeping with Anselmo and naively causing him to spill his seed by touching him. Ultimately her testimony differed from that of Anselmo, also checked for magical talismans, who confessed after being suspended three times over the course of an hour. He admitted to having sexual relations with Magdalena on a number of occasions in his house and in the surrounding fields. When asked to verify his confession the next morning – a practice typical of tribunals of the day – he recanted part of his testimony, saying that the couple had not had sex in the open fields.[31] The fact that the tribunal did not return to Magdalena to expand on her confession suggests that it was more concerned with the conduct and punishment of the priest than with those of his alleged lover.

When the interrogations were completed, the accused had the right to present his or her defence. This usually involved calling witnesses who supported the version of events offered by the accused or vouched for his or her good character. Thus, on 10 February 1590, Bernardino Baldano of Marano in the vicariate of Varallo Pombia appeared before the tribunal to answer questions about his curate, Tomasso Lazarini. He declared that he was asked to testify by Lazarini's brother, Giovanni Pietro, although he was not himself related to the accused and did not know the charges against him. He stated that as far as he knew, Lazarini always attended to the care of souls and took the sacraments to the sick. He knew that he carried a short sword (*storta*) but only for his defence and to harm no one.[32] On 23 January 1591 Lazarini was sentenced to a fine of ten scudi – to be paid to the nuns of the convent of Sant'Agostino at Novara – for carrying weapons and for negligence in the care of souls. A number of parishioners were said to have died without the sacraments. But these were probably the least serious of the charges against him. He was released from accusations of incest with his sister-in-law, burning the house and vines of one Battista Adotati, and demanding money for the administration of the sacraments.[33]

In the period 1591–8, when the tribunal was in its most active phase and when the book of sentences is available, only a third of the cases concluded in sentences. Although some of the cases may have been dropped for lack of evidence, in others the accused made a private confession to the curia or to the bishop, who agreed to grant absolution and waive or mitigate punishment in return for the promise of improved behaviour. For example, in early 1593, when the diocese was without a bishop, Bartolomeo Guerrino, canon at Intra, threw himself at the mercy of the cathedral chapter of Novara after he was accused of improper dealings with a woman named Domenica Buzelina. He was encouraged to do so after languishing at Novara for two weeks without being examined and after he was advised that it would be less expensive to pay a fine than to call witnesses and prepare his defence, especially since he did not know who was sending reports about him. He was released by the cathedral chapter, after being fined one hundred lire and being given an order not to see Domenica. In September 1594 he was charged with violating the order.[34] This time the vicar general absolved him from his offence and released him with a new injunction to have no further dealings with Domenica under threat of a fine of one hundred scudi.[35]

The book of sentences for 1591–8 includes seventy-two items, a number inflated by the inclusion of a dozen cases that led to fines for failure to appear when summoned by the tribunal. Members of the clergy were involved in forty-four of the cases: thirty-nine priests, four clerics, and one friar. The sentences were remarkably lenient: fifteen of the forty-four ecclesiastics were absolved from the charges and released, while eighteen were fined. Most of the fines were in the range of two to ten scudi, although fines for failure to appear were from one hundred to two hundred scudi, well over the annual income of most curates. It seems probable that the curia never intended to collect the greater sums, but used them to force the contumacious to appear. If we overlook those who spent time in the episcopal jail before and during their trials, only four of those convicted were incarcerated, none of these for sexual infractions but for cases involving assault, possession of weapons, and theft. Two curates were temporarily suspended from their duties, both of these after processes involving some form of neglect of the care of souls.[36] One curate, Michele Maffezone of Galliate in the plains vicariate of Trecate, was deprived of his parish in 1594 and fined two hundred scudi for failing to appear on charges of having sexual relations with a number of women. He was not one of the curates of Galliate during the visit of 1595.[37]

Another type of penalty, most commonly applied to the vagabonds and beggars who from time to time appeared in the city, was expulsion from the diocese. Thus on 26 March 1563 a beggar named Ercole of Ferrara was expelled from city and diocese, never to return, on a charge of begging under false pretences. When seeking alms outside the cathedral he claimed to have an injured arm. The ruse might have worked had he not been recognized that night at a local inn, playing cards freely with both hands.[38]

Tribunal Activity: The Charges against the Clergy

Recent studies have suggested that the post-Tridentine church had a singular focus on policing the sexual conduct of both clergy and laity, and that bishops' tribunals won a veritable hegemony over matrimonial questions and a growing control over the sexual practices of ecclesiastics and laity at the expense of the activity of secular judges in these matters. The work of the ecclesiastical courts in the resolution of matrimonial questions, the suppression of the sexual activity of clerics and priests, and the prosecution, within bounds, of types of activity which deviated from the norm, was imposing and well documented.[39] In Italy, refusing absolution and excommunication were the weapons used to combat sexual sins of the laity, with the support of parish priests who, willingly or not, seemed more and more absorbed in the tasks of control in the course of the seventeenth century. At Siena, the courts of church and state cooperated in handling sexual matters: the civil power helped in the apprehension of fornicating priests and the reform of clerical customs, while the ecclesiastical courts helped in the pursuit, arraignment, and imprisonment of concubinaries and those given to 'deviant' sexual practices.[40] Others have explored questions of sexuality from the perspective of the sacrament of confession, noting how the very success of the post-Tridentine church in promoting the practice of confession led to the rising suspicion and reality that some confessors might use the sacrament to seduce female penitents. One offshoot of the problem was that the sin of solicitation in the confessional became an offence subject to the Roman and Spanish Inquisitions, it being argued that to defile confession in this way was a form of heresy because it negated or subverted the sacrament.[41]

The bishop's tribunal of Novara reflected the preoccupation of the Italian hierarchy with sexual matters in that the sexual conduct of priests, clerics, and for a brief time laypersons occupied a significant part of its time and attention. However, acts of violence by or against the clergy were a close second to sexual misconduct. Furthermore, the spectrum of activity extended far beyond sexual matters and violence to include everything from failures in the administration of the care of souls to conduct regarded as demeaning to the clerical estate, including drunkenness, gambling, and night-time carousing. Matters of faith, which broadly defined included heresy, blasphemy, illicit magic, and witchcraft, were also taken up by the vicars general and the tribunal because the bishops, Carlo Bascapè in particular, kept a watchful eye over the local inquisitors and sought to assert their own authority as the ordinary inquisitors of their diocese. Although statistical information from the early modern period is crude and often imprecise, the records of the tribunal can help establish a perspective for understanding the relative importance the curia attached to various problems.

In post-Tridentine Novara the majority of cases against the clergy tended to include multiple charges. That is, relatively few of the cases focused on a single issue, whether sexual misconduct, acts of violence, neglect of the care of souls, or public misconduct. Negligence in the care of souls appears to have been a lesser concern in the diocese than other offences. When accusations of neglect were made, it was almost always in conjunction with other transgressions of a sexual or violent nature. Perhaps this had to do with the lack of severity of the cases of neglect. The great majority of the Novarese curates resided in their parishes and performed the basic duties of celebrating Mass, preaching, teaching catechism, and administering the sacraments. Accusations of negligence in the care of souls were relatively rare, appearing among the charges against slightly over thirty curates and vice-curates in the period 1563 to 1614. Of these, twenty-five occurred during Bascapè's years as bishop, involving approximately 5 per cent of the priests who administered the care of souls. Most accusations of this type concerned failure to take the sacraments to the sick or neglect of the duty to teach catechism. The more extreme charge of absenteeism from the parish occurred in only six cases, three of these before Bascapè's appointment. For example, in May 1576 three witnesses accused Battista Pillone, curate of Suno in the central region of the diocese, of often being absent from the parish for periods of a week or two, even on feast days, so that two women were said to have died without the sacraments. He was also accused of drunkenness at banquets and of failure to denounce public sinners, especially for concubinage.[42]

The charge of absenteeism was also levelled against Cesare Fisrengo, curate of the tiny parish of Fisrengo in the plains region near Novara, who was accused of this fault a number of times in the 1580s and early 1590s. In December 1581 Fisrengo, who had received the parish through the patronage of his family which was prominent in the city and diocese,[43] was accused of living in Pisnengo rather than in the parish house in Fisrengo, of celebrating only on feast days and Sundays and missing a number of these, of not preaching or saying evening prayers, of negligence in ministering to the sick, and of going about without the proper clerical attire.[44] He avoided serious punishment and in 1589 was prosecuted again, this time for allegedly having a child by his housekeeper. Two priests spoke in his defence, however, saying that he was a good man who attended to his parish and to the sick.[45] It was shortly after this, in the summer of 1590, that Fisrengo was the victim of a vicious attack by a number of members of a nearby farm (*cascina*), suffering wounds to his head and the indignity of being unhorsed and forced to run for his life.[46] In 1593 a more decisive process was conducted under Bascapè, with the old charges of non-residence and failure to celebrate Mass reappearing. This time Fisrengo was also accused of being vexatious towards his parishioners, irreverent when celebrating the Mass, avaricious to the point where he worked in the fields, and insulting and physically attacking his colleague, the curate of Pisnengo. The last charge attracted the most attention, for it resulted in his excommunication and suspension from celebrating the Mass. By a sentence of 12 February 1594, he was suspended from the care of souls and ordered to seek absolution from Rome for the assault. He was also to provide his parish with a vice-curate during his suspension and to apply the balance of the income of the parish to the maintenance of the church buildings and grounds.[47]

The last two cases in which absenteeism was involved concerned Giovanni Berella, curate of Ara in the vicariate of Romagnano Sesia, and Giovanni Mercandotto, curate of Lovario and Ferruta in the vicariate of Borgosesia. Both cases were marginal. In September 1605 Berella was accused of absences from his parish with the result that a deceased infant remained three days without burial. Berella claimed that he had only been absent for one day, and denied threatening the priest who came to bury the baby. Of far greater interest to the tribunal were accusations that Berella had become involved in a conspiracy to kill one of his enemies in a case involving long-standing family rivalries.[48] Mercandotto's case was marginal as far as absenteeism was concerned because he was involved in a dispute between the communities of Lovario and Feruta. Ordered to reside in Lovario in 1606, he was accused of being absent from the village in May and June 1608 and on later occasions for up to a week at a time. Mercandotto denied this, claiming that he was only away when he had permission from the rural vicar to travel to Milan to purchase ecclesiastical vestments. Other charges, which he denied, included serving as a tailor, keeping a hostelry, and berating his accusers in public, calling one of them 'foul mouth.'[49] He was no longer curate of Lovario in the visit of 1617.[50]

The majority of the other curates accused of neglecting their duties managed to incur the wrath of their parishioners without deserting them for prolonged periods. One of these was Pier Paolo Burro, curate of Buera, whose case is mentioned in the introduction to this volume. Another was Francesco Boniperto, curate of Mezzomerico in the central vicariate of Oleggio, who drew the wrath of Bascapè in December 1593. Already, in February 1583, Boniperto had appeared before the vicar general to respond to allegations that he had fathered a child by his mistress, failed to teach catechism, failed to celebrate two weekly masses at the chapel of Santa Maria as contracted, and demanded the outrageous sum of three scudi from the Company of the Blessed Sacrament for celebrating their annual Mass. Boniperto, who had only recently been appointed to the parish, which was in the gift of his family, was also accused of going about in disguise day and night and abandoning his parishioners after a procession to neighbouring Momo so that he could go to a tavern.[51] While it is not known whether Boniperto was fined or otherwise punished, he was still parish priest when Bascapè came to the diocese in 1593. On 23 December of that year Bascapè sent him a scathing letter to correct abuses brought to his attention by the people of his parish. He was accused of rarely celebrating Mass on weekdays and, when he did celebrate, beginning so late that those with other business could not attend. As well, he was said to be harsh in dealing with his parishioners and making comments during the Mass which always descended to his own personal and particular designs.[52] In this case, as in many others, a letter was not enough. In July 1594 Boniperto was summoned by the tribunal to respond to accusations that he kept his own son in his house, that he missed catechism lessons so that he could hunt and fish, and that a parishioner died without the sacraments because of his negligence. As so often happened in the trials, he denied all the accusations.[53] Boniperto did not receive a formal sentence in 1594, perhaps throwing himself at the mercy of the bishop. He was still parish priest when Bascapè visited Mezzomerico in 1595, now said to celebrate Mass almost daily, to teach catechism on feast days, and to preach on occasion (*quandoque*). However, the bishop found him to be poorly trained (*parum versatus*) in cases of conscience – despite his claims to have spent years studying at the seminary of the Island of San Giulio and the Brera College in Milan – and instructed him to study specific chapters of the *Summa Navarri* and the Roman catechism and appear for examination in three months time.[54] Boniperto survived this test as well and was still parish priest at Mezzomerico during the visits of 1618 and 1628, by which time he was over seventy years old.[55]

Another priest prosecuted for abusing his parishioners was Ottavio Tornielli, curate of Agnellengo on the Novarese plain, who in September 1594 stood accused of demanding money for the sacraments, of allowing two persons to die without the last rites through his negligence, and of preaching only when he had an audience. He was also accused of stating in one of his sermons 'that women are all good as long as they are not asked to do what is bad,' which he was asked to explain to the tribunal. Some of his parishioners appear to have taken this poorly.[56]

Among the charges made against Novarese priests and clerics in the post-Tridentine period, the most common concerned sexual matters and physical and verbal assaults of varying degrees of severity. Sexual offences formed at least part of the cases against almost half of the 275 priests, clerics, and religious arraigned by the tribunal at one time or another. Of those accused of sexual impropriety, the majority were involved in the care of souls: over 80 were curates and another 10 vice-curates or coadjutors.[57] To focus on the estimated 500 priests of Bascapè's episcopate who were directly involved in the care of souls, approximately 70 (14 per cent) were arraigned for sexual transgressions at one time or another during his years as bishop.

Recent studies of the penitential and legal systems in Italian dioceses have underscored the sexual misconduct of the clergy in two areas: frequenting prostitutes and concubinage or cohabitation with women over prolonged periods. At Siena, dealings with prostitutes by clerics and priests of a variety of ranks were said to be so pronounced that there was a virtual hunt for fornicating clerics by the officials of the communal watch. Meanwhile, it has been almost axiomatic that the concubinage of rural parish priests was so common in the sixteenth and seventeenth centuries that curates long escaped denunciation because of the high degree of tolerance for this type of offence. The people kept silent as long as pastoral duties were performed, and denunciations occurred only when a curate was guilty of serious shortcomings in the care of souls or began to jeopardize good order by acts of violence or attempts at new sexual seductions.[58]

Due to the cryptic nature of interrogations conducted at the episcopal tribunal, it is not always possible to determine the precise relationship between an accused priest, cleric, or religious and his or her sexual partners or, in some cases, victims. What is clear, however, is that the Novarese vicars general took action over a broader range of activity, with a wide variety of colours and shades. The Novarese cases covered a spectrum from suspicious contacts with women, attempted seductions, inappropriate touching, affairs, and dealings with prostitutes, to concubinage, the fathering of children, and less frequently, sexual assaults and allegations of homosexual activities.

Unlike the situation at Siena, where clerics and priests were often targeted for frequenting prostitutes, the records of the Novarese tribunal rarely referred to the women involved as prostitutes. This may be due to the contrast between urban and rural environments. A noteworthy exception occurred in August 1594 when Pier Paolo Ronchetto, the curate of Carpugnino in the vicariate of

Lesa, confessed to having sexual relations with Margarita or Magdalena of Alessandria in his house and was sentenced to a fine of twenty scudi and a year's exile from Carpugnino and Baveno. He was also to have no more to do with the woman under penalty of one hundred scudi and the threat of deprivation of benefice. The woman, meanwhile, was expelled from the city and diocese for five years.[59] In an offshoot of the same trial, Margarita accused Antonio de Margheritis, the provost of Baveno and rural vicar of the region, of having sex with her four times while she was in custody in his house and of paying her pimp, Francesco Rampone, fifteen ducatoni. De Margheritis, who was over sixty years of age, denied the charges, but the woman maintained her story under torture.[60] It is doubtful that the provost was convicted, and there is no mention of the incident in the pastoral visitation of 1595. When Cardinal Taverna visited Baveno in November 1617, de Margheritis, eighty-two years of age, was still serving as provost and rural vicar.[61] However the woman's name came up in 1595 in a second case involving Ronchetto, still curate of Carpugnino, who was accused of a variety of offences, including striking a woman of his parish, carrying weapons, pilfering from the alms box, allowing people to die without the sacraments through negligence, and sexual relations with Elizabetta, a woman of the parish. On this occasion Ronchetto was declared innocent and absolved from punishment.[62]

In contrast to dealings with prostitutes, cases of concubinage appeared frequently in the Novarese records, occurring in at least thirty of the trials, twenty-five from the time of Bascapè. In over a dozen cases, a long-term relationship of a priest with a woman was virtually the only matter raised. For example, on 2 December 1594 Gian Mario Vignolo, who had been curate of Grignasco in the vicariate of Romagnano for one year, stood accused of fathering a child by a forty-year-old woman. He denied the charge and was released with an order to have nothing to do with the woman.[63] Another, more complex, case was that of Antonio de Bressa, who was first prosecuted as a cleric under Bishop Cesare Speciano for impregnating Antonia Togna, a woman of his home village in the Antrona valley. He confessed his offence and was dismissed with a fine of fifteen scudi and an injunction to have no more dealings with her. In 1597, however, when he was curate of Schieranco in the Antrona valley, he was prosecuted again for resuming relations with Antonia and carrying a forbidden weapon. He denied the accusations. Although it is not known what penalty if any he received, he was prosecuted again in 1609 when he was serving as vice-curate of Intra on Lake Maggiore. This time he was accused of continuing relations with Antonia, keeping his son in his house, and seducing and impregnating a young girl after telling her that he would arrange her marriage with his son. Again he denied the charges.[64]

In other cases, concubinage was one of a series of charges levelled against a parish priest. One example is the case of Domenico Zuffo, the curate of Crodo in the Antigorio valley, who appeared before the vicar general on 25 February 1595 when he was forty-eight years of age, and declared candidly that in previous years he had sent a petition to Bishop Speciano asking pardon for fathering two children by a widow named Maria de Primetto or del Sartore, a poor woman who had originally come to his house seeking grain. Speciano had absolved him but fined him twenty scudi and required that he promise to have no more dealings with Maria. One of the sons died, but the second, then five years of age, was in his house to learn grammar, which Zuffo taught to him as well as other boys. What interested the court most was that Zuffo also confessed to having relations with Maria at later dates, claiming to be unaware of any subsequent children.[65] He was turned over to the jailer, but was later dismissed without further punishment when he accepted an injunction to have no more dealings with Maria under threat of imprisonment and deprivation of benefice. He was also ordered not to keep his children in his house. The tribunal kept him under close surveillance, and in December 1601 he was again interrogated and confessed to having his children in his house, but only when the curate of Baceno, who normally instructed them, was unable to keep them or when they were ill. In tears he denied violating the injunction not to have dealings with Maria, and alleged that the denunciations came either from Cesare de Dugno, whom he had denounced for selling grain at twice the normal price, or from his co-curate, Domenico Palluda, who had invented the story that he was living with Maria to get revenge because Zuffo had testified against him in his own trial. A year later, in January 1603, he was again arraigned and this time questioned under torture, suspended by the strappado for the amount of time it took to say the Psalm *Miserere*. He maintained his innocence.[66] When Bascapè visited Crodo in October 1603, Zuffo was roundly criticized by his parishioners because of his alleged dealings with men of bad life, excessive drinking, dissipated lifestyle, neglect of preaching and catechism lessons, and frequent absences from the parish.[67] In March 1605 he made another appearance before the tribunal, answering charges that after leaving Novara in 1603 he continued to have dealings with Maria, eating and sleeping with her and placing her in charge of his patrimonial lands at Cisore near Domodossola. He denied these charges, claiming that they were lies spread by his enemies, naming Antonio Rigolo who had previously administered his patrimony. It was July before he was released from prison so that he could obtain funds for his defence. He eluded the bishop's men at this point, alleging that his agents had pocketed much of the money he had raised. Captured, he was again brought before the tribunal in December 1605.[68] It is not known what punishments he received, but he was still one of the curates at Crodo in 1616, criticized by parishioners for past dealings with Maria del Sartore, who was said to have resided publicly in his house for many years and borne him as many as nine children, the majority of whom died. He was also accused of sexual liaisons with Domenica d'Orso and two or three other unnamed women. He was rumoured to have had recently impregnated Maria, daughter of Domenica d'Orso, who was frequently seen at his house, and was accused of keeping his two sons and daughter in the parish house against specific orders not to do so. It was said that he was at odds with his co-curate Antonio Celera, vexing him as he had vexed Domenico Palluda and another co-curate named Cesare Guidotto years before. It was noted that Zuffo and Celera had not talked to one another in years, to the harm and scandal of the people. Celera was himself accused of keeping a concubine and having children, and it is possible that Zuffo had a hand in advancing these charges.[69] A final list of accusations included that he was known to harbour bandits, was a habitual blasphemer, and was held by some to be a wizard or caster of spells. In the aftermath of the visit of 1616, Zuffo was again cited to appear at Novara but he presented a physician's note alleging that he was ill and could not travel without risk to his health. He was then said to be aged seventy-one.[70]

The record of Zuffo's appearances before the tribunal and the litany of accusations against him from his parishioners and fellow priests lead one to wonder what good he might have accomplished in the care of souls at Crodo. One possible explanation might be that some of the accusations were exaggerated. There had long been bad blood between Zuffo and his co-curates and between Zuffo and many of his parishioners. In 1596 he advised Bascapè that he had many powerful enemies, some of whom threatened his life. He was himself quite ready to denounce parishioners for their faults. In the same year, he commented that a number of women had been abused by devils and others were suspected of sorcery (*sorteligio*), giving a list of their names to the bishop.[71] In the visit of 1603 Zuffo complained about other abuses found in the parish: conversations and *rumori* during Mass time and especially during the sermon, lack of observation of feast days, a number of unmarried couples openly living together, husbands and wives living apart from one another, usurious transactions, and failure to pay tithes.[72] Originally entrusted with the parish in 1585, it is also clear that Zuffo met certain minimum standards in the performance of the care of souls. Despite the torrent of criticism during the visit of 1616, he appears to have given sermons and catechism lessons. Legacies and Mass obligations appear to have been fulfilled and duly noted in the parish registers. Confessions were heard. Orders from episcopal visitation were said to be executed, most notably instructions to establish companies of the Rosary and the Blessed Sacrament.[73]

One also wonders what might have prompted Maria del Sartore to remain with Zuffo for so many years, bearing so many children. The fact that she first came to his door in search of food suggests that economic dependence was a major factor. The longevity of the relationship suggests, perhaps, a degree of tolerance for Zuffo's concubinage in the parish. Tolerance was not necessarily the same as approval, for given Zuffo's position within the community and willingness to denounce his parishioners, many of the same parishioners must have been reluctant to provoke the curate by making denunciations. Zuffo also found ways to mask his conduct, by sending Maria away at strategic times and by constantly promising to change his ways. Even Bascapè, as zealous as he was for reform, seems to have been taken in to a degree by Zuffo's promises. And as Bascapè so often stated, it was difficult to find suitable candidates for the mountain parishes of the diocese.

Members of the Palluda family, named by Zuffo as his enemies, also figure prominently in the records of the court. In 1595 Domenico Palluda, then Zuffo's co-curate, was fined two hundred scudi and excommunicated for failing to appear to answer charges.[74] Four times the annual income of many curates, the fine was probably never enforced. Possibly the case involved some sort of sexual dalliance, for Palluda later conceded that he was prosecuted for having an illegitimate son. Transferred to the parish of Cavallirio in the vicariate of Romagnano Sesia, he was prosecuted again in 1606, 1608, and 1612 on charges ranging from keeping his son in the parish house in violation of an injunction not to do so, keeping a female servant (*fantesca*) without proper permission from the curia, offering remedies to cure people from witchcraft, and berating his parishioners from the pulpit for making accusations against him.[75] Although Palluda's sentence, if any, is not known, he was no longer at Cavallirio in the visit of 1617.

Lorenzo Palluda, probably the brother or cousin of Domenico and one of the curates of Baceno which neighboured Crodo in the Antigorio valley, also appeared before the tribunal on a number of occasions. On 8 March 1595, when he was in his mid-thirties, he was absolved for wounding another person and dismissed with an injunction not to carry any weapon except a short sword (*storta*).[76] Three years later he again appeared before the vicar general, this time taken from the bishop's jail, accused of having children by at least three women including a certain Domenica of nearby Premia, Catterina Bernardi of Baceno, and Maria, the widow of his brother. Palluda denied these charges and played down other accusations that he had taken part in a drunken wedding party and that he went about disguised with a false beard and carrying a short harquebus. He had missed Bascapè's synod of 1594 and explained this and other erratic behaviour by claiming that his enemies were plotting to assassinate him in order to install one of their own relatives as curate of Baceno, for 140 years under the care of a member of the Palluda family.[77] Whatever the result of this trial, Lorenzo Palluda continued to serve as curate at Baceno and for a long period as rural vicar of the Antigorio valley, an indication of the difficulty faced by the bishop in finding suitable agents in northern regions. He was still one of the curates when Cardinal Taverna visited Baceno in 1616, and was harshly criticized with his co-curate for negligence in teaching catechism and failing to take the sacraments to the sick. The complaints came mainly from the residents of outlying communities, eager to attain parish status for their oratories. Palluda vehemently denied all charges and offered to stand trial again, if need be.[78]

In almost forty cases, the majority involving curates and vice-curates, there were references to children fathered by the accused as in the case of Domenico Zuffo. This reflected the long-term relationships which developed between a number of priests and their partners. In twelve of the cases, the accused, again like Zuffo, acknowledged their offspring. In other cases, paternity was denied. For example, in December 1595 Giovanni Battista Ottolino, a deacon at Stresa on Lake Maggiore, vehemently denied impregnating Susanna, the daughter of Francesco Gallia Ferrari of the same town, saying that she was a liar and an idler (*poltrona*) and that her father was an enemy of his family. When told that his own mother had testified that he had kept track of the day he began to have sexual relations with Susanna, he professed astonishment that his mother would say such a thing.[79] Unfortunately, it is not known how this case was resolved.

Three cases involved infanticide or attempts to induce abortions. For example, in May 1595 Domenico Franzosino, a chaplain at Pombia and at Castelletto Ticino, was charged with having sexual relations with two women, having a son by one and procuring an abortion for the other. He was acquitted of the charge of abortion but sentenced to a fine of forty scudi for his sexual transgressions and given an injunction against having anything to do with the women.[80] He also appears to have resigned his chaplaincy at Pombia.[81]

In a similar case, in October 1605 Alberto de Alberti, curate of Cuzzago in the central vicariate of Intra, was detained and interrogated about his visits to Giacomina Madena, his former servant, now under death sentence in the secular prison at Vogogna for killing her child. De Alberti, then in his early fifties, was accused of fathering the woman's child and counselling her to kill the baby after a drug he gave her failed to induce an abortion. His visits to Giacomina were interpreted as an attempt to procure her silence. While Giacomina maintained her story under torture, de Alberti continued to protest his innocence. It is not known what punishment, if any, the priest received, but he was still curate at Cuzzago during the visit of 1618, at that time sixty-three years of age.[82]

The third case of infanticide involved Girolamo Bertolio, curate at Rocca in the vicariate of Varallo Sesia, who in the summer of 1598 was accused of having a child by the widow Margarita de Borlotto and having her abandon the infant in an oratory with the result that it died. The woman was imprisoned at Varallo and the priest was ordered to stay away from his parish under penalty of two hundred scudi and loss of his benefice. Bertolio violated the decree two years later and was excommunicated. He fled from his home, spending some time in the Franciscan house at Varallo and some time wandering in France and Savoy, begging to provide the necessities of life. He visited churches and said his office, but did not celebrate Mass except during a two-month period when he claimed to be absolved from excommunication by Rome. In June 1603, without funds to prepare his defence, he surrendered to the authorities in Novara.[83] It is not known how his case ended.

Approximately eighty of the cases involved suspicious dealings with women of one sort or another, without clear evidence of cohabitation. Over twenty of these involved accusations that priests or clerics were involved in affairs with married women. Often the denunciation was made by the husband. Thus, on 15 March 1563, Giovanni Maria de Ploto of Novara complained to the vicar general of Cardinal Serbelloni that Paolo de Barengo, curate of San Paolo at Novara, had appeared at his house at two in the morning wearing secular clothing and had struck him several times causing him to bleed. The attack was provoked by de Ploto's allegations that the priest had been committing adultery with his wife, Toquata Tamborini. While the assault took place, Toquata stood at the window shouting to the priest, 'Stop beating him, or tomorrow morning he will go to the vicar.' According to de Ploto, the relationship between the priest and his wife had been going on for about four years and efforts to stop it by appealing to Serbelloni's predecessor had failed. In fact, Barengo later accosted de Ploto again in the vineyards, calling him a 'damned cuckold' (*cornudazo*).[84]

Few of the cases involved paedophilia, or the sexual abuse of underage girls or boys. One arose in August 1590 when Alessandro Visconti of the archdiocese of Milan accused his teacher, the priest Giovanni Pietro Salatino, canon of Intra, of trying to seduce himself and a number of other boys that Salatino was educating in his house. At least three other students (*scolari*) supported this testimony. The end of this inquiry is not known, although Salatino and his colleague Martino Rigolo, also a canon at Intra, were accused of attempting to bribe Giovanni Paulo Caccia, canon of Novara, who was sent to inquire into the incident.[85] Although nothing more is heard of Salatino in the records of the tribunal or the acts of visitation of Intra, Rigolo remained a canon at Intra, prosecuted a number of times over the next decade because of altercations involving his prebend and scuffles in church.[86]

Another case of paedophilia occurred in 1599–1600, the period when the records of the tribunal are lacking. On 19 May 1600, Bascapè wrote to Cardinal Aldobrandini at Rome that the curate of Soriso in the area of the Riviera d'Orta had confessed to abusing four or five young boys (*fanciulli*) over a period of about nine months. Although a bull of Pope Pius V (r. 1566–72) called for the curate to be degraded and turned over to the secular authorities for execution, Bascapè feared that a jurisdictional problem might arise because although the Riviera d'Orta was under his temporal control, judgment had been passed at Novara. Bascapè asked if the Holy See would approve changing the punishment to life in the galleys, especially since the vice was so distant from the clergy and people of the diocese of Novara that a great display of judicial rigour was not necessary.[87] It is not known how the case ended.

A third case involving abuse of children occurred in November 1604, when Ottaviano Mercandotto, curate of Rassa in the mountain vicariate of Scopa, was charged with the attempted rape of a ten- to twelve-year-old girl when he was passing through Balmuccia, a nearby town. The girl was saved by passersby and the curate was cited and interrogated.[88] Mercandotto seems to have delayed the proceedings. In 1608 he remained curate at Rassa, now accused of habitually hearing the confessions of women in the sacristy with the door locked and of attempting to molest the young (*piccola*) daughter of Giacomo de Viatto of the parish when she came to confession. He protested his innocence, calling Giacomo 'that vituperative heretic' (*quel vituperoso heretico*) and alleging that his parishioners had removed the confessional to make room for a painting of the Madonna. He was also accused of eating too much at a hostelry and vomiting in public, of beating a young girl and a woman who acted as custodian at the church, and of having a son by a woman named Catterina, whom he sent away to have her child. Mercandotto denied all charges.[89] Although it is not known how the trial ended, he was still serving as the curate of Rassa in 1616, when he admitted only to being prosecuted in the past.[90]

Accusations of homosexual activity were also rare. There was a hint of this in the interrogation of Cristoforo Margherina, cleric and canon of the collegiate of San Leonardo of Pallanza, who on 14 August 1601 was accused of masquerading as a woman while attending balls and singing and playing the guitar during the time of carnival. Margherina admitted playing at the hostelry of a friend, but he denied playing at balls or singing in the streets at night. He spent some time in the episcopal jail before being interrogated a second time on 10 November 1601, this time accused of sleeping at the house of the priest Cesare Pizzolo, a canon and grammar teacher at Pallanza, and sharing the same bed with Pizzolo and the *podestà* of Pallanza. He admitted doing so in the past year and offered the explanation that it was raining and he could not conveniently return to his room at his uncle's house. The court continued to press him about other charges, to wit that he had threatened the life of Cristoforo Morigia with a pistol after the latter had given him a nosebleed, that he had harsh words for the provost of San Leonardo who had accused him of not attending catechism lessons on feast days, and that he had exposed himself in the presence of women at the house of Giovanni Battista Moltano, a carpenter at Pallanza. Although Margherina was detained in the episcopal jail through his interrogation, it is not known how his case ended.[91] Cesare Pizzolo, who was not charged, it seems, for sexual misconduct, was still a canon at Pallanza in 1617, when he informed the visitors that he had twice been prosecuted in the past but that nothing could be proved against him.[92]

There were also sexual dimensions to the two cases in which nuns were arraigned after fleeing from their convents, the first of which occurred in the last year of the Council of Trent. On 24 March 1563, three nuns of the convent of Sant'Agata of Novara, under the direction of the Canons Regular of St Augustine, were accused of fleeing their convent two years earlier to the great prejudice of their souls and the great scandal of their community, 'living dissipated lives' (*vivendo semper luxoriose*), and 'leading bad lives in the manner of prostitutes' (*malamque vitam ducendo more meretricio*). The nuns – Suor Magdalena of Trecate, Suor Veronica of Canalio, and Suor Prudentia also of Canalio – were identified as '*converse*' or lower-born women who were admitted to the convent to act as servants for the nobly born '*velate*' or 'nuns of the veil.' Since two of them had professed their final vows, their abbess, Suor Lucia of the noble Caccia family, did not protest when they exited the house to do the laundry at the irrigation ditch as was their wont. This time they did not return but fled to Vercelli where they were said to have had dealings with soldiers. They had recently returned to Novara where Suor Magdalena had lived in the house of Genesorio Calegate, by whom she had a child. The other two were said to be living in the city having a good time (*a far bon tempo*). According to the abbess, when asked if they wanted to return to their convent and do penance, one had replied: 'If I had left an eye there [in the convent], I would not return there to retrieve it' (*se li havessero un occhio, che non li sarebbero a pigliarlo*). Although the abbess was hardly eager to have the three return because they were too deceitful (*dishoneste*) and unpredictable, the vicar general decided to proceed further, citing the nuns to appear. The end result is unknown.[93]

A generation later, in 1593, Margarita da Cerano, another *conversa*, this time of the Humiliati convent of the suburb of San Lazzaro, was apprehended after fleeing from the convent and – as she herself admitted – becoming pregnant. Much of the investigation surrounding her case concerned the men she might have contacted and the degree of knowledge they had of her status. Those interrogated included the miller of the suburb and his wife, who admitted seeing Margarita come to the irrigation ditch by their mill to wash clothes with other women, wearing a dress made of material used by the nuns for their habit. Also interrogated was a Milanese widow named Marselia who had given Margarita a room to stay in for two weeks but claimed not to know of her pregnancy. She claimed that she had accommodated Margarita in the belief that she was a good and spiritual woman, only later learning that she was pregnant. When she chided Margarita for not telling her, the nun responded that she lied about herself for fear of being turned away and that Marselia should be happy because she had performed a work of charity by giving her a place to stay. Marselia denied knowing anything about the father of Margarita's child, to which her interrogators responded with the gratuitous observation that her ignorance on this point was strange 'since it is the custom of women to confer and discuss among themselves in similar matters' (*cum sit mos mulierum ad invicem similia inter sese conferre, et enarrare*).[94]

While the end result of Margarita's case is unknown, what is clear is that cases of grave impropriety, sexual or otherwise, of nuns were rare in the diocese of Novara. Sensitive though the bishops were to such matters, they spent more of their time enforcing the rule of cloister, ensuring that the convents of their diocese had sufficient funds to maintain a viable religious life and cajoling the nuns to observe the vow of poverty more strictly.[95]

Among the categories of charges against the clergy, cases of assault or violent behaviour of varying degrees of severity were the second most common. The fact that these appeared frequently before the bishop's tribunal suggests that the secular authorities respected the right of the clergy to be tried by the ecclesiastical courts, even for the most serious of crimes. As well, the correspondence of Bascapè includes no references to violations of this principle. Assaults, including homicides and planned homicides, appeared in 116 of the cases, involving over 100 different priests and clerics, over a third of the 275 individuals accused. Approximately forty of those accused of assault were parish priests or vice-curates, over thirty were identified as chaplains, priests, and canons, while over twenty were clerics in tonsure or in minor orders. More than forty of the assaults involved the use of a weapon, from staffs and knives to firearms. In almost twenty cases the attacks were accompanied by abusive or insulting language. The high number of assaults heard by the tribunal is not surprising because in most cases the aggrieved party was willing to file a complaint and demand justice. The assault cases reflect the involvement of the clergy in the life of their communities. Family feuds, altercations at local taverns, and property disputes were commonly at the root of assault cases.

In several of the cases the attacks appear to have arisen from minor altercations, often involving younger clerics. For example, in June 1594 a number of boys attacked Gaudenzio Salecino, a cleric of Novara, and he retaliated by injuring two of them, aged thirteen and fourteen. After appearing before the vicar general, he was released after promising to appear again, but the end result of the case is not known.[96] On 27 November 1596 Giovanni Battista de Franchi, cleric of Novara, was accused of insulting his fellow cleric Marc'Antonio Cattaneo and pelting him with rocks. De Franchi attempted to downplay the charge, saying that striking Cattaneo with the rocks was accidental. He was turned over to the bishop's jailer, but was later released into the custody of his father. Again the end result of the case is unknown, but it seems unlikely that there were serious repercussions.[97]

Other cases give evidence of greater severity or a more violent temperament and behaviour. Banditry, associating with bandits, and carrying prohibited weapons were often a part of these. Seven cases involved homicide, five of these implicating parish priests in murders. One example was the case of Domenico Gambara, one of the curates of Galliate in the plains vicariate of Trecate, who in June 1586 was accused of poisoning the husband of a woman with whom he was involved.[98] Although the end of the process is not known, he seems to have escaped serious punishment. In 1589 he was again denounced before the tribunal after being involved in an acrimonious conflict with his co-curate, Giovanni Giacomo Fara, whom Gambara accused of sexual improprieties, assault, and setting fire to his house.[99] Again Gambara escaped punishment, for in Bascapè's visit of 1593 he continued to hold the parish at age fifty-three. Not surprisingly he was described as ignorant (*illiteratum*) and criminally inclined (*criminosus*), and provision was made for a coadjutor since he was weak in the knowledge of cases of conscience and did not or could not preach to the people.[100] He died in 1599.[101]

One exceptionally violent individual was Girolamo Colonna, a deacon who possessed a prebend in the chapter of Gozzano in the bishop's feudal holding of the Riviera d'Orta. On 4 December 1593, he was convicted *in absentia* of wounding the provost of the chapter of Gozzano with a short sword (*storta*) and sentenced to excommunication, deprivation, and imprisonment at the discretion of the vicar general. In March 1594 he was apprehended in Milan, a vagrant wearing secular garb. He was returned to Novara where under interrogation he confessed to his assault on the provost of Gozzano, suggesting that he was enraged against the provost because the provost had seduced and impregnated Colonna's niece. The vicar general did not follow up on this accusation, probably because the accuser lacked credibility. The court also heard testimony that since the time of Bishop Serbelloni, Colonna had been accused of assaults against five other members of the clergy and fined for a number of them. He had also been prosecuted for purchasing his benefice with money. The trial and confinement appear to have been too much for Colonna, who hanged himself in his cell on 23 June 1594. His body was buried outside the city in unhallowed ground.[102]

Another priest accused of crimes of violence was Pietro Burro of Crevola, who served as chaplain and then curate of Caddo in the Ossola valley. In 1603 he was accused of attempted murder, associating with bandits who murdered a man during one of their nocturnal soirées, and discharging a firearm so that a horse bolted off the road and was killed. Burro was also accused of keeping a married woman as a concubine. He denied all charges and seems to have avoided serious punishment, still serving as parish priest of Caddo in 1617.[103]

Accusations of banditry or at least involvement with bandits were made in a half dozen other cases as well. Such charges often arose from family relationships of the accused. Two of these were Niccolò Applano and Bartolomeo Guerrino, canons at Intra on Lake Maggiore, who in 1598 were accused of associating with the brothers of Applano who were reputed to be bandits. The two canons were also accused of keeping weapons and of plotting to murder their provost. Other charges included a variety of thefts, eating meat during Lent, and attending a masked ball. In July 1598 they were acquitted of all charges except attending the ball and released without penalty because of time served in detention.[104] In Applano's case, the incident does not appear to have prevented his advance in the ranks of the clergy of the diocese, for in 1605 he again appeared before the vicar general, now as the provost of Pallanza, entrusted with the care of souls in that town. The new charges concerned reports that he had fathered a child by Bernardina Cappa of Pallanza, resident in Intra, and that he had intercepted letters of complaint that his rival, Canon Baglione, had tried to send to the bishop.[105] Applano denied the charges, and the end of the trial is not known.

Family ties also had a negative impact on Giovanni Antonio Bonino, a cleric who possessed a canonry at Gozzano in the territory held in feud by the bishop of Novara. In June 1612 Bonino appeared on his own volition before the tribunal to answer to charges that he had aided and abetted Ercole Gemelli and his cousin Francesco Bonino, both reputed to be bandits in the territory. The cleric was accused of giving them food and shelter, carrying prohibited weapons, and complicity in an armed attack they made on Giulio Cesare Manino, who was resisting their efforts to arrange a marriage between the Bonino and Manino families. Specifically, he was accused of allowing the bandits to hide in a house where he taught school while they lay in wait for Manino. Bonino denied the charges, claiming that the two bandits had abducted him and held him prisoner for five days, until he escaped and made his way to Novara.[106]

Another homicide case involved Martino Craco of Rocca, cleric in the order of porter, who in April 1613 was accused of killing his cousin Marta by dropping a pole on her head from a chestnut tree that he was helping to harvest. Although Marta's death seems to have been the result of negligence or of a boyish prank, he had at first fled the diocese but was then called to account for his role in the tragedy.[107] The result of the process is unknown, but it is unlikely that the punishment, if any, was severe given the accidental nature of the offence.

Also accidental was the fatal shooting of a woman from Novara in May 1605. Giovanni Battista Rabbatino, coadjutor in the cathedral of San Gaudenzio, was accused of returning home after eating and drinking at a tavern, putting powder in a gun, and goading his friend into discharging the weapon in the direction of several women, killing one of them. Rabbatino denied being at a tavern and claimed that his friend had taken up the weapon, already loaded, on his own, despite his protests. In addition to his complicity in the homicide, he was accused of having sexual relations with a woman.[108] It is not known how the case ended, but it is known that Rabbatino was still serving as coadjutor at San Gaudenzio in August 1607 when the notary Pier Francesco Scarabaratio was cited for striking him during a heated argument.[109] He was still listed among the canons of San Gaudenzio in 1618.[110]

In September 1605 Giovanni Berella, the curate of Ara in the central region of Romagnano, appeared before the tribunal on a variety of charges, including conspiring with a man named Bartolomeo Solio to murder Bernardino di Sala. The plot was evidently the result of feuding between the Solio and di Sala factions of the region, for it is known that efforts were being made to make peace between the parties. On 25 November of the same year, Giacomo Tosallo testified that he had been promised fifty scudi to lead the intended victim to his assassin, Giacomo Rizzolino, who was also to be paid fifty scudi. Tosallo kept to this story even under torture. Under examination the curate confessed to knowing about the conspiracy and being invited to join it, but said that he had not participated, maintaining this story under torture.[111] He was freed by the end of the year, but on 1 May 1609 was again examined for a third of an hour under torture after Rizzolino confessed his involvement in the plot. Again Berella maintained his innocence.[112] While it is not known how the case ended, he was no longer curate at Ara at the time of the visit of 1617.[113]

Another homicide involved Giovanni Pietro Bovio, one of two curates at Bellinzago in the vicariate of Oleggio. In November 1612 he was taken to the episcopal jail and questioned three times, the last time under torture, on a charge of killing his relative, the soldier Francesco Bovio, after the latter had discovered that the curate was sleeping with his wife. A bloodied cap and murder weapon were found in his house. He denied the charges and was absolved in July 1613 but received an injunction not to return to Bellinzago and not to have any dealings with Lucia, the woman involved in the affair. However, in May 1614 he was apprehended again, this time accused of violating the injunctions, of carrying a stiletto, going about in secular garb, lodging bandits in his house, and impregnating a young woman.[114] The vicar general absolved him, but his enemies appealed, and he fled. In 1615 Bovio appealed to the Congregation of Bishops and Regulars at Rome, saying that he was being persecuted by his enemies so that he had spent twenty-eight months in jail at Novara. He asked the Congregation to review his case and order the vicar general not to molest him further.[115] It is not known whether the Congregation acted on his request.

In the majority of cases, violent behaviour stopped short of homicide. An especially irascible individual was Francesco Folieta, a priest of Novara who appeared before the tribunal on 3 June 1590, accused by Catterina Marana of striking her on the head with a cudgel when she and her daughter were gathering wood on the road near the priest's vines. The woman was treated by the surgeon Bernardo de Villa who described her injuries as non-life-threatening, although she was confined to bed for a fortnight.[116] Folieta again appeared before the tribunal in July 1595, accused of resisting Giovanni Battista Fratino, the agent of the episcopal curia who had been sent to collect a small sum owed to a poor woman. Folieta denied greeting Fratino with threats and insults.[117] In February 1597 Folieta was again summoned, this time for wounding a man named Bernardino on the arm when Folieta discovered Bernardino taking wood from his land. The priest alleged that it was Bernardino who wounded him on the hand, but the court replied that the injury to Bernardino's arm would have prevented this.[118] In November 1601 he was again accused of assaulting a woman, hitting her face and biting her arm during an altercation in the fields. Folieta was not in clerical garb at the time and was weeding and gleaning grain during the harvest. Asked why he engaged in this physical labour, he replied: 'It seems to me that in such times it is worthwhile for everyone to help out, so much more because of the danger of storms and other misfortunes.'[119] In 1607 Folieta appeared for yet another offence, this time accused of insulting and throwing a lump of dirt at Giovanni Maria Tettoni, canon of the cathedral and from a noble family. Although he admitted to some of the charges, it is not known how this case ended.[120]

A number of the assault cases involved squabbles over property. In September 1590, for example, Giuseppe Toscano from the suburb of San Gaudenzio complained that Gaudenzio Taegio, a priest from the same district, had attacked him with his fists and a rod because Toscano had complained that

Taegio's brothers had cut the crops on a part of his field that bordered the brothers' vines. The attack was triggered when the complainant said to the priest: 'Monsignor, I am as good a man as you are and you should be careful how you speak to me.' Other witnesses testified that the priest's blows were accompanied by a torrent of insults, including calling Toscano a liar, with no more soul than a dog.[121] It is not known how the case ended, but Taegio was arraigned again in July 1595, accused of assisting his nephews in running a shop where they sold cheese, lard, and soap. Taegio conceded that he had helped his youngest nephew weigh goods and keep accounts, but denied minding the store alone.[122]

Another interesting case was that of Giovanni Viscardi, the curate of Cravegna in the Antigorio valley, who in March 1595 was tried for wounding Taddeo del Molino on the head with a rock during an argument over payment for goods enjoyed by Taddeo. Viscardi, who was in his forties and had studied philosophy and canon law at Bologna, attempted to avoid prosecution by the vicar general by paying the local surgeon to treat Taddeo and help cover up the incident, but to no avail. It is not known how the case ended, although it does not appear to have gone to sentence.[123]

Not all the examples of assault by clerics were directed against laypersons. It was also common for clerics to scuffle among themselves over rights or matters of precedence. In July 1608 Gottardo de Monte, chaplain at Isola Superiore, was interrogated after coming to blows with Battista Magnetti, the curate of Stresa, when the two were returning by boat from the monthly congregation at Lesa. The fight was over the question of whether de Monte, a chaplain, could say Mass and preach without the permission of his parish priest. De Monte claimed to have a decree of the bishop permitting this on the first Sunday of the month for the Company of the Rosary.[124]

More serious were the activities of Giovanni Pietro Caccia, a subdeacon from Trecate and a member of a prominent noble family of the diocese who was arraigned on a number of counts in 1610. He was accused of grappling with Don Valerio Giuliano, one of the curates of Trecate and a member of the Canons Regular of St John Lateran, on the roadway and throwing him down in anger with a torrent of abuse. Caccia replied that the incident was instigated by Giuliano, whom he accused of keeping a mistress for the last two years and having a child by her. The tribunal seems to have taken the charge as unfounded and did not prosecute Giuliano, who was still curate at Trecate when Cardinal Taverna visited in 1617.[125] Caccia, who acted as a notary before entering the clerical estate, was also accused of trying to force two witnesses to accuse a notary of extortion and going as far as to threaten one of them with bodily harm. He denied this charge. When accused of serving as an advocate before the secular courts in violation of the canons and a specific injunction given to him in 1601, he replied only that his work did not really constitute legal service because he did not have the knowledge to do so. Finally, Caccia was accused of causing great scandal by verbally abusing and physically attacking the Lenten preacher Padre Steffano Meloni of the Augustinian order because in his sermons the preacher attacked the vices of money changers, the profession known to be that of Caccia's brothers. Caccia denied this story, saying it was concocted by Don Valerio and the preacher.[126] Whatever the results of the process, Caccia, who held a lucrative chapel at Trecate, finally made progress through the orders, attaining the status of deacon and priest in 1626. By then he was in his late fifties or early sixties.[127]

A further indication of the degree to which the secular clergy remained involved in day-to-day concerns and foibles can be found in accusations concerning the theft, destruction, and alienation of church property. These were much rarer than those of sexual misconduct or assault, with only twenty-nine cases appearing in the criminal files of the tribunal. An extreme example was that of the cleric Giovanni Giacomo Cestinello, who was caught red-handed stealing from the alms box of the parish church of Ogni Santi at Novara by one of the curates on 30 September 1590. For this he spent some weeks in the episcopal jail, only to be apprehended a second time for robbing the alms box of the cathedral on 22 November 1590. This time his principal accuser was Piero de Borgosesia, a boy whom Cestinello tried to convince to stand guard while he raided the alms box.[128] Cestinello's case was unique because it focused entirely on his theft. Most thefts were accompanied by other charges. For example, on 18 July 1595 Girolamo Settala, the vicar general, sentenced Giuseppe Mazzolio, a cleric from the region of Romagnano Sesia, to two months incarceration, three days of each week on bread and water alone, for a variety of offences which included theft of two hundred scudi from the cathedral of Novara, playing illicit games, and fornication. Mazzolio was also declared unfit for ordination and was banished from the city at the discretion of the vicar general.[129] Mazzolio's career in the clerical estate was revived, however, for in July 1609 he appeared before the tribunal after an altercation with the rural vicar of Borgosesia over whether he had absolved parishioners from reserved cases. On this occasion, Mazzolio was identified as curate of Colma. He was accused of making his differences with the vicar public by criticizing him at the Mass held for the meeting of the rural congregation, an action which was scandalous and shameful (*cosa indecente et indegna*). The curate was also accused of remonstrating with his people on another occasion, asking for higher payments for funerals. When a parishioner named Jorio Giulietto told him to get on with the Mass, Mazzolio called him arrogant and insolent for making such a remark when he was at the altar. The confrontation continued into the churchyard after the Mass, with the curate alleging that Giulietto had lifted a gun to his shoulder as if to shoot him until he was restrained by others. Mazzolio's interrogators rejected his version of events, saying that the injurious words he used at Mass were disgraceful and that other witnesses claimed that it was the curate who had provoked Giulietto after the Mass.[130] Although it is not known how this process ended, Mazzolio was still curate at Colma, a small village of four hundred souls, during the visitation of 1617.[131]

Another example involved Giuseppe Tettone, curate of Granozzo in the plains vicariate of Cameriano, who on 31 May 1603 was accused of cutting an oak tree on church property, as well as working in the fields, neglecting to say weekday masses, failure to teach catechism, being given to drink, playing cards at the hostelry of a relative, having sexual relations with a married woman who was his parishioner, and making improper advances towards the wife of the church custodian. In a scathing remark, the vicar general deemed him 'more suited to the hoe' (*più atto alla zappa*) and more suited to servile work in the vineyards than to his office as curate. Tettone admitted cutting the oak but claimed this was permitted because the tree was not bearing acorns. He also defended his refusal to say prayers to ward off inclement weather on the grounds that the threat was remote, and justified playing cards at the hostelry because it was an occasional recreation. He denied having relations with the woman and pursuing the wife of the custodian, as well as making the indecent remarks attributed to him.[132] The end of this process is not known, but it is known that Tettone appeared before the tribunal again on 13 August of the same year, accused of assaulting a chaplain with a sword and saying Mass the next day while in a state of excommunication. Again, the end of this process is unknown.[133]

Less serious than the homicides, assaults, thefts, and sexual practices were a variety of other activities that appeared in the records of the tribunal because the hierarchy deemed them to be prejudicial to the clerical estate. These included attendance at dances, night-time carousing, participation in carnival festivities, frequenting hostelries, drunkenness, and gambling.

What appeared to be a minor case arose in March 1597 when Francesco Pizetto, vice-curate at Bolzano, then in his early thirties, was accused of roaming the streets at night during the time of carnival with several young men and playing the guitar, which was described in the tribunal records as unbecoming to the clerical estate. What was more, when his playing interfered with a dance being held by another group, he refused to stop, thus setting the stage for a public disturbance. As so often happened in similar cases, Pizetto pleaded ignorance.[134] There was more to his case than appeared in the court records. He was very much in Bascapè's bad books during the visit of October 1601, by which time he had been appointed rector or titular parish priest of Bolzano by papal authorization. The reason for Bascapè's displeasure was that Pizetto had been fined for sexual relations with a woman and for keeping his daughter in his home. He was fined again and given a series of orders against gambling, living outside the parish rectory, and keeping his daughter. In August 1604 and again in May 1611 he was fined after it was noted that he had violated the injunctions and had not paid previous fines.[135] Nevertheless, Pizetto, who had been a student of the Jesuits' Roman College and the Brera at Milan, survived as rector of Bolzano, appearing in the visitations of 1617 and 1626 conscientiously, it appears, administering the care of souls by celebrating Mass daily, preaching, teaching catechism, and tending to the sick when called upon. Although he was severely criticized for not using clean altar cloths when celebrating the Eucharist, there seem to have been no prosecutions after 1611.[136]

Accusations of gambling, usually at cards, came up in seventeen of the cases, eleven involving curates and one a vice-curate. In 1595, in an example of compulsive gambling, Francesco Balbo, curate of Vignarello in the plains vicariate of Vespolate, admitted to playing cards at a neighbouring town and losing the alms he had received from performing a funeral, a hoe he had brought to the town for repair, a knife with scabbard, two years' rent from a piece of land, and his breviary, which he traded to another priest for a ring.[137] Balbo still exercised the care of souls when Bascapè visited Vignarello in 1596. A thirty-five year old from the diocese of Alessandria, Balbo was poorly regarded by both bishop and people. He was criticized not only for his gambling, which appears to have netted a fine of twenty-five scudi, but also for going about poorly dressed and without tonsure and for hunting with a firearm. Although he taught grammar to boys of the town, he was said to be poorly prepared in cases of conscience and in the ceremonies of the Mass. He was given a number of warnings, including one to cease engaging in games forbidden to clerics and another to refrain from hearing the confessions of people from outside his parish.[138]

Gambling at cards was also one of several accusations levelled against Giacomo Galina, curate of Cameri in November 1604. While admitting to paying an earlier fine of six ducatoni because of card playing, a fine also paid by two other priests of the town, he denied accusations that he gambled in taverns with laymen causing scandal and on occasion the loss of a good deal of money. In the opinion of his judges, he might have better spent his time in study because his ignorance of cases of conscience had led to suspension of his faculty to hear confessions.[139]

As in cases of theft, most accusations of scandalous behaviour were made in conjunction with other, more serious charges. For example, in early 1594 Cesare Guidotto, curate of Crodo in the Antigorio valley for only one year, was arraigned on a series of charges including seducing a woman after hearing her confession, greeting women at his door clothed only in a nightshirt, being ordained a priest before attaining the legal age, drinking excessively and vomiting in public, including after Mass, going about singing at all hours of the night, and abandoning the Rogation Day procession of his church. On 7 April 1594, he was acquitted of all charges.[140] The fact that he was no longer curate of Crodo when Bascapè visited the parish in October 1596 suggests that his sentence might have been the result of a private arrangement with the bishop that he resign the parish.[141]

At least fourteen of the trials, ten of them involving curates, involved the charge of exercising occupations normally performed by laypersons, a practice expressly forbidden by the first provincial council of Milan and by Romulo Archinto in his synod of 1576. Bascapè for his part promised to enforce the rule, noting that he had overridden exemptions granted by Rome for two curates to practice the office of notary.[142] Several priests were accused of keeping hostelries. One was Gaudenzio Marcandotto, curate of Vocca in the region of Varallo Sesia, who in 1594 was accused of keeping an inn and encouraging a drunken customer to expose himself in the presence of women. Other charges included having a child by a former housekeeper and seducing another woman in the confessional.[143] It is not known how this case ended, for no sentence has been found. Another priest accused of maintaining an inn was Alberto de Alberti, curate of Cuzzago, who in 1605 was implicated in a case of infanticide.[144] More unique was the case of the cleric Bartolomeo Laria of Cerano, arraigned in October 1594 for setting aside his clerical habit to join the army and for assault. This time Bascapè himself recommended leniency and Laria was given an injunction not to bear arms and to continue in habit and tonsure.[145]

Although it is not known if the local inquisitor heard many cases involving heretical beliefs or practices on the part of members of the clergy, the bishop's tribunal heard only a handful of such cases in this period. On four occasions in the 1580s and 1590s priests were accused of possessing prohibited books, and in 1598 eating meat and other prohibited foods in Lent was one of many charges filed against Niccolò Applano and Bartolomeo Guerrino, canons of Intra. In the latter case, heresy was by no means the main issue of the bishop's tribunal, which was more concerned with the other charges against the canons, which included plotting to murder their provost. As noted, the two were acquitted of all charges except attending a masked ball.[146]

Heresy also came up as one charge among many in 1593 during the trial of Bartolomeo Cagnola, Curate of Bannio in the Antrona Valley. Cagnola, twenty-eight years of age, was accused of numerous crimes while serving as vice-curate at Cimamulera, including a sexual relationship with and children by Catterina de Vallantrona, possessing prohibited weapons, having prohibited, erotic books, being ordained on the basis of false documents, celebrating Mass rarely, and not teaching catechism. Almost as an aside, he was accused of having a poor concept of the faith since he was educated among the heretics of Geneva and his father had been tried as a heretic. Cagnola was questioned under torture for a quarter of an hour about his relations with Catterina but not over his alleged heresy. He maintained his innocence and was absolved of most of the charges against him, including heresy. Instead he was fined six scudi for possession of weapons and disguises in his house and was given strict injunctions to avoid suspicious contact with women and to teach catechism as required.[147] The sentence, it seems, was the result of a settlement negotiated with the bishop. In a subsequent trial, in March 1603, Cagnola, who was still the curate at Bannio, admitted that while maintaining his innocence in court, he had in fact confessed to Bascapè so as not to give new means to his enemies to cross him. He had in fact had five children by Catterina. In 1603 he was prosecuted for irregularities in his efforts to arrange a marriage for his daughter, who was alleged to be less than twelve years old at the time. Other accusations included a new series of weapons violations, assaults, robberies, and affairs with two other women, all of which he denied, once again under torture.[148]

Among the trials of priests and clerics in the period 1563 to 1614, accusations of involvement in magic occurred more frequently than accusations of heresy, with ten priests, including several curates, accused of using incantations and spells, especially for seducing women. Thus, in May 1595 Girolamo Frello of Varallo, who had exercised the care of souls at the village of Fobello for over a year, admitted to having carnal relations with a girl of the village and to using an incantation, made up in his head, to make her satisfy his desires. He claimed that he believed the words of the incantation were nonsense and could not be used to constrain people. Frello also admitted to making prognostications based on astrology, but denied reading palms, except on one occasion during the time of carnival when he did so as a joke and in disguise. Other charges included conspiring to pass counterfeit money and causing a melee at a church procession by smashing the candle given to him because he deemed it too small for a priest of his status. It was his use of incantations that received the most attention from the vicar general, however, and the question of whether he had seduced the girl in the confessional or at least after serving as her confessor. His trial continued until September 1595, when he was questioned under torture by the vicar general, Girolamo Settala, in the presence of the Dominican inquisitor, Domenico Buelli.[149] It is not known how Frello's case ended. Other cases occurred in the early 1600s. In April 1610 Francesco Ficia, a priest at Cameriano in the plains region of the diocese, was accused of professing to use magic to enable a certain

Maddalena de Magri to consummate her marriage and later to seduce her. He was also accused of attempting to seduce a number of other women and of at least one rape. He denied all of the charges.[150]

There was one case in which a member of the clergy responded to an allegation of black magic or witchcraft. Between May and September 1601 Giovanni Antonio Montano, a priest alleged to be widely known for witchcraft at Mergozzo in the mountainous region of Pieve Vergonte, was interrogated on charges of providing cures from spells cast by his sister on four women, of using magic to cause impotence, and of casting a spell to choke a man of the village when he visited his home. The inquisitor of Novara attended two of his interrogations, the second of them under torture, during which Montano maintained his innocence. It is not known how the trial ended.[151]

In conclusion, the bishop's tribunal of Novara had an uneven record in its effort to discipline the clergy of the diocese. It was put to great use during the first five years of Bascapè's time at Novara, but its activity declined during the bishop's last fifteen years. The reasons for the decline are not clear, but might have had to do with the distractions created for the bishop and his curia by the jurisdictional struggles with the secular government, by frequent trips he was required to make to Milan and to Rome, and by the fact that the limited personnel in the curia and on the ground level of the parishes caused activity to slow. When accusations did occur, the episcopal curia could, at times, show a dogged determination in pursing problem priests and clerics, especially those involved in the care of souls. Prosecution by the bishop's tribunal could be a significant deterrent to clerical 'crime,' as the cases of Giovanni Anselmo, Domenico Zuffo, and Girolamo Bertolio demonstrate. To be summoned to Novara, endure time in the episcopal jail, withstand interrogations and possibly torture, and pay for the expenses of a legal defence and a substitute in the care of souls were major hardships for the accused and for the most part worse than the sentences which the vicars general imposed on those found guilty. However, in the majority of cases the accused managed to avoid the worst the bishop's tribunal had to offer. Many cases that did not come to sentence were terminated due to lack of evidence or curtailed when the priest or cleric privately confessed his guilt and received absolution and a penance. When sentences were passed, the punishments were remarkably light and ineffective, with many involving small fines and injunctions to avoid occasions of sin. A number of historians have observed that in the early modern period there was a tendency for the Roman Inquisition to overlap with and intrude in the work of the confessor, most notably by forbidding confessors to grant absolution to those who confessed heresies and demanding that such penitents present themselves to the inquisitor.[152] In the case of the bishop's tribunal of Novara, it more often seemed that the spirit of the confessor penetrated into and mitigated the judicial process.

The records of the episcopal tribunal demonstrate that approximately one-fifth of the Novarese priests were prosecuted at least once during Bascapè's episcopate, a surprisingly high number. The fact that the parish priests and chaplains were thoroughly integrated with their communities, for the most part born and raised in the diocese and sharing the sensibilities of their neighbours, ensured that the tribunal would be fighting an uphill battle in dealing with what the hierarchy regarded not just as sins but crimes against the order of God and of the church. Many secular priests simply did not have the sense of religious zeal and commitment demanded of them by reforming bishops and their curial officials. Negligence in the care of souls was not a major problem in the diocese. Most curates performed their basic duties and accusations of negligence were usually confined to failure to take the sacraments to the sick, to celebrate weekday masses, and to teach catechism. Prolonged absences from parishes and gross neglect of duties were rare. The Novarese hierarchy paid considerable attention to suppressing sexual activity on the part of the clergy, a problem which appeared in approximately half of the cases and covered a wide range of activity. Prostitution was not as prominent in the diocese of Novara with its large number of rural parishes as it was in more urban dioceses such as Siena. Most of the cases concerned dealings with local women in more or less lasting relationships, with cases of clerical concubinage appearing frequently in the books of the tribunal. It has been argued that parishioners had a high tolerance of clerical concubinage in the early modern era and that accusations against parish priests would only be made if other serious problems appeared, including such things as neglect of the care of souls, incidents of physical violence or verbal abuse, and new attempts at sexual seduction. While there is ample evidence of this at Novara with many cases involving blanket accusations including concubinage, there were also a good number of occasions when sexual misbehaviour was the only accusation brought against a priest. Was it possible that there was less toleration for sexual offences at Novara than in other dioceses? The fact that women would stay in relationships with curates and chaplains which lasted years on end suggests that there was a degree of community acceptance of their conduct, or at least a reluctance to make an accusation and incur the displeasure of a parish priest. It should also be borne in mind that sexual cases were only one part of a broad spectrum of charges which occupied the time and energy of the bishop's tribunal. Charges of assault, up to and including homicides, were almost as common as accusations of sexual misconduct. The fact that they were dealt with by the bishop's tribunal suggests that the principle of clerical immunity from prosecution by the secular courts was upheld in the diocese of Novara and underscores the independence which the hierarchy enjoyed in policing their own. Allegations of theft, gambling, drunkenness, and unruly behaviour also appeared with frequency, as did involvement in illicit magic. The bishop's tribunal was deemed necessary to keep some members of the clergy on a straight path and appears to have played a role in the attempt to mould the clergy into the professionalized body envisaged by the reforming hierarchy. Still, because of the tribunal's lack of personnel and resources, the poverty of many parishes and the shortage of capable priests, the bishops of post-Tridentine Novara were forced to temper their use of the law with clemency. Thus the fallen were allowed to recover and to continue in the care of souls over the years in spite of their repeat offences.

4 The Bishop's Tribunal and the Laity, 1563–1615

Although the post-Tridentine hierarchy emphasized its judicial prerogatives, it remains to be seen how large a role the bishop's tribunal played in the reform of the laity in the second half of the sixteenth century and the early years of the seventeenth. The bishops of Novara, imitating the work of Carlo Borromeo in this as in so many other areas, pursued a number of strategies for the spiritual development and moral reform of the people of the diocese. Included in their plans was the possibility of employing the tribunal as a means of control. Whether or not it was a strong instrument of moral reform or social control in the diocese would be revealed in its records in the period 1563 to 1615.[1]

The bishops of Novara took many steps to improve the spiritual lives of their flocks by implementing policies and programs called for by the provincial councils of Milan. The hierarchy's work was not primarily judicial and punitive but developed around a positive core designed to improve the spiritual life of family, parish, and confraternity.[2] The measures to reform the clergy, which were meant to provide the diocese with a cohort of upright and learned parish priests, were to be the foundation for a more spiritual society, which included the laity. During pastoral visitations, special attention was paid to whether parish priests celebrated Mass, preached on Sundays and feast days, held vespers, taught catechism, and brought the sacraments to the sick and dying in a manner that would truly edify and minister to the people.

Other steps focused more directly on the laity and lay leadership. Fathers of families were especially bound to ensure that their children and servants prayed, attended catechism lessons, and followed the Ten Commandments.[3] Special attention was paid to the development of religious confraternities. Bascapè and his fellow bishops encouraged the foundation of new confraternities in order to promote key devotions and knowledge of the faith within the parish structure. Each Novarese parish was to have a Company of the Blessed Sacrament to promote devotion to the Eucharist, a society of the Virgin or the Rosary to foster Marian devotions, and a School of Christian Doctrine to assist in catechizing.[4] In larger centres Bascapè encouraged the foundation of companies of the dead to provide masses for the souls of deceased members.[5] Older confraternities of the 'disciplined' were also placed under the watchful eye of the clergy.

Episcopal attempts to enforce standards of public morality were another aspect of Tridentine reform. As noted in the introduction to this volume, the ecclesiastical courts, especially in Catholic lands, made little distinction between sin and crime, between morality and violent crimes against persons and the public order. Members of the hierarchy attacked sin in all its manifestations, but they were especially interested in suppressing sins that they felt caused scandal and had the potential of undermining the spiritual health of the community. Adultery, concubinage, usury, blasphemy, the excesses of the carnival and the dance, and matters of faith ranked high on their list. They proceeded against these in a number of ways, from demanding more rigour on the part of confessors to attempting to curb carnival and enforce the observance of feast days to threatening concubinaries, blasphemers, usurers, heretics, practitioners of magic, and witches with prosecution by the bishop's tribunal.[6]

As in Borromeo's Milan, the bishops of Novara emphasized the proper administration of the sacrament of penance as a means of disciplining the people of the diocese. In their seminaries, the study of 'cases of conscience,' or the weighing of sins and penances, was the centre of the curriculum. The bishops ordered parish priests to purchase summas of cases and rural priests to congregate monthly to continue their studies.[7] They tested and licensed confessors, issued instructions (*avvertenze*) covering the proper administration of the sacrament, and insisted, among other things, that habitual sinners not be absolved until they had demonstrated their sincere desire to change.[8] In a bureaucratic process that was potentially a threat to the seal of confession, the rule of annual confession and Easter communion was enforced by a system of passes given by confessors to penitents and retrieved by parish priests at communion, with the process for each parishioner duly noted in a register called the 'status of souls.'[9]

In a further test of the secrecy of confession, absolution for serious sins was reserved to the bishop and curia at Novara. This was to ensure the uniform treatment of sins and to increase the disciplinary effect of the penitential rite.[10] Bishops Archinto and Bascapè, following the provincial councils of Milan, reserved absolution for murder, rape, abortion, concubinage, premarital sex, blasphemy, usury, eating meat during days of fast and abstinence, the use of magic to harm others, and other offences.[11] In practice, the enforcement of reserved cases was shared by the bishops with their vicars general, rural vicars, and the more trusted of the diocesan confessors, who in the late 1590s numbered approximately sixty. According to an instruction from Bascapè to his rural vicars, when a confessor encountered a reserved case but did not enjoy the faculty to absolve it, preference was given to writing to the bishop or the vicar general rather than sending the penitent in person, lest suspicions be aroused and the seal of confession jeopardized. In his letter the confessor was not to name the penitent or even the specific sin, but to cite the number of the sin from the tables circulated by the episcopal curia. At the same time it was recommended that the confessor send information about the quality of the penitent, the degree to which he or she persisted in the sin, and whether public scandal was involved.[12]

When a sin was public or especially dangerous because it presented a threat to the faith, or when a parishioner avoided the annual obligation of confession and communion, he or she was, in theory at least, subject to denunciation to the bishop's tribunal. However, the records of the bishop's tribunal between 1563 and 1615 suggest that the tribunal was neither a preferred nor an effective instrument for disciplining the laity. The proof lies primarily in the numbers. In the years 1563 to 1615 the names of slightly over 200 laypersons appear in the records of the tribunal on charges ranging from sexual transgressions like adultery and concubinage to matters of faith which included blasphemy, heresy, illicit magic, and witchcraft. The number of laypersons arraigned by the court was low when compared to the 350 prosecutions of priests and clerics in the same period and minimal when compared to the total population of the diocese, approximately 185,000 souls in 1616–18.[13] Further, unlike some members of the clergy, laypersons rarely appeared before the tribunal on more than one occasion, and most of their trials kept to one or two issues. It was unusual for accusers or prosecutors to make more than one charge against a layperson. The exceptions were when failure to appear before the tribunal led to a second citation for contempt, or an assault on a member of the clergy was accompanied by a blasphemous outburst. Incomplete or not, the Novarese statistics also pale when compared to those of the ecclesiastical courts of England in the Elizabethan and early Stuart eras. For example, accusations before the archidiaconal courts of the county of Essex, made in large part by elected churchwardens, numbered in the thousands.[14] Thus while the episcopal tribunal may have been a common way of dealing with the deviance of clerics in post-Tridentine Novara, sheer numbers suggest that this was not true for the laity.

Further, the staff of the Novarese episcopal court was never large enough to process both clerical and lay cases in a systematic fashion. As noted, the tribunal was composed of the vicar general, the prosecutor, chancellor, and jailer. As well, the tribunal could call on the services of twenty-five rural vicars who communicated and enforced episcopal policy in the parishes of the diocese and who were often asked to gather information. The Novarese bishops do not appear to have developed a group of armed retainers (*famiglia armata*) to apprehend the accused. For this they relied on the cooperation of secular officials (*podestà* and *sbirri*) on an ad hoc basis. Like other tribunals of the day, the ecclesiastical court from time to time interrogated the accused and in some cases accusers under torture, which occurred in fifteen of the lay cases found in this period, the majority of them during the episcopate of Bascapè when records for interrogations of the accused are most complete.[15] Although Novarese parish churches had syndics to see to the maintenance of the church buildings and grounds, they lacked the mechanisms for lay involvement and control found in England. The system of churchwardens, synodsmen, and other officials in Elizabethan England was not found in the Novarese countryside. Lack of personnel may partly explain why a high number of the accused ignored the summons to appear. Of the twenty-one lay cases found in the book of sentences for 1591–8, six were fines for failure to appear.[16] In most of these cases there is no evidence that the tribunal was able to pursue the matter. Although the threat of prosecution before the tribunal may have been a deterrent to types of sin and crime, the limited resources of the tribunal demanded that it focus on the clergy first and leave the laity to the internal tribunal of the confessional and the system of reserving absolution for certain sins to the bishop.

Nevertheless, it is interesting to examine the nature of the trials and the light they throw on the shifting priorities of the bishops, especially Carlo Bascapè, who was a figure of some weight in the unfolding of Tridentine reform in the archdiocese and province of Milan. Not surprisingly, three-quarters of the 200 laypersons who appeared before the tribunal did so during Bascapè's twenty-three-year episcopacy, as chart 4.1 demonstrates. Chart 4.1 reports cases by the lowest common denominator of persons denounced before the episcopal tribunal and reflects the mixed nature of the surviving documentation. As in the case of the clergy, in 1563–4 and 1576–90 the documents include testimony of accusers and witnesses, with only a few of the accused known to have been arraigned. It is only in the period following 1593, when the interrogations of the accused are available, that the numbers are based on persons arraigned by the tribunal. It is not known how many others may have been accused in this period but not arraigned because of limited resources or the policies of the curia. In the first years of Bascapè's episcopate, between twelve and thirty laypersons were arraigned annually, with the peak attained in 1594. The yearly average for the first five years of Bascapè's episcopate was fifteen arraignments. Prosecutions of laypersons fell off dramatically in the period 1600 to 1614, to an average of only six a year. Even this low average was inflated by spikes in 1601–2 (seven and fifteen persons cited annually) and 1609–11 (between eleven and fifteen persons arraigned annually). The spikes coincided with three trials in which

Chart 4.1. Laypersons Accused by Year

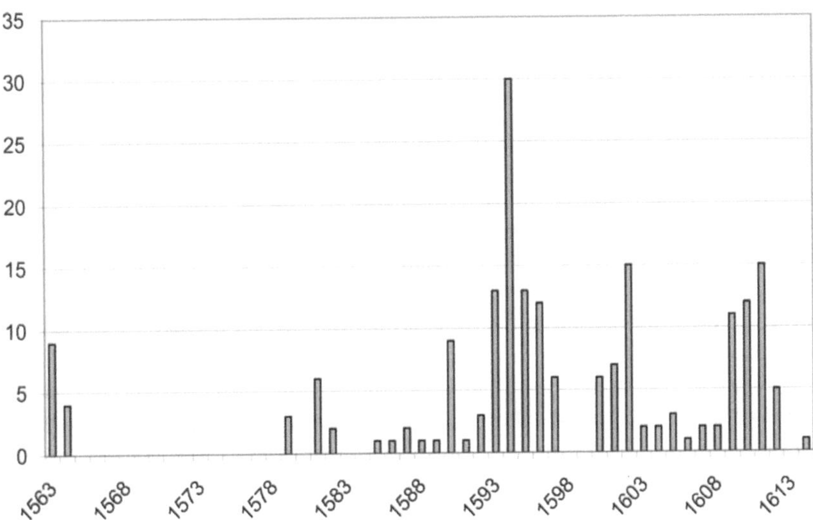

large numbers of persons were brought to Novara. Eight persons stood accused in a single process for dealing with a suspected heretic in 1601–2, sixteen were arraigned for allegedly attending a witches' sabbat in 1609–10, and another nine were brought to Novara in a related case in 1611.

As noted in chapter 3, accusations against priests and clerics also spiked in the early years of Bascapè's episcopate. However, while there was also a notable decline in processes involving ecclesiastics in the period 1600 to 1614, the pace of these remained much steadier than those of the laity, averaging approximately ten a year in that period, as chart 3.2 demonstrated.

The array of accusations against laypersons included a handful of cases involving usury, perjury, violations of sanctuary, and theft or destruction of ecclesiastical property. The majority of charges fell into four broad categories of 'crime': assaults against the clergy and agents of the court, accusations of sexual misconduct, cases of heresy and blasphemy, and illicit magic and witchcraft. Approximately three-quarters of the accused were males who were preponderant in all types of investigation, with the notable exceptions of illicit magic and of witchcraft.

Lay assaults against members of the clergy were the most common cases found in the Novarese records, with fifty-five processes involving over sixty persons standing accused. During Bascapè's episcopate there were twenty-seven such processes in the period 1593 to 1599 and a further sixteen between 1601 and 1614, with the great majority of the perpetrators male. The assaults reflect the degree to which the clergy of the diocese was involved in the day-to-day activities of the people despite the efforts of the hierarchy to set them apart. Most cases involved petty attacks, random blows, shoving, rock throwing, and insulting language. According to Bascapè there were nine homicides of members of the clergy in the years 1593 to 1609, but none of these were tried by the episcopal tribunal.[17] The same holds true of attempted murders and assaults that left grave injuries, leading to the conclusion that the more serious cases of lay violence against ecclesiastics were left to the secular courts. Nevertheless, the number and ongoing nature of the charges before the episcopal tribunal reflect the preoccupation of the post-Tridentine hierarchy with defending the dignity of the clergy. As well, each case of assault left in its wake a person willing to make a denunciation before the court, namely the offended cleric or official. Finally the sanctity of the clerical estate was such that attacks on a priest or cleric resulted in the excommunication of the perpetrator. For the eternal well-being of the soul of the guilty, this had to be resolved by the ecclesiastical authorities.

A number of cases involved disputes over property and the collection of parish revenues. On 3 August 1590 Cesar Fisrengo, the curate of Fisrengo in the plains near Novara, appeared before the vicar general to show wounds he had received at the hands of a group of workers of the Cascina of Mirabella in the territory of Gargarengo. The priest had left his parish on horseback with his servant on foot to visit a miller, but when he passed by Mirabella he was accosted by a group of three men and two women wielding staffs and throwing rocks. Led by Domenico, called '*il Giarla*,' they threw him from his horse and wounded him on head, face, shoulders, and arms. The priest fled on foot, followed by his servant and the small mob calling 'Kill, kill the priest!' (*Ammazza, ammazza il prete*). The attack seems to have been related to legal proceedings, which Fisrengo had launched for the collection of parish tithes.[18] It is not known if any of the perpetrators were formally arraigned.

A property dispute was behind another assault which happened in 1602. On 24 May of that year, Prospero Morigia of Pallanza on Lake Maggiore appeared before the vicar general on a charge of wounding Cesare Pizolo, a priest of the same town. Morigia admitted to quarrelling with the priest over which of their families had a right to a piece of land and scuffling with him with a sword in his left hand, cutting him on the ear. He was allowed to leave after promising not to receive communion under a penalty of two hundred scudi.[19] The end result of the incident is not known, but it is probable that Morigia was granted absolution.

A number of assaults involved attempts to intimidate or interfere with parish priests in the exercise of their duties. For example, in the fall of 1594 two brothers of the Piscatore family of Fara in the vicariate of Romagnano were arraigned for an armed attack on their newly appointed curate after he had declared them under interdict for not performing the Easter duty. It was alleged they were keeping concubines. One of the brothers was accused of ransacking the priest's bedroom and destroying documents. The brothers replied that the curate was staying at a house they owned, and they wanted him to leave.[20] The tribunal's records contain no indication that the brothers were prosecuted for concubinage as well as assault.

On other occasions priests provoked attacks by their own bad behaviour. Thus, in September 1585 Antonio Maria Besutio appeared before the vicar general on a charge of firing a gun at Antonio Ferabino, the curate of Cavaliano. The priest had been keeping Besutio's wife as his mistress. The offshoot was that the priest was himself arraigned, with two of the witnesses stating that it was commonly held at Cavaliano that the curate had fathered children by a second woman. Besutio himself appears to have escaped rather lightly, for a note in the margin of his process states that 'it was expedited by a decree of grace' (*fuit expeditus per decretum gratiae*).[21] A second case concerned Pietro Bellula of Borgosesia, who in December 1603 appeared to answer charges that he assaulted a cleric named Pietro Godio. Bellula had gone to the cleric to collect payment for some grain which he had given to the cleric's mother, only to be told that he was lying and threatened with a trained hawk! Bellula admitted that in the ensuing scuffle he may have struck Godio, thus incurring excommunication. However, he maintained that he was acting out of anger at being called a liar when he was only trying to recover what was his. He was a married man and an honourable man who valued his soul above any other thing (*perchè mi è più cara l'anima mia di ogni altra cosa*). He had reconciled with the cleric and begged the vicar general to grant him absolution if he had been excommunicated.[22] Given his penitent demeanor, it is likely that the vicar general complied.

Up until 1600, sexual matters rivalled attacks on the clergy as the most common cases brought before the bishop's court. This should not be surprising given the emphasis that the Council of Trent had placed on ecclesiastical control of the sacrament of matrimony and related attempts to systematize diverse marital practices and combat clandestine marriages and concubinage.[23] The cases found in the judicial records were those which the curia regarded as criminal: adultery, concubinage, bigamy, and incest being the most prominent.[24] On the other hand, requests for annulments and legal separations do not appear in the criminal records. If they were made at Novara, which appears likely given the activity of tribunals in other dioceses, they would probably have been included in files of '*cause matrimoniali*,' which were quite commonly saved in other diocesan archives but not at Novara.[25]

A key question here is the extent to which such matters occupied the time and attention of the ecclesiastical tribunals. It has been argued that sexual transgressions such as concubinage and prostitution assumed a central position in the penitential and judicial systems of post-Tridentine Italy. In the case of Siena, it has been said that for decades after Trent there was an atmosphere of denunciation which bordered on hysteria, and that the justice of the church had deviated from its 'pastoral orientation' and adopted a punitive way of proceeding which was similar to that of lay tribunals, with emphasis on fines, imprisonment, and corporal punishment.[26] Denunciations for concubinage peaked at Siena between 1590 and 1650, with 291 made between 1604 and 1628 alone.[27] In the city and diocese of Naples, the hierarchy made sporadic, largely unsuccessful efforts to restrict concubinage in the first decades following the closure of the Council of Trent. However, the first half of the seventeenth century witnessed a great increase in prosecutions of couples found in concubinage in the city of Naples, with an emphasis placed on the excommunication of those who refused to conform. The peak years were 1633–41 when 730 procedures for excommunication were recorded. After initial interventions and resistance by lay tribunals and authorities, the ecclesiastical courts of Naples are said to have enjoyed a monopoly in this area of activity. Still, it seems the repressive measures taken by the curia at Naples succeeded only in part, if at all. Factors such as the passive resistance of many couples and the lukewarm response of parish priests and confessors to episcopal directives ensured that concubinage remained a major factor in the social fabric of Naples as elsewhere.[28]

Preoccupation with sexual matters was a European phenomenon in the early modern era, and denunciations and trials of 'immoral offenders' were by no means confined to Italy. During the Elizabethan era the archidiaconal courts of the county of Essex, England, saw between 10,000 and 15,000 men and women denounced for sexual charges including premarital sex, bridal pregnancy, adultery, and prostitution. These numbers arose from a population base of 35,000 to 40,000 adults. The prominence of sexual offences at these low-level ecclesiastical courts was so high that the courts were known as the 'bawdy courts.'[29]

At Novara, in the half-century following the closure of the Council of Trent, cases of lay concubinage were not nearly as common as at Essex, although it is possible that these increased after 1615, if northern Italy followed the trends evidenced at Siena and Naples. Approximately fifty lay cases, a quarter of the lay cases, involved sexual offences, and the majority of these occurred before 1600. Most of these were heterosexual in nature. Approximately thirty appear to have been long-term relationships: concubinage, adultery, and bigamy (three cases).

Sexual charges involving laypersons were especially common in the first six years of Bascapè's episcopate, with twenty-four appearing on the books between 1593 and 1598, fifteen of which involved either concubinage or adultery. The majority of the accused were men, with only six women cited to appear on sexual matters. In the case of the women, even these numbers are inflated since two of the six were summoned because of alleged relationships with their parish priests. Such was the case of Catterina, the widow of Antonio Fracola, who in December 1608 was accused of having children by Domenico Palluda, then the curate of Cavalirio. Catterina alleged that she had initially been raped by Palluda, maintaining her story under torture.[30] None of the trials dealt with premarital sex or bridal pregnancy – which was a common charge in Elizabethan Essex – although premarital sex was deemed serious enough to rank among the cases reserved to the judgment of the bishop of Novara.[31]

The Novarese accusations were usually made by spouses. For example, on 26 August 1564 Agnese, wife of Battista de Cagnone of Ponzana, notified the vicar general that her husband had for six years kept the wife of a man from Pavia as a concubine. Orders were given to gather information, but the end result is not known.[32] On other occasions. abandoned spouses enlisted the aid of parish priests. In August 1582 Baldessaro Barciocco, curate of Camariano in the Novarese plains, informed the vicar general that Battista Cremonese, who also went under the name Vincenzo, had been living in the village for over a year with Helisabeta Mantuane who was not his wife but had borne him several children. Neither Battista, who was described as a tailor who also worked the fields, nor Helisabeta had received communion, and Battista never attended Mass in the church. Barciocco had heard from Lucretia, the man's wife of nineteen years, that Battista was a blasphemer who 'lived as a bestial man without fear of God' (*vive da huomo bestiale et senza timor di Dio*). The parish priest claimed that he had not heard Battista say anything heretical. Lucretia and Helisabeta were questioned, the former alleging that Battista had beaten her on many occasions. Helisabeta testified that she would never have taken up with Battista had she known about his marriage. The vicar general ordered her to leave Battista, possibly with some effect, for the woman testified that she had stopped relations with the man after learning of his marriage to Lucretia.[33]

On occasion the principal accusers were neighbours operating with varying degrees of credibility. On 5 May 1590 Giovanni Andrea Scarono of Novara appeared before the vicar general to accuse his neighbour the tailor (*sartore*) Giovanni Battista della Bella, called Santecca, of conducting an affair with Jacomina della Secondella virtually under the nose of Santecca's own wife. Although Scarono had never seen the two in bed together, he made his denunciation on the public knowledge that Jacomina was a woman of bad quality and a whore (*atteso la mala qualità di lei che è puttana*) who was rumoured to have had two children by Santecca and others by Gioseffo Cavalotto and the barber Giovanni Tomasso, who was by then deceased. Scarono added that the two were known to eat and drink together, and that Jacomina lived in a room in Santecca's house. He alleged that on the morning of the octave of Easter, when Santecca's wife Lucia had gone to the first Mass at the cathedral, Santecca, dressed in his nightgown, had gone to the bedroom where Jacomina slept, a room which protruded onto the plaza of the Castello, and was seen peering from the window to check that all was clear. On cross-examination Scarono admitted that Santecca owed him the sizeable sum of sixteen scudi. He named five other witnesses, but unfortunately for his case they did not offer solid support for his contentions. His neighbour Domenica da Vignola claimed to know nothing about the alleged relationship and Michella de Boschi, another neighbour, had seen the two eating and drinking together but could not judge if they had sexual relations. Michella added that she herself had little to do with Jacomina but fled her company 'more than the devil fled holy water' (*più che il diavolo dall'aqua sante*) because Jacomina was a woman who spoke poorly of others and made things up about them (*fa mille inventioni ancore se non siano vero, et a starne lontano sto meglio*). She had heard of the possibility of concubinage between the two, but knew nothing about it, suggesting that the vicar general speak to Santecca's wife Lucia, the person who should know best. Unfortunately, it is not known whether this suggestion was followed or how the matter ended.[34]

Whether the initial accusations were made by jilted spouses, parish priests, or neighbours, it was the desire of the bishops of Novara to ensure that long-term relationships outside the sacrament of marriage not turn into occasions of scandal. This was especially true when the offenders were from the higher sectors of society. Thus, in March 1595 Bascapè wrote to the curate of Orta that a certain Doctor Antonio Martelli of Borgomanero, who had already been fined the incredibly high sum of one hundred scudi and threatened with excommunication for failure to appear before the court, must turn his mistress out of his house. Bascapè added that he had up to now proceeded in the office of a father but if need be would act in the office of judge.[35] The bishop's intervention appears to have had some effect, for he returned to the subject a fortnight later, telling the curate to insist that Martelli find a good house for the woman and pay for her meals, for no other way could be found to remove the scandal. For the time being, Martelli was denied the sacrament.[36]

In most cases the thrust of the court was to separate the offending couples and have them return to their rightful partners. Fines were used to that end, as in the process of the notary Giovanni Maria del Monte of Cuzzago, who on

9 December 1596 admitted to paying a fine of twelve or thirteen ducatoni to obtain pardon for his relationship with Madalena d'Ornavasso, by whom he had two children. Now accused of violating the terms of his sentence by continuing the relationship and fathering another child, he denied the charges.[37]

Other cases appear to have involved shorter term relationships, in some cases bordering on prostitution. Thus, on 20 April 1579 Anna Camossa, daughter of Agostino, who lived in the hostelry of the Croce Bianca at Novara, was arraigned after fleeing her husband, who she claimed was older than she, treated her poorly, and beat her. Although the testimony was not clear, she seems to have spent time with two different men, failing to confess at Easter. A week in the episcopal jail appears to have had an effect on her, for on 28 April she declared herself ready to return to her husband 'and to live as a good woman and to set aside the bad life which [she had] led in the past' (*et vivere da donna da bene et lasciare la mala vita che ho fatta per il passato*).[38]

Allegations of incest, which included relationships by consanguinity (bloodline) as well as affinity (relationship through marriage) appeared in nine of the cases.[39] One process involving consanguinity began on 12 February 1579, when Cristoforo de Joannis, a rural worker from the parish of Morghengo on the Novarese plain, was accused by his sister Maria of fathering a child which she left at the hospital (*la Carità*) of Novara. The trial dragged on into the middle of March, with Cristoforo held in prison and questioned under torture, but protesting his innocence.[40] Two cases of affinity involved Giovanni Bartolomeo Tornielli of Borgolavezzaro and Giovanni Giacomo Maio of Cerano. Tornielli was summoned to appear before Girolamo Settala, the vicar general, on 21 April 1595 on suspicion of having sexual relations with the wife of a deceased relative. Although he conceded that there was room for suspicion, Tornielli denied the charge.[41] Maio, who was one of the few laypersons accused of a variety of charges, was arraigned in May 1600 primarily on a charge of blasphemy. He was also accused of having an illegitimate child by the widow Magdalena della Mora after standing as godfather for one of her older children. While evidently conceding that he had committed adultery, he denied knowing that he had run afoul of canon law by violating the spiritual relationship established by the baptism.[42]

Few laymen were accused of homosexual acts or of paedophilia before the Novarese tribunal in this half-century. There were two cases, both involving older men accused of forcing themselves on young boys. The first occurred in 1563 when Giovanni Antonio de Barris accused his master Francesco d'Arezzo of attempting to sodomize him when they shared a bed at a hospice at Novara with a third partner named Pedro who was also in the service of Francesco. Francesco and his companions were itinerant beggars who had been seeking alms through northern cities, ostensibly for a pilgrimage to the Holy Land, making stops at Pavia, Cremona, Vercelli, Biella, and elsewhere. Although Francesco claimed to be a hermit from the mountain of Sermoneta near Rome, he was not a member of a religious order but a poor man who could neither read nor write. Francesco alleged that Giovanni Antonio was taking his revenge after he had kicked the boy for coming to bed with dirty feet. The lack of convincing testimony, including the fact that Giovanni Antonio waited through the whole night before making his complaints, was enough for the deputy of the vicar general to set Francesco free, on condition that he leave the diocese of Novara within the day, never to return.[43]

A second trial concerned the farmer Giacomo Lombo of Ponzana in the southern region of the diocese, who in December 1601 appeared before the court on a charge of failing to perform his Easter duty and remaining under a sentence of excommunication for over a year without acting to remove it, thus incurring suspicion of heretical views because he held excommunication in such contempt. Despite Lombo's protestations of ignorance, the prosecutor soon revealed that over a year before, a young boy in his household, Battista of Ponzana, had fled from his employ, alleging that Lombo had sodomized him in a rye field. While begging for the excommunication to be lifted, Lombo vehemently denied the charge of sodomy, saying that his attackers – with the exception of the prosecutor of course – were lying (*si mente per la gola*). The end of the process is unknown.[44]

After 1600 the number of cases involving the sexual transgressions of laypersons declined significantly, with only nine appearing between 1601 and 1614. Most of these were atypical in the sense that they either included other charges as well or concerned offences which were regarded as especially reprehensible. Three of the nine persons accused were Giacomo Lombo, who was accused of sodomy, Giovanni Giacomo Maio, who was also accused of blasphemy, and Maio's alleged mistress. One was the custodian of the cathedral of Novara, accused of having sexual relations with a young woman entrusted to his care.[45] Another was Antonio Maria Bronzino of Ghemme, who in August 1609 was captured and arraigned after he was found having sex with a woman in the garden of the church of San Stefano at Novara.[46] Two were women involved in illicit relationships with priests, including Catterina Fracola, cited as the alleged mistress of Domenico Palluda, curate of Baceno. One possible explanation for the decline is that the jurisdictional squabbles of the period 1596 to 1615 discouraged an aggressive policy towards sexual transgressions by laypersons. During the controversies Bascapè argued that undermining the ecclesiastical tribunals would also undermine public morality, and it is possible that he wanted to avoid confrontation at a time when negotiations for a concordat were still at play.[47] However, the fact that trials of laymen for assault continued with little reduction suggests that this was probably not the only reason. A second and perhaps better explanation behind the decline in cases involving sexual transgressions of the laity is that matters of faith were taking more of the tribunal's time. Blasphemy, heresy, illicit magic, and witchcraft had long been concerns of the tribunal, but after 1600 they assumed a new weight in its work, making more demands on its limited resources. No doubt, abandoned spouses and irate neighbours continued to make accusations to their parish priests and to the bishop's vicars, but now the tribunal had less time to investigate and move on these matters. Combating concubinage was still, no doubt, on the curia's agenda. In 1616, shortly after Bascapè's death, Canon Antonio Tornielli reported to Rome that some laymen in the city caused scandal by keeping concubines and that their refusal to correct their way of life resulted in a number of ugly incidents with parish priests. It was equally difficult to have all parish priests, fearful for their safety when powerful individuals were involved, publish lists of those who failed to confess and communicate at Easter.[48] It seems possible that the bishop's tribunal resumed its activity against sexual offences after 1615, but equally possible that their success would not be any greater than that of the curia at Naples.

As noted in chapter 2, a new dimension was present in matters of faith, for the bishop's tribunal shared the field with the local inquisitor. During Bascapè's episcopate, after initial exchanges over the harshness of the inquisitor Domenico Buelli and attempts by the bishop to assert his rights as 'ordinary inquisitor,' inquisitors and vicars general appear to have cooperated in the prosecution of cases of faith. For example, as required by papal constitutions, the bishop's vicar general and the inquisitor both participated when the accused were interrogated under torture and when sentences were pronounced.[49] It is not known how active the Holy Office was at Novara during the episcopate of Bascapè. It is possible that the Inquisition's activity was slowed by the aging of Buelli, who died in 1603, and by the transition to a new inquisitor, the Dominican Gregorio Manino of Gozzano. It is also possible that the Inquisition itelf lacked resources and would have accepted the involvement of the episcopal tribunal in matters of faith at that time.[50]

Approximately six of the trials in matters of faith involved allegations of blasphemy, linked to heresy because sacrilegious words were deemed not only scandalous but also injurious to God and to religion. Thus in 1591 Giovanni Antonio Grignasco of Intra was tried over comments he made while drinking that he would renounce God and the celestial court and follow the devil before agreeing to the construction of a bell tower at the local church. The case was heard by the vicar general and the local inquisitor who, in their sentence of 17 December, determined that the words were not heretical but 'badly sounding' (*male sonant*) and scandalous. Grignasco was ordered to pay the substantial fine of ten scudi to the nuns of Intra within two weeks or face excommunication.[51] Blasphemous words often arose during violent altercations, but the court's concern that heresy might be involved remained the same. On 25 November 1603 Giovanni Battista de Rubeo of Romagnano was accused of using blasphemous words when he struck a priest in an altercation over a piece of land. When his interrogators informed him that he had fallen into excommunication because of the attack, he denied the charges. Accused of calling the priest a 'whore of God' (*puttana di Dio*) – words deemed 'atrocious and heretical, attributing to God something so alien as to say whore of God' (*atroce, et hereticale, attribuendo à Iddio cosa tanto aliena, come dire puttana d'Iddio*) – he again maintained his innocence.[52] The end result of the trial is not known, but it is unlikely the tribunal pushed the insinuation of heresy too far.

Cases which involved more substantial heresies were relatively few in spite of the fact that the Novarese bishops were on the alert for signs of it in the decades following the Council of Trent. One incident is mentioned in Bascapè's correspondence but not found in the records of the episcopal tribunal, perhaps because it was dealt with by the Inquisition. In the years before Bascapè's episcopate, several persons from Pallanza on Lake Maggiore abjured 'Lutheran' heresies while others were burned in effigy after fleeing.[53]

In 1591, just before Bascapè's episcopate, the tribunal began the trial of Gianni Gulielmotto of Loreglia in the mountain vicariate of Vallistrone. Gulielmotto was accused of frequenting areas of France where he attended Protestant sermons, praising them and compelling members of his household to attend. He was also accused of eating meat on Fridays and during the Lenten season and forcing his family and workers to do the same. After appearing voluntarily before the tribunal at Novara and presenting his defence, he was absolved of the charges by Ludovico Boido, the vicar general of Bascapè, and Domenico Buelli, the inquisitor of Novara, on 7 February 1594.[54]

In a similar process, in 1614 Fabrizio Moriggia of Vogogna was accused of saying that the religious orders had invented purgatory and masses for the dead in order to make money. Moriggia denied holding these views and claimed he was only repeating the words of a Servite friar.[55] The result of Moriggia's trial is unknown, but it is unlikely that he would have received a severe punishment such as a death sentence, for Bascapè's correspondence is without reference to his trial. Further, although the prosecution of religious dissent marked a sad stage in the history of the church, the records of Inquisitorial tribunals in other areas of Italy were not as sanguinary as once believed. The Inquisition was responsible for between twenty and twenty-five executions at Venice between the 1540s and 1600.[56] The Inquisition is said to have executed ninety-six persons in the city of Rome in the sixteenth century and another thirty in the seventeenth, but the Holy Office tended to call the more serious cases to Rome, and this inflated its number of executions.[57]

While heresy had not made many inroads in the diocese, Novara's location on the borderlands of the duchy of Milan and the threat of infiltration of Calvinist ideas from Switzerland remained serious problems in the eyes of the hierarchy. The diocese was within twenty kilometres of the Protestant canton of Bern, and on its northwest frontier shared an extensive border with the Valais, a Catholic canton under the bishop of Sion but open to Calvinist preachers in the last half of the sixteenth century.[58] Bascapè sought to enforce a number of papal and provincial edicts regulating travel to northern lands. The edicts forbade Catholics to settle in areas where the Mass was not celebrated or to trade or purchase property there. Anyone who travelled to areas where Protestantism and Catholicism coexisted was expected to return annually to perform the Easter duties of confession and communion or to send written proof that they had done so abroad. Bascapè also discouraged the residence of Protestant merchants in Novarese territory and placed those who visited the diocese under strict surveillance. They were not to discuss their beliefs and were not to be served foods forbidden to Catholics on days of fast and abstinence.[59]

The edicts proved difficult to enforce in northern regions where trade with Switzerland and seasonal migration in search of employment were necessary for economic survival. On several occasions Bascapè ordered rural vicars to investigate rumours that people had left the diocese for Protestant lands. For example, in 1600 Bascapè ordered the vicar of Domodossola to make inquiries about rumours that two brothers of Formazza in the northern tip of the diocese had emigrated to Aslea, in the canton of Bern, and may have become Protestants. If true, the rural vicar was to confiscate any property they had left in their homeland.[60]

In November 1601 the tribunal opened a process which illustrates both the prevalence of economic links between the people of the northern valleys and Switzerland and the fears of the curia over contact with Protestants. Lorenzo Palluda, curate of Baceno and the bishop's vicar for the Antigorio valley, the northernmost region of the diocese, denounced Domenico Pignolo, an elderly agricultural labourer, shepherd, and cheesemaker, as a heretic. In two interrogations before the vicar general at Novara, Pignolo admitted that he was born a Catholic but had spent fifteen or sixteen years in the Bernese village of Aslea without receiving Catholic sacraments and that he was following the religion of that region, for which he asked the pardon of God and the saints. His own knowledge of religion appears to have been minimal. He claimed to know part of the Lord's Prayer but not the Apostles' Creed or the articles of the faith. He also named a number of workmen and merchants of Baceno who frequented Aslea. The tribunal responded by calling for a curate to instruct Pignolo in the faith and by sending Bartolomeo Zucchinetti, the episcopal chancellor, to the Antigorio valley to gather information about Pignolo and his contacts. Although there was no evidence that Pignolo had attempted to spread unorthodox beliefs, beginning in February 1602 the tribunal arraigned eight merchants and shepherds of Baceno on charges of dealing with a known heretic. In socio-economic status, the eight ranged from Antonio del Bodaro, who described himself as a poor man and a labourer who travelled here and there in the Valais seeking work, to members of the Chiapino family, which included some of the more prosperous merchants of Baceno. Giovanni Chiapino, who drew most of the attention of the tribunal, admitted to hiring Pignolo after meeting him on the way to Switzerland. Chiapino was a moderately wealthy merchant, owning six horses and making approximately eight trips a year to Swiss towns, some of them Protestant, to trade in grain, cheese, wine, cattle, and all sorts of other merchandise. He also traded with southern towns including Omegna, Domodossola, and Pallanza in the diocese of Novara, and as far as Milan, which he had not done for the last three or four years. Although Chiapino and the others admitted familiarity with Pignolo, they denied discussing religion with him or knowing that he was a heretic. Three of them, including Chiapino and Bocaro, maintained this story under torture with the elderly inquisitor of Novara, Domenico Buelli, in attendance. Their process continued at least to the end of May, after which a sentence was issued. Although terms of the sentence are not known, it is doubtful that it included more than a penance or time served because Bascapè's letters are silent on the matter. Even so, the merchants and workmen of the Antigorio valley endured considerable hardship because of the expense of travelling to Novara, imprisonment, and being removed from their normal occupations through the spring of 1602. Pignolo himself endured a longer confinement. He was interrogated again in June and August 1602 to resolve inconsistencies in his testimony about the length of time he had spent in Protestant Aslea. He also faced new questions about the sacraments and responded simply but correctly, saying that he had learned much from the curate assigned to instruct him. His sentence remains unknown.[61]

If the trial of Pignolo and the men of Baceno was meant to intimidate the people of the Antigorio valley, its effects were short-lived. The northerners depended on ties with Switzerland for their livelihood, and no amount of surveillance could make them sever these. In 1608, merchants from the valley complained that their trade was hampered by a recent order that they obtain written permission from the bishop's rural vicars before travelling north. In reply, Bascapè compromised to ensure tranquility in the diocese: he did not wish to threaten the livelihood of the merchants and guaranteed that permits for travel were to be issued free of charge and for a period of time sufficient to conduct their business.[62] The merchants of the valley continued to take a relaxed attitude in their dealings with the Swiss. In 1617, Cardinal Taverna, Bascapè's successor at Novara, launched an inquiry into the conduct of several merchants of Baceno, who were accused of lodging 'Lutheran' traders from the canton of Bern and the Vallais who came to the Antigorio valley, as many as forty or fifty at a time. They were also accused of serving them meat on days of fast and abstinence. At the same time a number of Catholics were accused of believing that five Swiss Protestant victims of an avalanche had gone to heaven because they lived good lives, following their religion.[63] Thus, in the Antigorio valley edicts regulating relations with Protestants enjoyed limited success. There was little that could really be called heresy in the Antigorio valley and in other areas of the diocese. The greatest danger in the north was not that the people would convert to the Reformed faith, but that familiarity with Protestants could lead to indifference towards episcopal regulations, towards the distinction between Catholics and Protestants, and towards religion itself. Domenico Pignolo, when asked if he preferred to live as a Catholic in Baceno or in the Swiss Catholic town of Suit or as a Protestant at Aslea, replied ambivalently: 'When I was staying on this side of the mountains and in Suit, this way of life and that of Suit pleased me more, and when I was in Aslea the way of life over there pleased me more, and now that I am here, this pleases me more.'[64] Pignolo later gave a reply more favourable to the Catholic religion, but his first naive response was probably the better expression of his sentiments, and his words would probably have been seconded by many of his fellow labourers and shepherds and by the merchants who plied their trade with the Swiss.

By the end of the sixteenth century the episcopal tribunal of Novara, like tribunals of the Inquisition in other parts of Italy, was more involved with illicit magic and witchcraft than with heresy.[65] Illicit magic generally involved using spells to enamour, to predict the future, and to cure from disease and the effects of black magic (*maleficium*). Although its practitioners usually protested their good intentions, the courts often linked their activities to the more serious charge of witchcraft, which was held to involve the invocation of the devil and harming one's neighbour. Cases of illicit magic and witchcraft appear in the records of the Novarese tribunal as the bishops took both seriously as threats to the faith. In May 1590 Bishop Cesare Speciano issued an edict to condemn a number of local practices, including refusing to walk alone in a house where a corpse was being kept, taking the songs and flight of birds as portents, and praying to the moon to protect chicken coops against wolves. Speciano felt that such superstitions were a form of heresy: at best they dishonoured God with vain ceremonies, at worst they led the faithful to invoke the aid of the devil.[66] Bascapè, like the majority of his contemporaries, accepted as true stories of witches' sabbats and pacts with the devil.[67] It is possible that he acted as confessor to several witches burned in the Mesolcina valley in the 1580s under Carlo Borromeo.[68] As bishop, Bascapè ordered the clergy to study the legislation of Milanese provincial councils, which called for the extirpation of witches and magicians from the society of the faithful, and his vicars general proceeded diligently against those who engaged in this form of heresy.[69]

Although an early denunciation of illicit magic occurred on 3 May 1563, when Battista della Mora of Cerano accused Giacomo de Barberio, a carpenter, of using magic to render him impotent,[70] the greatest number of cases fell during the episcopate of Bascapè. Thus in 1596 Eusebio Isorno, a surgeon from Intra on Lake Maggiore, was convicted of possessing superstitious books and of using sorcery to cure from sickness and impotence. He was tortured in the presence of Girolamo Settala, the vicar general, and the Dominican inquisitor Domenico Buelli, but he maintained that he never used magic with evil intent. He was sentenced to recite the seven penitential psalms and a litany on his knees every week for a year at the shrine of Santa Maria at Suna, and was ordered to cease using superstitious remedies under penalty of a beating (*sub pena fustigationis*).[71]

In the next year, 1597, similar accusations were made against Francesco Poletto, an elderly notary from Villette in the Vigezzo valley. Poletto was accused of using prayers and a mysterious powder in an attempt to cure a bewitched woman of Suna. He visited Bernardo Pagane, the curate of Suna, asking him to bless the powder, which the priest refused to do, saying that it would be sinful on his part. Poletto informed the curate that he required the woman to say one Our Father and forty-one Hail Marys. Asked to explain why he required forty-one Hail Marys, he replied by asking why the rosary included decades of ten Hail Marys or why confessors required penitents to say ten or fifteen Our Fathers. The curate grew angry and ordered Poletto not leave the town under threat of a fine, but Poletto refused to obey. In all, Poletto was interrogated by the tribunal on five occasions about this and other attempted cures and about his possession of a recipe for transforming dung to a love powder. He was finally released from the bishop's jail on 1 April 1597 because of his age and with the condition that he not leave Novara under penalty of one hundred scudi. He was also ordered to pay seventy lire for meals received while in jail and fifteen lire for court costs.[72]

Other trials focused on using spells to enamour. For example, in fall 1602 Tibaldo Caccia, a grammar student at Novara, and Lucia de Balestrina of Intra were accused of preparing a charm to make Giovanni Battista Caccia, Tibaldo's relative, do whatever Lucia desired. The charm was in the form of a paper (*bolletino*) prepared by Tibaldo and placed in Giovanni Battista's bed for a night. Lucia was to burn the paper and mix the ashes into her target's food or drink. She maintained this story under torture, but the final outcome of the case is not known.[73]

In other cases a more open link was made between illicit magic and witchcraft. In 1595 Catterina di Compertonio, formerly of Milan, confessed to providing magical cures in the regions of Novara and Trecate. She signed people with the rosary and used other methods to cure stomach ailments but denied mumbling words that no one understood. If anyone was cured, it was not because of her but because of God and the Madonna. When she was unable to explain why she asked her clients to contribute money to charity and to say forty Our Fathers and forty Hail Marys, her interrogators accused her of giving a strong indication of superstition and witchcraft (*manifesto segno di superstitione, et arte maleficia*).[74] A more serious case was opened in 1610, when the widow Catterina de Albertino of Calasca in the Anzasca valley and her daughter Bartolomina were accused of causing one of their enemies to sicken and die after an argument. Reputed to be witches, they were also accused of using food, drink, and the evil eye to bewitch other persons.[75] It is not known how this trial ended.

Several Novarese trials for witchcraft involved a wide number of women and to a lesser extent men. One of these appears only indirectly in the existing records of the bishop's tribunal. According to testimony given in November 1609 by Comina Taramora of Baceno, herself accused of witchcraft, a number of women from the Premia and Antigorio valleys had been prosecuted forty years earlier by the inquisitor of Novara and a certain Fra Alberto. Comina and others had been exiled from their villages, although the inquisitor pardoned Comina with a document notarized on 21 May 1576.[76] Catterina de Franzino, also arraigned in 1609, gave a similar account of this incident, adding that one of her guards had informed her that two women had been burned as witches.[77] According to records of the Roman Inquisition, now found at Trinity College, Dublin, and not in the records of the episcopal tribunal of Novara, in 1580 twenty witches were tried by the Inquisition at Novara. Of these, two were retained in prison for further examination, ten were released after providing security, seven were acquitted, and only one was convicted and sentenced to perpetual imprisonment, which probably meant a confinement of six months to three years.[78]

The most spectacular trial of Bascapè's episcopate occurred between 1609 and 1611 and involved accusations of witches' dances or sabbats, demon worship, and ritualistic cannibalism. The focus was again on the Antigorio valley, which had long been under the scrutiny of the Inquisition and which had more recently drawn the attention of the episcopal tribunal during the trial of Domenico Pignolo and the frequent processes against the curates Domenico Zuffo and Lorenzo Palluda, neither of whom were on good terms with their parishioners. It is possible that both parish priests had a hand in the denunciations. In 1596 Zuffo had already advised Bascapè that a number of women in his parish were involved in sorcery. In November 1609 a twenty-year-old woman of Baceno in the Antigorio valley, Elizabetta de Julio, called '*la bastarda*,' was brought to Novara after testifying that she had attended a witches' ball. After prompting by her interrogators, Elizabetta described how two widows of Baceno, reputed to be witches, taught her the lessons of witchcraft, compelling her to assist while they prepared an ointment for casting spells. The devil appeared, with black and leathery skin, a tail, and goat's horns. Devil and witches took Elizabetta to the top of Mount Cervandone, where they were joined by eight other demons and where the devils and witches danced, had sexual intercourse, and feasted on roasted infant. Elizabetta's testimony was taken extremely seriously by the court. Six other suspects from Baceno and neighbouring Croveo were called to Novara in 1609, and an additional eight in June 1610. Two other 'witches' confirmed Elizabetta's story, and several admitted that they had been accused of witchcraft in the early 1570s, in the case mentioned by Comina Taramora.[79] In 1611 nine more were cited from the Antigorio valley, and in a similar process Pietro della Gueda of Macugnaga was accused of taking a young boy to a ball with three other witches.[80] It is not known how the processes of 1609 to 1611 concluded, although it is unlikely that any death sentences were meted out, for Bascapè's letters and other Novarese sources do not mention executions, and it was rare for Italian inquisitors to call for capital punishment in such cases.[81] Unfortunately, the prosecution of the women stained the record of the tribunal, for twelve of the accused died of fevers after imprisonments of up to one year.[82] Bascapè was aware that the women of the Antigorio valley were suffering ill health in his jail and considered freeing them in August 1611, but decided not do so because there were new reports of witches in the valley.[83]

The records of the episcopal tribunal suggest several things about the role of the tribunal in the reform of society in the period 1563 to 1614 and about theories of confessionalization. Citations for sexual offences appear less frequently than they do in the records of other ecclesiastical tribunals. The majority of these cases arose because of the allegations of deserted spouses and not because of a systematic effort by the episcopal curia or the clergy to bring them forward. Although sexual charges appeared with moderate frequency up to and including the first five years of Bascapè's episcopate, their incidence declined after 1600 when the churches of Lombardy were locked in their jurisdictional controversy with the Milanese state and when the bishop's tribunal was confronted with a number of serious cases in matters of faith. For the time being at least, sexual matters were increasingly left to the internal forum of the confessional and, if need be, the system of sins reserved to the bishop. Usury, perjury, theft of ecclesiastical property, and failure to perform the Easter duty appeared infrequently in the records of the tribunal.

Still, the bishop's tribunal remained active in dealing with minor assaults on the clergy and with matters of faith. Over a quarter of the charges dealt with assaults on the clergy. Serious crimes such as homicides remained in the hands of the secular authorities. The cases before the bishop's tribunal were relatively minor and had more to do with the dignity of the clerical estate, the reconciliation of enmities, and the removal of the penalty of excommunication than they did with the reform of laypersons. Questions of faith were given an intense scrutiny by the tribunal to the point that even words spoken from the bottom of a cup or in the heat of argument had to be weighed for their heretical implications. The tribunal examined several substantial allegations of heresy during the period 1563 to 1614, but by the 1600s heretical opinions appear to have been of lesser concern than the threats posed by travel to northern areas and fraternizing with Protestants. Because of the dependence of the northerners on trade with Switzerland and on finding work outside the safe confines of the diocese, even an ardent reformer like Bascapè was prepared to compromise when enforcing his own regulations. Accusations of illicit magic and witchcraft were found throughout the period of this study but appear to have been on the rise in the late sixteenth and early seventeenth centuries and led to the most spectacular and tragic trials in the history of the bishop's tribunal. Belief in witches and their evils may have had popular roots, but the credulity of the episcopal officials and the actions of the episcopal tribunal played a role in advancing them.[84] Be that as it may, if we accept theories about the use of the penitential system as a means of confessionalization and social control as valid and attempt to apply them to the diocese of Novara, it must be with the caveat that the ecclesiastical tribunal played a marginal role in the process, and that its main focus was the disciplining of the clergy. The tribunal was not a primary or a preferred way of asserting control over the laity.

5 Shifting Patterns of Activity: The Bishop's Tribunal, 1745–1799

Little is known about the activity of the bishop's tribunal of Novara in the century and a half following Carlo Bascapè's death in 1615. After a few cases in 1618–9 pertaining mainly to the sale of goods on Sundays and petty infractions of regulations governing the visit of nuns, the records of the tribunal were either lost or at least no longer maintained in a separate category of archival documents.[1] What little remains must be gleaned from the records known as *Acta Curia* and the *Licentiarium*, voluminous collections of routine documents filed by year without further sorting or indexing.[2] Be that as it may, the bishops of Novara of the seventeenth century remained active pastors and maintained high standards for the clergy, despite a general downturn in the role and activity of Italian bishops in the middle decades of the century. When episcopal activity and prestige improved in Italy in the late-seventeenth and early eighteenth centuries, the Novarese church continued on its steady course of action. However, it is only in the period from 1745 to 1799 that records of the tribunal have survived in a systematic fashion to permit comparisons with the earlier, post-Tridentine trials. By that time conditions in the diocese had changed in two important ways. First, Novara passed from the control of the duchy of Milan to become part of the dominions of the house of Savoy, now elevated to the status of kings of Sardinia. In the first half of the eighteenth century, the royal government had been especially assertive in establishing its rights and powers in ecclesiastical matters, including the question of ecclesiastical jurisdiction. Second, like so many other areas of Italy, Novara had experienced a tremendous growth in the numbers of priests, especially chaplains and other priests who were not directly involved in the care of souls. The bishop's tribunal played a reduced role in the period from 1750 to 1799 compared to its activity in the post-Tridentine era, not only in dealing with the laity but also in disciplining the clergy. While this may in part have been due to the more aggressive attitude of state authorities, it also suggests a turn in the work of the episcopal curia towards a more informal, less legalistic approach in dealing with problematic members of the clergy. The tribunal was clearly in decline as a legal entity in the diocese, as the bishops and their officials moved away from the aggressive stance taken in the earlier period of Tridentine reform, and especially during the first years of Carlo Bascapè.

The middle years of the seventeenth century have been viewed as a period of stagnation or decline for the church in Italy. Although plague and a return to warfare played roles, the greatest manifestation was a recurrence of the problem of absenteeism of bishops from their dioceses, as many bishops preferred to pursue advancement by service to the Roman curia or made requests to stay away from their dioceses for personal reasons. In 1635 a congregation was established under Pope Urban VIII (r. 1623–44) to enforce the residence of bishops in their dioceses, but ironically its main function seems to have been to grant dispensations from residence for reasons such as ill health and the inability to cope with banditry and threats of violence. The congregation, which functioned until 1668, granted seventy dispensations from episcopal residence in the first year of its activity, thirty-five of these to bishops from the kingdom of Naples. This reflected the growing difficulty of the southern bishops in asserting their rights when confronted by powerful barons and also the great violence which characterized many of the provinces of the kingdom.[3] The lack of resident bishops was not the only problem in this era. Episcopal power was also eroded by the centralizing policies of Rome and the pensions that Rome imposed on Italian dioceses. Other problems were the lack of diocesan seminaries, the expanding role of the religious congregations in the fields of education, preaching, and missionary work, and the extensive involvement of the Roman Inquisition in disciplinary matters.[4] It was only in the battle against the cohabitation of unmarried couples that a number of dioceses developed new, aggressive policies of reform, which had limited success.[5]

The pontificate of Innocent XI (Benedetto Odescalchi, r. 1676–89) is regarded as a turning point in the history of the Italian episcopacy. Odescalchi was a former bishop of Novara (r. 1650–6) who ironically left relatively little imprint on the diocese and is said to have used the position to advance his career at Rome. As pope he was influenced by developments north of the Alps, in the Gallican Church and in areas of Germany which involved a revival of episcopal endeavour and prestige. Steps were taken to appoint strong bishops and to free bishops from burdens placed on them in the past, most notably by curtailing the pensions taken from their revenues. In the period between the 1670s and 1750s, Rome oversaw the appointment of a high number of culturally prepared and morally upright bishops, dedicated to pastoral care and a great improvement over the episcopate of the previous fifty years. The improvement in the calibre and status of Italian bishops had a variety of results: the development of diocesan archives to establish documentary control and to place the rights of churches on a firm basis, new construction focusing on cathedrals, episcopal palaces, and seminaries, a return to the practice of holding diocesan synods, and finally the development of seminaries to prepare a corps of dedicated priests.[6]

Although Benedetto Odescalchi may have left only a modest imprint on Novara during his short tenure as bishop, and although the diocese shared in the miseries created by the recurrence of military invasions and plagues, the Novarese episcopate appears to have avoided the decline that weighed so heavily on the church elsewhere in Italy in the middle decades of the seventeenth century.[7] There was bound to be some fall off after the intense activity of Carlo Bascapè, but the bishops continued to reside and perform their pastoral duties, as evidenced in the numbers of pastoral visitations conducted, diocesan synods held, and seminarians attending Novarese institutions. More or less complete cycles of visitation of the parishes of the diocese were conducted by Cardinal Ferdinand Taverna (r. 1615–19), Giovanni Pietro Volpi (r. 1629–36), Antonio Tornielli (r. 1636–50), Giulio Maria Odescalchi (r. 1656–66), Giovanni Battista Visconti (r. 1688–1713), and Giberto Borromeo (r. 1714–40). Synods were held by Taverna in 1618, Tornielli in 1639, Odescalchi in 1660, Giuseppe Maria Maraviglia in 1674, and Visconti in 1707.[8] Although the seminaries, with the possible exception of the main seminary at Novara, continued to be strapped for funds through the seventeenth century, they remained a steady factor in the life of the diocese with modest increases in the number of students. The seminary of Novara housed fifty students annually from the 1620s through the 1650s, and between sixty and seventy students from the 1670s to the end of the century. The level of instruction was elevated in the 1620s when the Jesuit order assumed control of the Cannobian School in the city and the seminarians began to attend their classes. The minor seminary at the Island of San Giulio continued to accommodate in the range of twenty students of grammar and letters, while the college of Santa Cristina at Borgomanero held a similar number of older clerics who studied cases of conscience under the oblates of San Gaudenzio and San Carlo.[9] The seminaries enjoyed further growth and stability in the first half of the eighteenth century, with the number of clerics at the main seminary rising to over one hundred in the 1750s. Here the more advanced students of the diocese received lessons in rhetoric, philosophy, moral theology, and scholastic theology. The seminary of Isola had grown to thirty-six younger students of grammar and the humane letters, while Santa Cristina provided lessons in moral theology, and the seminary of Varallo Sesia continued to teach a handful of poor boys from the region.[10]

By the 1740s, when the records of the tribunal were once again consistently maintained, the activity of the curia had changed significantly. The staffing of the tribunal continued to consist of a coterie of vicars general, prosecutors, chancellors, jailers, and rural vicars, and the tribunal continued to be responsible for both civil and criminal matters.[11] However, the Novarese hierarchy had all but abandoned its efforts to use the court as a means of policing lay conduct, and gave it a reduced role in the disciplining of the clergy. Although the surviving documentation gives no rationale for a change in policy by the hierarchy, there was a trend on the part of the curia to deal with clerical offences in an informal, extra-judicial manner, with more emphasis on admonition, penance, and correction than on the force and intimidation of the formal legal proceedings, which were so prominent in the post-Tridentine epoch. The tribunal itself was in a state of decline in the last half-century of the Old Regime in Italy, and the decline could be attributed to both the hand of the state and to a more mature attitude on the part of the hierarchy when dealing with problem clergy. Even when proceeding judicially, the curia used milder techniques. Torture was no longer employed to secure confessions and verify testimony. Rather than calling the accused to the episcopal jail for extended periods at great cost to themselves in terms of time and money, there was a greater tendency to gather information on site in the rural parishes using the services of rural vicars and officials sent from Novara, usually prosecutors and chancellors. Fines were still used as punishment, but in lesser numbers than in the days of Bascapè. Deprivation of benefice, suspension from sacred functions, and imprisonment or at least confinement in a religious house were surprisingly more commonly applied than in the late-sixteenth and early seventeenth centuries. However, the punishments were supplemented by the remedial practice of having wayward priests and clerics undertake spiritual exercises with the oblates of Novara or in the houses of the religious orders. At the same time, rising standards of education and an abundance of priests made it easier for the bishops of Novara to find suitable candidates for the parishes of the diocese and to remove curates and priests found wanting in the administration of the care of souls or caught in flagrant violation of the lifestyle expected of the clerical estate. Matters of faith remained a concern for the hierarchy but left little impact on the activity of the tribunal, which declined in this area to a minimal level at a time when its sister institution, the Roman Inquisition, was also experiencing a downturn in activity through much of Italy and probably at Novara as well. In the few cases of faith that did arise, the emphasis had shifted from illicit magic, witchcraft, and Protestant infiltration to the threat posed by the new ideas of the Enlightenment.

The shifting role of the bishop's tribunal was in part a reflection of the changing parameters facing the diocese of Novara and its clergy. Two features were prominent: the transfer of Novara from the duchy of Milan to the new kingdom of Piedmont-Sardinia and a spectacular increase in the numbers of diocesan clergy.

By 1736 Novara and its territory had been completely absorbed by the house of Savoy, which from 1713 enjoyed the added status of kingship, winning first the kingdom of Sicily, later exchanged for that of Sardinia.[12] Until 1791 the bishops of Novara were still legally nominated by the papacy, but with the approval of the court at Turin.[13] With the transfer in political allegiance there also occurred a rise in the desire and ability of the secular authorities to establish firmer control both over the clergy and over judicial processes in their state. Under Victor Amadeus II (r. 1675–1730) and Charles Emanuel III (r. 1730–73), the Savoyard state, in advance of the great reform efforts of other Italian states in the second half of the eighteenth century, engaged in protracted struggles with the papacy in order to gain greater control over such matters as ecclesiastical appointments, the taxation of church property, and the work of ecclesiastical tribunals.[14] Concordats signed in 1727 and 1742 strengthened the position of the secular authorities in the areas of ecclesiastical appointment and taxation of church property. Victor Amadeus II was known for the care he took to appoint bishops he could trust, and he developed a body known as the 'royal congregation of secular ecclesiastics' (also known as the Congregation of the Superga after the cathedral of Turin) to help mould and select the higher clergy, a project which failed to provide the state with the anticipated number of bishops.[15] Be that as it may, by the second half of the eighteenth century the episcopacy and the upper echelons of the senate and magistracy enjoyed close relations and were often from the same families. In the eighteenth century, in contrast to the sixteenth and seventeenth centuries, royal policy was that bishops were to restrict their activities to their dioceses and were to remain outside the sphere of high politics and diplomacy.[16]

Jurisdictional matters remained to be resolved, but the balance had shifted in favour of the state as it asserted its rights over all legal affairs in its territory and over all of its subjects. By the second half of the eighteenth century, these and other matters were usually resolved by negotiation and compromise instead of a more formal and binding concordat, and in the process a degree of harmony between the royal officials and the ecclesiastical hierarchy in Piedmont and even at Rome replaced the jurisdictional conflicts of earlier periods.[17] In the absence of a department or committee dealing exclusively with ecclesiastical matters, leadership was assumed by the magistrates of the senate of Piedmont, the most important of the supreme courts of the diverse dominions of the house of Savoy. The heads of the senate, endowed with administrative as well as judicial powers, defended the sovereign in the relations with the Roman curia and developed new strategies for involvement in the affairs of the church, involvement which limited the authority of the ecclesiastical tribunals.[18] Their efforts were manifest in a number of areas. They insisted that the ecclesiastical courts, including the Inquisition, must demonstrate their reasons to the court at Turin before they could call on the 'secular arm' for the apprehension of laypersons; they limited the right of sanctuary; they required that the clergy obey state laws against carrying weapons and against counterfeiting currency; and they intervened in cases where the award of ecclesiastical benefices was in dispute.[19] In the case of justice applied to priests and members of the religious orders, there had been an attempt, at least, under Victor Amadeus II to restrict 'privileged crimes' (*crimini privilegiati*) or more serious crimes such as homicide, carrying prohibited weapons, and attacks on public authorities to the secular courts while leaving only 'common' crimes to the ecclesiastical courts. Approximately forty cases involving members of the secular and religious clergy, ten of these with the clergy standing accused of crimes, are found in the records of the senate of Chambéry, which had authority over the territory of the duchy of Savoy beyond the Alps in the eighteenth century.[20] Although the numbers were relatively low, the cases were an erosion of the principle of the *privilegium fori*, or the right of ecclesiastics to be tried by the ecclesiastical courts and not the secular courts, a principle dear to the Italian bishops of earlier centuries. The relationship of the secular and ecclesiastical tribunals was in a fluid state in the eighteenth century, with the secular courts encroaching on the ecclesiastical courts.

The diocese of Novara, like those of Tortona, Vigevano, and Bobbio, was a newly acquired territory of the Savoyard state and not subject to the same laws and administrative procedures as the older territories of the kings of Piedmont-Sardinia. For a time, it was allowed to follow the old usages of the duchy of Milan in ecclesiastical matters.[21] However, it was slowly but surely being brought into the Savoyard system of ecclesiastical governance, and this would have an impact on the work of the tribunal.

The first of the bishops appointed after the transfer to Piedmont-Sardinia was Bernardino Ignazio Rovèro (r. 1741–7) who was born in Asti and was a lecturer in philosophy and theology in the Capuchin order before becoming bishop of Sassari on the island of Sardinia in 1730. Transferred to Novara, he assumed control of his new diocese with the best of intentions, announcing a round of pastoral visitations in 1744. However, ill health prevented him from proceeding any further than the vicariate of Oleggio, and he died at the episcopal residence at Trecate in October 1747. His immediate successors were Giovanni Battista Baratta, provost of the Congregation of the Oratory, who died in April 1748 while travelling to the diocese, and Ignazio Rovèro (r. 1748–56), who was a canon of Turin, laureate in law, but also a servant of the Holy See, acting as governor of Sabina, Città di Castello, and Fano in the Papal States. Although he issued a number of directives on the education of the clergy and the liturgy, ill health prevented him from visiting more than a small part of the diocese, including the more remote areas of the Valsesia, Ossola, and Verbano.

The history of truncated episcopates and lack of steady attention that characterized the first decades after the Council of Trent seemed to be repeating itself at Novara, when Marco Aurelio Balbis Bertone, aged thirty-one, was appointed to the diocese in January 1757. Born in 1725 to a noble family at Chieri near Turin, he was laureate in theology at the University of Turin in 1749 before continuing his studies in liturgy and ecclesiastical history at Rome. He was involved with the priests of the Oratory and of St Vincent de Paul and participated in the catechization of the poor. His episcopate lasted until his death in 1789. He conducted a complete cycle of visitation between 1758 and 1765 and began a second in 1779, which did not cover all parts of the diocese and did not include the city. After some delay, he held a diocesan synod in 1778 and gave steady attention to the diocese and especially its priests, overseeing a new phase of seminary construction in the 1760s and 1770s. Alleged to have Jansenist leanings, he set high standards for morality and the administration of the sacraments, and in his theological discourses resisted the lax moral theology of probabilism, insisting on the need for contrition, a perfect sorrow for sin, in confession. Not surprisingly, he was not on good terms with the Jesuits and eventually removed the theology students of the seminary of Novara from the Cannobian School, run by the order. The Jesuits themselves lost control of the school in 1772, shortly before the order's dissolution in 1773.[22] Balbis Bertone's relationship with the Savoyard court appears to have been cordial, and in 1767 he and King Charles Emanuel III agreed on a convention which transferred control over the feudal territory of Riviera d'Orta to the crown in exchange for the honorific title of 'prince of San Giulio and Orta.' This was part of a redimensioning of feudal jurisdictions in Piemont-Sardinia during the second half of the eighteenth century.[23]

Balbis Bertone's expectations for the conduct of the clerical estate were high. As in the post-Tridentine era, priests and clerics were to conduct themselves in a manner that would distinguish them from and provide leadership to the laity. According to his decree on the life and honour of the clergy, issued in the synod of 1778, they were to wear the proper clerical garb, exercise moderation in all they said and did, shun gambling, excessive drinking, and participation in dances, the theatre, and other public spectacles, refrain from carrying weapons, and at all costs avoid excessive familiarity and suspicious dealings with women. Since ignorant clergy were not only useless but a danger to the church, priests were to congregate regularly to study cases of conscience. They were to have books useful for the ecclesiastical estate and office, especially the Bible, the Roman catechism, and the decrees of Trent, the provincial councils, and diocesan synods. They were to reject books that were harmful to religion, discipline, and the fear and love of God. All priests, but especially those entrusted with the care of souls and the power to hear confessions, were exhorted to undergo spiritual exercises every year or at least once every three years.[24]

The second great change in the Novarese church in the eighteenth century was the greatly inflated number of priests. A head count based on the *status personalis* of priests in the pastoral visitations of 1758 to 1763 reveals that numbers of secular priests in the diocese had more than tripled in the century and a half that followed the death of Bascapè. This reflected a trend evident throughout the Italian peninsula in the early modern era.[25] By the mid-eighteenth century, based on reports made during pastoral visitations, the population of the diocese had increased by approximately 23.8 per cent, from over 186,000 to over 230,000,[26] perhaps reflecting the increased economic activity noted for the smaller towns of northern Italy between the mid-seventeenth and the eighteenth centuries.[27] In the meantime, the number of secular priests had almost tripled from 485, or one priest for 384 souls, to 1460, or one priest for 158 souls.[28]

Reforming states of the eighteenth century, critical of the rising numbers of priests, often blamed the phenomenon on the fact that clerics and priests enjoyed the privilege of being free from prosecution by secular tribunals.[29] A number of other explanations can also be advanced. First, schools dependent on the church and the religious orders were recruiting grounds for the clergy, both secular and religious. In the diocese of Novara, the majority of secular priests of the seventeenth and eighteenth centuries had received at least part of their training at one of the diocesan seminaries or at the Cannobian School, founded in 1603 and controlled by the Jesuit order from 1624 to 1772. In 1764 the main seminary housed 120 clerics and provided instruction in rhetoric, philosophy, speculative theology, and moral theology, while smaller seminaries operated at Borgomanero, Suna, Varallo Sesia, the Island of San Giulio, and Gozzano. As well, many clerics were able to round out their education at colleges outside the diocese, most notably the Jesuit Brera College in Milan and the Roman College at Rome.[30] Second, the proliferation of masses for the dead and chaplaincies provided a comfortable niche for many sons of the middling classes of the towns and villages of the diocese and were another incentive to a priestly vocation.[31] The majority of 'new' priests were not parish priests but chaplains with a variety of Mass obligations, canons without the care of souls, and priests living on their patrimony or family property and on occasion saying masses to fulfil legacies.[32] Since the sixteenth century, numerous families, lay confraternities, and communities had established collegiate canonries, lifelong and perpetual chaplaincies, and legacies for the souls of the departed. Although such arrangements reflected the devotional and spiritual aspirations of families and corporate groups, they were also, from an economic perspective, a way for families to shelter part of their holdings from state taxation. From a social perspective, they were also a means to provide family members with a more or less elevated and stable position, and more generally to advance the prestige of one's family, confraternity, or community by demonstrating a degree of patrimonial wealth and stability.[33]

The diocese no doubt benefited from the presence of the canons, chaplains, and simple priests, for they added to the splendour and availability of liturgical functions and served as catechists and, when qualified, confessors. As well, many acted as grammar teachers in villages and towns, providing an unofficial system of primary education. In Balbis Bertone's visitations of 1758 to 1763, at least 129 chaplains and 9 parish priests were engaged by their communities as schoolmasters. They covered more than a third of the parishes of the diocese, and in some vicariates of the plains, lakes, and mountains there was at least one schoolmaster for almost every parish.[34] The rise of chaplain-teachers in the diocese paralleled developments in other regions and cities in the early modern era. For example, at Siena there was a movement away from secular schools and teachers towards a greater degree of ecclesiastical involvement, it is said with greater emphasis on orthodoxy and a loss of freedoms enjoyed previously. The trend to greater ecclesiastical control was resisted by leading sectors of the city of Siena, a development not in evidence in the Novarese rural parishes.[35]

Nevertheless, the high number of priests, especially those not involved in the care of souls, attracted increasing attention in eighteenth-century Italy, at first from the writers of the Enlightenment and eventually from reform-minded states, concerned that young men chose the ecclesiastical life in order to escape the jurisdiction of the secular courts and to avoid the burdens of secular society, often leading idle lives and committing acts against good order and the public peace. In 1771, King Charles Emanuel III, acting in conjunction with Pope Clement XIII, gave these as his reasons when he issued a proclamation which declared that all candidates for first tonsure were to have title to a benefice, a perpetual chaplaincy, or an ecclesiastical pension sufficient for their support. As well, they were to be at least ten years old and have spent three years in a seminary or church school, or spent three years committed to the service of a church while wearing ecclesiastical habit. Having received tonsure, they were to remain in their seminary, school, or the church to which they were assigned, and to observe the rules of the church as to clothing and separation from secular occupations. If they met these conditions, they would continue to enjoy immunity from prosecution by the secular courts.[36] The promise of immunity may have been a hollow one, as the records of the bishop's tribunal would demonstrate. From the perspective of discipline, the rising numbers of priests had both advantages and disadvantages. On one hand, the bishops of the eighteenth century enjoyed a substantial pool of candidates with seminary training to draw upon when selecting priests for the care of souls and could more easily remove those found wanting. On the other hand, the diocese possessed a large body of marginally employed priests and clerics who often lived with their families and were often entangled in local activities and rivalries. These represented a potential source of trouble for ecclesiastical discipline. Their negative potential was often reflected in the work of the bishop's tribunal.

The surviving records of the eighteenth-century tribunal, which cover the years 1745 to 1799, demonstrate that the bishop's curia had almost completely abandoned the use of the tribunal against the moral and criminal infractions of laypersons. Of the over 450 separate cases, only 36 concerned laypersons, a figure inflated by the inclusion of 9 men from Vergano who were denounced by their curate in 1771 for failure to perform the Easter duty of confession and communion.[37] Only one case involved a laywoman: Giovanna Grolli, investigated for alleged heretical or blasphemous statements in 1787. Assaults on priests or clerics were the basis for thirteen of the thirty-six cases, and these appear to have been on a declining curve: nine of these date from the 1760s, two from the 1770s, and only one from each of the 1780s and 1790s. The majority of these cases were trivial. For example, in April 1782 Biaggio de Angelis, a young layman, was accused of hitting a cleric with a snowball on the steps of the church of Gnogno. De Angelis claimed that he did not recognize his victim as a cleric because he was not wearing clerical attire.[38] More serious was the case of Raimondo Gippini, who in May 1797 was accused of insulting the priest Francesco Invorio with the words 'Wicked, quarrelsome, reckless pig' (*Birbante, litiggioso, temerario porco*), punching him in the stomach, and threatening him with a knife. The inquiry was quickly dropped, perhaps because of the unsettled political environment with the French invasions of northern Italy, perhaps because the priest was crossing a line himself by acting as an advocate before the secular courts.[39] There were two cases of lay threats against priests, both from the 1760s. There was one case of a layperson infringing on church property by cutting trees on church land.[40] There were three cases involving violations of the rule of sanctuary, all from the 1750s and 1760s, and none thereafter.[41] In 1763, by a letter dated 3 September, Pope Clement XIII had extended the rules of sanctuary agreed upon in the concordat of 1742 to the diocese of Novara and other territories formerly part of the duchy of Milan. This severely curtailed the right of sanctuary, which was denied to the majority of those pursued for serious crimes including homicides (except accidental), arsons, forced entry, selling poison, and treason.[42]

The almost total disappearance of trials of laypersons accused of assaulting priests suggests that such cases were now almost entirely under the purview of the secular courts. In the time of Bascapè, the prosecution of laypersons for homicides and serious assaults against the person of priests already rested with the secular authorities.[43] The same was certainly true in the eighteenth century. Thus, in June 1770, when the tribunal considered the case of Antonio Ferrari of Oleggio, accused of killing the priest Giuseppe Maria Mireto with a pistol shot, there was no indication that the court intended to apprehend or try the accused, only to note that he had incurred the penalty of interdict and excommunication from which only the Holy See could absolve him.[44]

In the absence of records of matrimonial cases (*cause matrimoniali*) such as requests for annulment and separation, only four lay cases involved sexual or marital matters, two of these before 1765, and neither involving accusations of adultery or concubinage, which had been relatively common in the late 1590s, the first years of Bascapè's episcopate. By the eighteenth century, it seems, the Novarese hierarchy preferred to leave these cases to the confessional and possibly to the lay courts. One case arose from a complaint filed in February 1759 by Lorenzo Galletti, keeper of the artillery (*guardiano dell'artiglieria*) of the city, against Vincenzo son of Domenico Aiazza, the Captain of the Gates, that the young man had broken into his house and seduced his daughter, giving a false promise of marriage. Galletti demanded that the young man both honour his promise and compensate the offended family given the public nature of the offence and given that his family was not of lower status than that of the culprit. A lengthy inquiry by the bishop's prosecutor ended in a declaration that the young man was guilty. He was ordered to pay the expenses of the process and to either marry the girl or provide a suitable dowry, to be determined by the vicar general.[45] A second case was less spectacular, involving a clandestine marriage conducted at Arola by a physician from Milan in 1762.[46] How this case ended is unknown. The next case involving marital matters did not occur until 1787 when Filippo Grazioli of Gozzano was apprehended for beating his wife, Angela Pastoro, after she had delayed going to harvest rye in a field that they rented. She was three months pregnant at the time, and much of the court's concern seems to have been about whether this would cause her to lose the baby.[47] The end of the case is not known. The final marital case occurred in 1795, when Giovanni Battista Ceruti was accused of polygamy. It is unknown whether the tribunal proceeded with the case.[48]

Matters of faith remained a concern of the tribunal for both laypersons and the clergy, but with reduced incidence and a notable shift in emphasis. There were no clear cases of illicit magic or of witchcraft in the Novarese records of the mid to late eighteenth century, although the bishops of the early 1700s continued to issue edicts, which included clauses against magic and invoking the devil.[49] In contrast, in other regions of Piedmont-Sardinia the Inquisitions dealt with a number of cases of using magic to obtain money or love, and a number of men were tried on suspicion of sorcery after the death of the favourite son of Victor Amadeus II.[50] At Novara, the closest case was that of Giuseppe Gramo of Villa, accused of invoking the devil with a series of blasphemous outbursts such as 'May the devil come to take me in soul and in body' (*Diavolo vieni a prendermi in anima ed in corpo*).[51] The case seems to have been dealt with as blasphemy rather than a serious invocation of the devil. Although the bishops of Novara continued to reissue regulations about travel to heretical lands until late in the eighteenth century, there were few cases related to such travel and to dealings with Protestants.[52] The most serious threat to the faith was now felt to come from the new philosophers of the Enlightenment. The bishops were acutely aware of the dangers presented to the faith by the new ideas. On the occasion of his synod of 1778, the first held in the diocese in seventy years, Balbis Bertone underscored the need to combat the false prophets of the age, as he put it, the philosophers who styled themselves the glorious defenders of human liberty and with their corrupt reasoning tried to subvert divine revelation, remove fear of the afterlife from the hearts of the faithful, and completely overturn the very foundation of religion. Parish priests were to be vigilant in defending their flocks and were to report those who blasphemed God, the Virgin Mary, and the saints, those who promoted immodesty and fornication, and those who ate meat on the days prohibited by the church.[53]

Despite the stern pronouncements of the synod, in the second half of the eighteenth century the bishop's tribunal dealt with few cases of faith, whether of heresy, magic, or the new ideas of the Enlightenment. The response of the curia was sporadic and muted, reflecting perhaps the pressures that the northern Italian states were placing on the Roman Inquisition. In the state of Milan, now under the watchful eye of Count Kaunitz (1711–94), the Austrian chancellor, the Roman Inquisition was increasingly regarded as a cruel, abusive, and antiquated institution which served a purpose during the days of the Protestant threat but was no longer necessary because the church was blessed with good bishops and educated priests. Kaunitz's strategy was to slowly undermine the Inquisition in the state of Milan by refusing to recognize the credentials of new appointees to the office of inquisitor.[54]

In the eighteenth century, Piedmont-Sardinia also attempted to limit the power of inquisitors appointed by Rome. Victor Amadeus II would have preferred to see matters of faith entrusted to the bishops in the manner of the French church because they were his appointees, enjoyed his confidence, and would not divert revenues to Rome. However, he did not press this issue and as a result the status of the Inquisition remained unresolved in Piedmont. The government followed the course of refusing to recognize new inquisitors nominated by Rome. In most cities of Piedmont, including Turin, Vercelli, Asti, Alessandria, Mondovì, and Casale, vicars functioned instead of proper inquisitors. Ironically, the local vicars may have been more dependent on advice from the Congregation of the Holy Office at Rome than titular inquisitors would have been. As well, the government insisted that vicars of the Inquisition provide a rationale when requesting the aid of the secular arm, and limit their activity to heresy only and not take up cases of blasphemy, polygamy, and sorcery.[55] Not surprisingly, in the Savoyard state cases of the Inquisition probably dwindled to three or four a year in the eighteenth century, in the same range as numbers at Venice, Friuli, and Naples.[56] In the second half of the eighteenth century the crown and the episcopal courts wavered between antagonism towards the Inquisition and collaboration with it, with the crown usually favouring the bishop's tribunals over the Inquisition. Thus, in 1751 the crown authorized the bishop of Alessandria to proceed against a number of men accused of sorcery, excluding the Inquisition from the process. The bishop's tribunal was regarded as more lenient in this matter.[57] In another case the bishop of Alessandria turned a priest who celebrated Mass with false patents over to the Inquisition because the Inquisition had better access to information from other jurisdictions.[58]

Unlike other regions of Piedmont-Sardinia, Novara and Tortona, the most recently acquired territories, were permitted to maintain their own titular inquisitors through the eighteenth century. As well, the inquisitors were not dependent on the secular arm to execute orders, but had their own officials licenced to bear arms. At the end of the 1730s, Charles Emanuel III declared in the course of negotiations with Rome that he did not intend to change the usages of the two regions.[59] It is unlikely that the inquisitors of Novara were as active in the eighteenth century as in earlier times. The records of the bishop's tribunal contain several fleeting references to their continued existence.[60] For example, in September 1753 Carlo Giuseppe Mazola, parish priest of the northern village of Zuccaro and a vicar of the Inquisition, accused the cleric Giovanni Battista Gentile, recently released from the prison of the Inquisition, of cursing him and threatening him with harquebus in hand because he blamed him for making false charges against him to the inquisitor at Novara.[61] Although isolated, the incident seems to point to a diminished respect for the institution in the diocese, and so too does the fact that the vicars general of Novara for the most part moved without the local inquisitors on the few occasions when they dealt with matters of faith in the eighteenth century, specifically in gathering information and at the crucial point of sentencing. Only in the case of the chaplain Gregorio Gnemma, discussed below, was there a reference to the local inquisitor being consulted on the validity of a sentence.

At Novara, documents survive for only six laypersons and a similar number of members of the clergy accused of heretical opinions, and most of these were dealt with as a penitential matter more than a criminal case. In most cases, those arraigned seem to have been quite ready to accept the penances assigned to them, suggesting that the accused may have appeared of their own volition or at the prompting of a confessor dealing with a reserved case.[62] The first layperson was Giuseppe Andrea Borgno, a merchant from Santa Maria Maggiore in the Vigezzo valley, who in March 1758 confessed to coming into contact with 'libertines' at a hostel when on one of his trips to France. It is not known how the curia dealt with his case, but given his confession, it is probable that he was absolved and given a penance.[63] A second was Giovanni Battista Vella of Galliate, denounced by his parish priest in 1777–8 for denying the immortality of the soul on several occasions, saying 'after death nothing' (*post obitum nihil*). The curia ordered that he should be gravely admonished and sent to his confessor for absolution. There is no indication that they consulted the local inquisitor on the matter.[64]

The remaining lay cases were clustered in the mid to late 1780s. One was that of the above mentioned Giuseppe Gramo of Villa, who in 1786 was prosecuted and sentenced for his blasphemous outbursts and also for refusing to perform the Easter obligation, causing scandal by eating meat in Lent, saying that he wanted to follow the Hebrew law, failing to attend Mass on feast days, and preventing his wife from doing so. After throwing himself on the mercy of God and of his judges and refusing legal counsel, he was sentenced to stand before the collegiate church of Domodossola during Mass with a candle in hand and to confess his errors before the canon curate, the rural vicar, and a delegate of the episcopal tribunal. As well, he was to sweep the parish church of Villa one day a week for six months. Once again, the inquisitor was not involved.[65]

In February 1787 Giacomo Antonio Albertazzi, who claimed to be acting as a good Catholic and as 'chancellor of the Holy Office,' denounced Giovanna Grolli née Pizardi of Vogogna and her husband, the advocate Filippo Grolli, to the tribunal for telling a group of friends and associates that Jesus Christ was a bastard and that those who said otherwise were trying to mislead the simple. After the charge led to an inquiry conducted by the rural vicar, Filippo Grolli wrote a number of lengthy, impassioned, letters to the vicar general. Less docile than Gramo and the others, Grolli argued that he and his wife had only intended to say that Christ was from an illegitimate line, a comment which they found in *De nothis spurisque filis liber singularis*, a sixteenth-century commentary on illegitimacy by no less a stalwart of Catholicism than the legal scholar Gabriele Paleotti (1524–97), who went on to be named archbishop of Bologna and Cardinal.[66] Grolli protested the innocence of himself and his wife and accused Albertazzi of vindictively spreading rumours that the couple had been taken in chains to the court of the Inquisition at Novara, something which had not occurred. Grolli also gave the vicar general copies of letters he had sent to the prefect of the province of Pallanza and to royal officials at Turin, allegedly to ward off further attacks by his foe, Albertazzi, but no doubt also to warn the vicar general to proceed with caution.[67] Given his vitriol it seems doubtful that the vicar general was inclined to move against him.

Another denunciation for heresy was made in September 1788 when Carlo Pianazza of the northern village of Scopa was accused of speaking ill of the religious orders, advising his associates not to listen to the parish priest and refusing to fast and abstain from meat during Lent. Once again, it is not known how this case ended.[68]

There was at least one case of sacrilege. In 1794 a soldier named Giovanni Battista Bonella of Prato from the provincial regiment of Novara stood accused, possibly through self-denunciation, of removing the host from his mouth after completing his Easter duty and concealing it. The host was retrieved after it fell from the window at his barracks. The accused, aged twenty-one, claimed that he had not confessed his sins before approaching the altar rail and that since he was too embarrassed to refuse the host, he decided that it was the lesser evil to receive and conceal it. The investigation appears to have ended at that point, suggesting that the vicar general accepted Bonella's story.[69]

In contrast to the low number of laypersons, priests and clerics continued to be the primary focus of the work of the bishop's tribunal in the eighteenth century. The good conduct of the clerical estate was deemed essential to the well-being of church and society, and in some cases stern action was necessary to maintain good conduct. In a telling statement, Francesco Gallo, the parish priest of Crusinallo in the vicariate of Omegna, wrote to the curia in November 1789 that since the death of Bishop Balbis Bertone, Francesco Antonio Viola, a chaplain of the parish, had been intolerable and more insolent than ever: 'Fraternal correction in the spirit of unity will not only be useless but also pernicious, if not done with a strong hand.' Gallo went on to describe the recent attacks and insults given by Viola, including a surprise attack on Gallo's brother who was virtually blind but thrown to the ground with blows and kicks. The chaplain was alleged to have had improper relations with Clara Giovanna Ceruta for a decade, causing her to be '*in illegitimo divorzio*' from her husband,

Chart 5.1. Clergy Cited, 1745–99

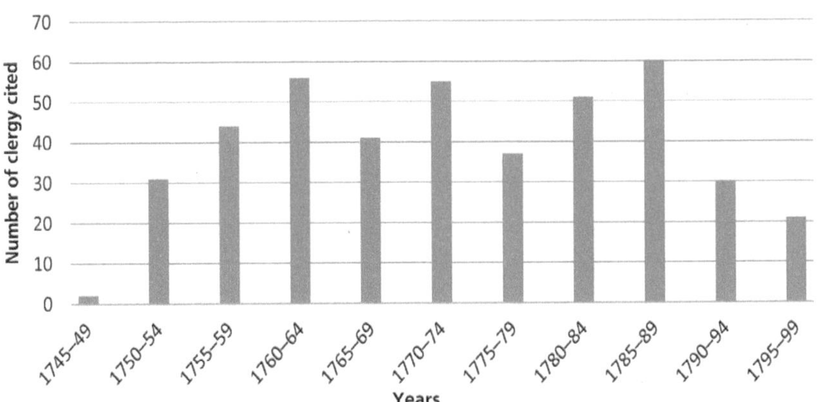

who in consequence refused to perform his Easter duty because he could not have justice from ecclesiastics. To add to the scandal, Viola rarely attended church functions and catechism lessons, but was agitating for the men of nearby Gattugno, where he was chaplain, to form their own parish.[70]

In the period 1745 to 1799, approximately 385 priests and clerics attracted the negative attention of the episcopal curia at one time or another, for a total of slightly over 430 separate cases. As chart 5.1 demonstrates, for each five-year interval of time (with the exception of 1745–9 and 1795–9), there were between thirty and sixty cases. Although the data for chart 5.1 largely comes from the files of the tribunal, the *foro ecclesiastico*, almost thirty are found in the miscellaneous letters, proclamations, and papers of Bishop Balbis Bertone. On average, approximately eight ecclesiastics were denounced to the curia each year between 1745 and 1799, or approximately nine a year between 1750 and 1799.[71]

However, the number 430 is inflated by the fact that not all of the cases resulted in formal inquiries. Of the 430 complaints against priests and clerics, approximately 230 are known to have led to inquiries, often delegated to the rural vicars of the diocese, who were instructed to operate with utmost discretion and secrecy. In slightly over 140 cases all that remains is a complaint, sometimes accompanied by an order for a priest or cleric to appear before the vicar general or to undergo spiritual exercises for a specific reason such as excessive drinking or excessive familiarity with women. In over fifty cases the only surviving document is a *precetto* or citation that the vicar general, 'moved by a worthy cause' (*dignis de causis animum nostrum moventibus*), wanted a priest or cleric to appear without a specific reason being given. In seven cases the only surviving

Chart 5.2. Inquiries Conducted of Clergy, 1745–95

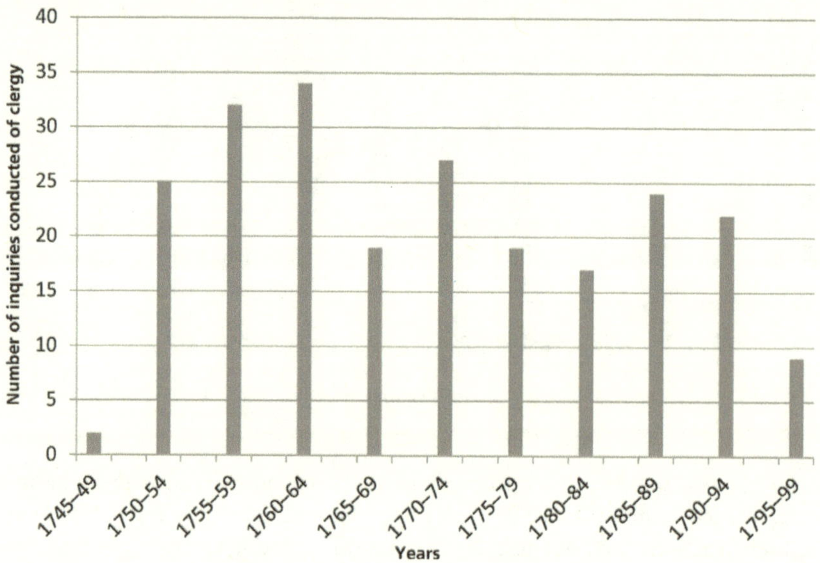

documentation is a confession of guilt. If the tally is restricted to the cases which are known to have resulted in a formal inquiry, the numbers are lower, as indicated in chart 5.2. The average number of inquiries for each five-year interval, minus the periods 1745–9 and 1795–9, fell to twenty-four, or fewer than five per year. This was remarkably lower than the totals from the first five years of Bascapè's episcopate, when the tribunal arraigned and interrogated an average of more than twenty-four ecclesiastics and fifteen laypersons each year. The number of trials conducted during the last fifteen years of Bascapè's episcopate was also higher than the eighteenth-century number: an average of almost ten ecclesiastics and six laypersons were arraigned annually between 1601 and 1614.

As noted above, the 430 total cases involved 385 different ecclesiastics. Of these, ninety, or slightly less than a quarter, were priests directly involved in the care of souls as curates, vice-curates, or coadjutors.[72] Approximately 220 of the 385 were identified as chaplains and simple priests, or over half of the accused. Slightly over 10 per cent (45) of the 385 accused were clerics, with only 17 canons, 10 friars, and 1 hermit. The records of the tribunal include no prosecutions of nuns in the eighteenth century, although one cleric, Giovanni de Marchi, was arraigned in 1759 for ignoring repeated orders not to visit the monastery of Sant'Agnese at Novara and for conspiring to take away one of the *converse*, a certain Suor Paola, who had long been his friend and who had received six or seven letters from him. On 19 February 1759 de Marchi petitioned for the right to set aside clerical habit. His request was granted, but it is not known whether Suor Paola was allowed to leave her convent.[73]

There were fewer repeat offenders in the eighteenth century than in the post-Tridentine period, when over a third of the parish priests prosecuted by the tribunal endured more than one trial. In the eighteenth century, in contrast, slightly over one-sixth of the accused were cited more than once. Of the 385 accused, 40 were called to appear before the vicar general twice, 11 three times, 4 on four occasions, and 1 five times. As well, only 15 of the repeat offenders were curates, perhaps because the bishops and the curia found better candidates for the parishes of the diocese or perhaps because curates had learned to act with greater discretion. The priest cited at least five times was the above mentioned Francesco Antonio Viola of Crusinallo whose name appears in the pastoral visitation of 1759 as a thirty-nine-year-old chaplain, already prosecuted on a number of occasions. Between 1759 and 1793, when he was in his seventies, he was frequently investigated by the tribunal for verbal attacks and assaults on his neighbours and for alleged affairs with married women of the town. For his offences he was required to undergo spiritual exercises on at least two occasions, as well as pay fines and court expenses.[74]

If it can be assumed that two generations of priests served the diocese between 1750 and 1800, over 800 parish priests, vice-curates, and coadjutors administered the care of souls in this period. In this group the ratio of accused to total priests had fallen to one in nine or ten (90 of 800), half of what the ratio had been in the years of Bascapè, when approximately one-fifth of parish priests were arraigned at one time or another. As well, the eighteenth century number was inflated by the inclusion of those simply accused or cited to appear, whereas the calculation made for Bascapè's years includes only those who were put through the formal processes of arraignment and interrogation.[75] If the diocese was populated by over two thousand canons, chaplains, and other priests during the same period, the ratio of accused from these categories (220 chaplains and priests, 17 canons, and 10 friars) amounts to approximately one in every eight or nine of the total numbers. Once again the ratio of accused to total clergy is far below that in the post-Tridentine era, which underscores the fact that the tribunal played a reduced role in the disciplining of the clergy in the eighteenth century.

It is possible that the files of the eighteenth century do not include all of the accusations and processes of this period because documents were misfiled, lost, or removed for one reason or another. As noted above, almost thirty of the cases come from the miscellaneous letters and papers of Balbis Bertone. The maintenance of archives could be extremely casual in the early modern period, and it is possible that other cases were completely lost or included in the unsorted papers of the curia that were gathered each year.[76] However, such losses would have had to occur on a substantial scale to change the conclusion that in the eighteenth century the ratio of known accusations and inquiries to numbers of priests and clerics in the diocese was far below what it had been in the post-Tridentine period.

Before discussing the reasons for the decline in tribunal activity, it is necessary to examine the nature of the accusations against the priests and clerics. Because a number of files involved only the notice to appear, specific charges are only known in slightly over 300 of the cases. As in the post-Tridentine era, charges of physical assault were common, appearing in over sixty-five cases, approximately one-fifth of the cases for which the charge is known. Three aspects of the cases of assault should be underlined. First, the majority of these charges were against clergy in the lower ranks – simple priests, chaplains, and clerics (eleven cases) – with only five of them against parish priests. In contrast to the parish priests, the chaplains, priests, and clerics were more likely to be living with their families and in their original villages, and more prone, perhaps, to frequent taverns and engage in card playing, dances, and other pastimes that might lead to quarrels and assaults. Second, the great majority of the assaults were against laypersons, a fact which further underscores the degree of involvement of the ecclesiastics with secular society. Third, and most significantly, the most serious of the assault cases heard by the bishop's tribunal, including six homicides, came in the years before 1765, after which they fell off dramatically. One assumes that homicides and serious assaults, especially assaults with weapons, would have continued to occur in roughly comparable numbers after 1765. If the bishop's tribunal was not prosecuting the offenders, it seems likely that the secular courts would have been doing so, which would have been an infringement on the principle that clerics should be tried by ecclesiastical courts in criminal matters. Although Charles Emanuel III had promised in 1771 to respect the immunity of the clergy from secular prosecution, the abolition of the bull *In Coena Domini* by the majority of Italian states in 1768 to 1769 and its abandonment by Clement XIV in 1770 point to the mounting encroachment of the secular courts on this aspect of ecclesiastical immunity.[77]

In the 1750s and early 1760s the episcopal court investigated accusations of homicide against three priests and four clerics. For example, on 21 June 1754 the cleric Carlo Caccia, son of the noble citizen Marc'Antonio Caccia, was convicted of the fatal stabbing of a sergeant of the garrison of Novara in front of the cathedral of San Gaudenzio. He was deprived of all benefices and sentenced to life in prison.[78] More fortunate was the priest Giovanni Battista Mauletti of Prato who was accused of killing Giorgio Genesio at Prato the night of 5 August 1760. Giorgio and his brother Carlo Maria Genesio had accosted members of the

Mauletti family on the road near Prato earlier in the day. At night they came to the Mauletti house threatening harm. The priest Mauletti, who later claimed to be acting in self-defence, fired a harquebus to frighten Giorgio when the latter was climbing a ladder to Mauletti's room to break into his house. His version of events was accepted, and on 25 September 1761 he was ordered to undergo spiritual exercises for one month and to stay away from Prato. This was followed by a testimonial of remission (forgiveness) signed by Giuseppe Genesio, father of the deceased Giorgio, on behalf of his family to Mauletti and his family.[79]

On the lighter side, perhaps, was the case of Baldessar Uglione, a cleric of Ghemme, accused in 1762 of causing the death of an eight year old by pulling his ears (*eccessivo tiramento d'orecchij*). A surgeon was sent to investigate and determined that the boy died of natural causes.[80] Uglione went on to be ordained a priest, leading a quiet and undistinguished life in his home town. In 1783, when he was aged forty-three, he was still without a benefice and the episcopal visitors described him as suited to 'priestly duties.' Although he was not said to be suited for service as a confessor, as others were, he claimed to minister to the sick when called, to avoid taverns and illicit games, and to devote time to his studies.[81]

In another case, not found in the files of the tribunal but in the records of Balbis Bertone, the curia conducted an investigation into the accidental shooting of Maria Pisella, a scullery maid in the service of Antonio Bottolo, by the priest Andrea Rasaro, at midnight on 27 May 1762. The priest, a chaplain at Cigogna in the vicariate of Intra, had been hunting with Bottolo, his friend. After the two dined together, the priest accidently discharged his firearm, striking Pisella in the neck while she was washing the dishes. The rural vicar of Intra sent his chancellor, a notary, and a surgeon to investigate, and they supported the claim of an accidental death. This was followed by an act of remission between Rasaro and Maria Pisella's father, duly recorded by a notary from Milan. Although the councillors of the community of Cussogno, where the incident occurred, were said to have been notified, there is no indication that Rasaro was called before the secular authorities.[82]

The tribunal dealt with other cases involving weapons and serious damage to the physical well-being of victims, again most of these before the mid-1760s and relatively few between 1765 and 1799. Thus, in April 1764 the cleric Valentino Giovanetti, called Tamelino, from the diocese of Pavia was accused of wounding Pietro Feria of Tornaco in the leg with a gunshot. The leg was later amputated. Giovanetti claimed that Feria had attacked him with a knife, and he won acquittal on the grounds of self-defence. On 25 March 1765 the affair ended when the parties conducted a formal act of remission.[83] Assaults by members of the clergy were directed not only against men but against women as well. In May 1763 Antonio Maria Cavallo of Granozzo in the plains region of the diocese complained that the chaplain Alessio Maraschi had beaten his wife after the two had a series of unpleasant encounters. The complainant added that he did not wish to litigate with the priest because he was a poor man and the priest had a lot of money, but he did want to prevent future attacks. Cavallo also complained that the priest's two dogs kept him awake at night. Legal action was terminated after Maraschi, then in his mid-thirties, agreed to undertake spiritual exercises and to pay expenses to Cavallo and his wife.[84] Another case from January 1763 bore even more serious implications. The priest Giuseppe Antonio Zanoia of Domo Vissulta was accused of invading the bedroom of Madalena Tadea, a married woman with whom he was evidently involved, beating her stomach and back, and throwing her down the stairs. Although she appears to have recovered from her serious injuries, Madalena died two months later from an unrelated illness. The reason for the attack appears to have been jealousy on the priest's part, for it was alleged that he did not want her to leave her house at night or to have dealings with persons of whom he did not approve, this despite an injunction issued in February 1762 that he not visit her or have dealings with her. There is no record of the result of the inquiry undertaken by the rural vicar of Domodossola, but a parallel process was before a lay tribunal.[85]

Charges of banditry and association with bandits were no longer prominent in the eighteenth-century records, although a number of priests and clerics were accused of committing armed robberies. For example, in February 1759 the cleric Marco Galarati of Sillavengo stood accused of stealing a chicken while armed, firing a shot at a man who saw him, and threatening a second man. He was also accused of scandalous behaviour and of cursing and threatening the curate and vice-curate when they remonstrated with him. In July 1759 he was ordered to pay a fine and a deposit to guarantee his good behaviour.[86] Another culprit was the chaplain Giacomo Antonio de Marchis of Mollia in the Sesia valley who was accused of armed robbery and of sexual relations with a woman in 1754.[87]

The willingness of the secular authorities to intervene in crimes involving the clergy may be partly explained by the lack of confidence in ecclesiastical tribunals. The concerns expressed by Antonio Maria Cavallo about the gap in wealth between himself and his antagonist, the priest Alessio Maraschi, were probably shared by others. On 28 September 1762 Giovanni Francesco Gavinelli complained that Giulio Bovio, a priest of Bellinzago, and a certain Giovanni Vandone had met him at a hostelry on the road to Oleggio, beaten him, and left him on the road. He went on to say that the priest always went about armed with a knife and led a scandalous life, especially in the manner of his clothing. On 8 November Gavinelli dropped the charges, saying that he had calmed down and that he was concerned about the the haughty nature of Bovio and the tardiness of the curia in proceeding.[88] Bovio appears to have continued his violent ways. In February 1770 Giuseppe de Vechio of Belinzago accused him of assaulting his wife and threatening to stab her. It is not known what action, if any, the curia took on this occasion.[89]

As Bovio's second process suggests, the tribunal continued to process serious cases of violence and theft in the years after 1765. For example, in August 1782 a priest named Giacomo Annovazzi of Cerano was accused of robbing a man at gunpoint in his home town.[90] Although it is not known how his case was handled in 1782, in 1786 Annovazzi again stood accused, this time for wounding his cousin in the left arm with a pistol shot in the course of an argument, allegedly with intent to kill. Annovazzi confessed to the attack and was sentenced to confinement in a monastery or religious house for three years and suspension from divine offices, as well as paying the costs of the process.[91] In another case, in 1786 the cleric Stefano Tosi was accused of wounding Antonio Maria Tagnone during an altercation at a tavern. He was held in jail until 1788, at which time his period of incarceration was declared sufficient punishment, and he was given an injunction to avoid taverns.[92] However, the disappearance of homicides from the files of the tribunal and the decline in the number of serious attacks suggests that the secular courts may have begun to act in such cases, to the detriment of the principle of clerical immunity at Novara in the late eighteenth century. The abolition of *In Coena Domini* points to this conclusion, as do the records found in the archives of the senate of Chambéry, and at least one case found in the Piedmontese book of *banditi* (fugitive criminals) for the 1780s and 1790s in the state archive of Novara. In 1791 a priest named Michele di Pietro of the village of Brazzo of an unspecified diocese was sought in the stabbing death of a man named Michele Brunetto on 7 August. The priest was to be given ten years' imprisonment and held liable for costs.[93] Another clue to secular involvement with clerics in criminal cases comes from the records of the Novarese episcopal tribunal itself. In 1766 to 1769 Pietro Antonio Tadeo of Cavaglia, a layman, appeared before the vicar general to accuse Pasquale Nicola di Aqua, a cleric of the parish of Cellio in the Sesia valley, of helping Stefano Spinelli, a layman, in a vicious attack that left him beaten, wounded in the leg with a gunshot, and half-dead in a country field. The case was also before a secular tribunal. On 20 December 1769 the ecclesiastical court appears to have deferred to the secular court, absolving the cleric of guilt because the process conducted by the secular tribunal had found him not responsible.[94] In short, there was a degree of acceptance of the powers of the secular courts that was unheard of in the post-Tridentine period.[95]

In the eighteenth century, as in the sixteenth and seventeenth, sexual offences were the most common found in the records of the tribunal, appearing in over a third of the 300 cases in which the charge is known. This was below the pattern of the period 1563 to 1615, when almost half of the charges brought against priests and clerics involved sexual matters. The vast majority of the cases involved dealings with women, none of homosexuality and only one of paedophilia. As in the post-Tridentine period, the majority of accusations involving women did not involve prostitution, something which was quite common in seventeenth-century Siena.[96] In the eighteenth century, however, instances of concubinage or long-term cohabitation of priests with women also appear less frequently than in the late sixteenth and early seventeenth centuries. Instead it was more common to see offending priests accused of 'suspicious dealings' with women without reference to cohabitation. At least twenty-five illicit encounters resulted in children, whom the priests were often later involved in supporting. The majority of those accused of this were chaplains and simple priests. Among priests exercising the care of souls, only four parish priests, one vice-curate, and one coadjutor were cited for fathering children.

In fact, only thirty-one of those accused of sexual impropriety were curates, while six were vice-curates or coadjutors. This amounted to roughly 5 per cent of this group of priests over the two generations. When one considers that during Bascapè's episcopate eighty curates and ten vice-curates were charged with sexual improprieties at one time or another, an argument can be made that decades of epicsopal activity and interventions had improved the behaviour of the parish clergy in this area. If not, it might at least have caused them to be more circumspect in their dealings with women. As well, the great majority of parish priests accused of sexual transgressions were prosecuted on only one occasion for this infraction, in some cases leading to their removal.

In the post-Tridentine era, approximately twelve cases of concubinage or adultery involved this as the only issue. In the eighteenth century, over 60 per cent of the accusations of sexual impropriety focused on this as the only matter. It seems possible that there was a lower degree of tolerance for this abuse. In many cases the persons accusing a priest were concerned parents or the husbands of the women involved. As in the post-Tridentine era, there were also cases where accusations of sexual impropriety against parish priests were accompanied by charges of negligence in the care of souls, assaults, and other offences. In August 1787, for example, Giuseppe Galleazzi, curate of Coiro (Coiromonte) in the region of Gozzano, was confronted with a list of thirteen charges including drunkenness, taking parish funds for his personal use, falsifying accounts, setting a fire in the parish rectory before a pastoral visitation so that the parish books were destroyed and could not be used against him, failing to observe the fasting and abstinence rules for Fridays and before Mass, and negligence in the administration of the sacraments so that a number of persons died without them. His sexual transgressions included scandalous dealings with two women of his parish, one married and the other a widow, even after his superiors admonished him to avoid contact. He was also accused of sexually assaulting a third woman who was unmarried at the time, hearing the confessions of the women with whom he was alleged to be involved, and celebrating Mass immediately after his encounters without confessing his own sins. In September of the same year, criminal proceedings were stayed when Galleazzi confessed to all the offences except the rape of the unmarried woman, renounced his parish, and received an injunction never to visit the confines of Coiro or to have dealings with the women named in the charges. A year later, in December 1788, a new process was initiated when the priest violated the injunction and visited the parish and the women.[97] It is not known how this case ended.

In the eighteenth century the majority of those accused of sexual transgressions were in lesser positions, not tied to the care of souls. Among these, forty-two were described as priests, fifteen as chaplains, nine as clerics, and seven as canons. Many of these were the lesser lights among the clergy and clearly the amount of time on their hands was not always put to good use. A particularly bad case was Francesco Bergatta of Nonio in the central region of Omegna. In 1786 he was tried on six charges, including possessing forbidden weapons, keeping obscene pictures in his house, which he showed to people of both sexes, married and unmarried, and not confessing his sins for several years. In addition to a life marked by shamelessness, scandal, and indecency – qualities deemed improper for a Christian let alone a priest – he was accused of fathering two illegitimate children. Bergatta confessed to most of the charges against himself, including impregnating a woman named Angela Maria Clerici. His sentence, signed on 18 July 1787, was a fine of fifty scudi for arms violations, confinement for three years in the house of a religious order for his sexual improprieties, and perpetual suspension from religious duties. He was also to have no more dealings with Angela Maria under threat of a fine of one hundred scudi for every violation. Finally, there was to be a further inquiry into allegations that he did not fulfil the Mass obligations he had undertaken.[98]

Another repeat offender in sexual matters was Giacomo Lorenzino, a priest from Beura in the vicariate of Masera (Pieve Vergonte), who first appeared before the vicar general on charges of improper dealings with a married woman in the 1750s. In 1759 he was accused of fathering twins, and in 1760 he was under investigation for fleeing the diocese. Fresh charges were laid in 1761 with his accuser claiming, in a tale reminiscent of Boccaccio's *Decameron*, that the priest used a ladder to climb to the bedroom of a married woman at night.[99] In June 1772 a new inquiry was launched into charges that he had impregnated the wife of Pietro Antonio Bernardolini while he was serving as chaplain at Viceno in the Antigorio valley. The husband demanded payment for the offence given.

In December 1772 Lorenzino was found guilty of scandalous dealings with women, adultery, and violating the orders of the bishop to correct his conduct. On 16 January 1773 he was suspended from sacred functions and ordered to undergo penance in the house of a religious order for five years. The penance seems to have done him little good, for in April 1777 Lorenzino was asked to respond to new charges with no fewer than eleven married women.[100] It is not known how this case ended, but Lorenzino's history demonstrates that the curia could be highly ineffective with some individuals, even when proceeding judicially.

Although members of the religious orders were normally subject to discipline by their superiors, from time to time they too came under the scrutiny of the episcopal court. In 1794 Giuseppe Maria Danda complained that Fra Alessandro da Borgomanero, a Capuchin of the house of Domodossola, was on terms of 'close friendship' (*stretta amicizia*) with his wife Margarita Agnese. Although the rural vicar had told Danda that it was nothing to be concerned about, the curia decided to gather more information and the bishop wrote to the superior of the Capuchin order on 5 June 1795 to report that the relationship was a cause of scandal, that the friar and the woman met at all hours and had been found together in her bedroom, and that they had spent the night of 2–3 December together. The bishop requested that the Fra Alessandro be transferred away from Domodossola and given a suitable punishment within thirty days, with a written report provided.[101]

One curate and three priests were accused of attempting to induce or procure abortions. One was Pasquale Nicola, a priest holding a benefice in the parish of Cellio, vicariate of Borgosesia, who in July 1780 was accused by Maddalena, daughter of Giacomo Nicola, of getting her drunk in order to have sexual relations with her, which he did three times. When she became pregnant he tried to have her abort the baby by procuring medicines from a surgeon at Borgosesia and then kneeing her in the stomach. She eventually bore a daughter, who later died of a cold.[102] The end result of this case is not known, but we do have a resolution for a similar case from 1799 involving Pietro Antonio Olgina of Quarna Sopra, a priest who held a chaplaincy at Cireggio in the central region of the diocese. In the 1780s, when serving as vice-curate at Lumellogno, he was already under investigation for frequenting inns and causing scandal through his dealings with young women, two of whom he was accused of impregnating. He was suspended from celebrating Mass and required to undertake spiritual exercises. Held in low regard by the people of his home village because he frequented inns, gambled, and meddled in village affairs, in the 1790s he was again charged with a variety of offences, including deflowering a young unmarried woman named Margarita Butola, 'not without a degree of violence' (*non senza qualche violenza*), having relations with her on other occasions, impregnating her, and giving her medicine to induce an abortion. Nevertheless, the woman bore a son. Although the priest dismissed the charges as calumnies, in July 1799 he was sentenced to suspension from divine functions for one month, detention in the house of a religious order, a fine of 100 lire to be paid to the parents of the girl, and court costs of 132 lire.[103]

The lone paedophile was Giacomo Penotti, who served as a chaplain in the parish of Cellio in the vicariate of Borgosesia. In 1791 he confessed to molesting at least ten boys over two decades. He had invited boys to spend the night at his house where he taught them how to masturbate and told them that sexual touching was wrong only between male and female and not among males. The case only came to light after a confessor who was conducting a mission to the area insisted that the young men, his penitents, denounce the culprit. Their reluctance to come forward probably reflected the shame felt by the victims of Penotti's crime. As was true of many of the sexual offences in this period, the response of the episcopal curia was remarkably lenient. The chaplain was ordered to spend time in the house of the oblates of Novara, and in December 1791 he successfully petitioned the vicar general for permission to return to his chaplaincy so that he could celebrate Mass during the Christmas season. He was to return to the vicar general on 20 January 1792.[104]

After cases involving sexual misconduct and assault, the most commonly found charges concerned unruly or inappropriate behaviour, which appeared in over sixty-five cases. The majority of these were made against clerics, priests, and chaplains rather than curates. Many involved frequenting taverns and inns, gambling, boisterous conduct during carnival, and drunkenness, the last of which was a factor in approximately twenty-five cases. One particularly irascible individual was Giovanni Battista Azari, chaplain at Folsogno in the Vigezzo valley who in 1787 was accused of acting in an imperious manner and refusing to pay the community the normal price for cutting trees for a house. He was also accused of holding a dance at his house for men and women from Malesco during carnival, and of striking several of his neighbours.[105] It is not known how this matter ended.

In some cases the charges concerned young men who were clearly not suited for the clerical estate. In 1761–2 Girolamo Negri, curate of Dormeletto, denounced his own brother, the cleric Carlo Negri, for frequenting taverns, drunkenness, going about armed with a pistol and knives, keeping company with soldiers, extorting money, and dealing in contraband tobacco. After eight years in clerical dress, Carlo had not applied himself to his studies and in the past year had completely abandoned his books. The matter seems to have ended when he was permitted to set aside clerical clothing.[106] In a similar case, on 23 February 1787

Paolo Lamberto D'Allegra, the provicar general, issued a sentence against Carlo Grazioli, a twenty-seven-year-old cleric from Pombia, beneficed in the parish church of the same town. The cleric had confessed to 'an idle, wandering life disgraceful to the ecclesiastical state' (*vita oziosa, vagabonda e indecente allo stato ecclesiastico*). He had not performed the Easter duty in the past year, nor had he said the divine office as required by his benefice. He kept prohibited weapons and engaged in smuggling tobacco. He had stolen six or seven hundred lire from a woman of Pombia and made false claims for support at the hospital of Novara at various times. Because of these and other dishonest deeds, Allegra sentenced Grazioli to be stripped of ecclesiastical habit by the *bargello* of the curia and his name striken from the register of clergy. However, Grazioli appealed for clemency, and as a result his sentence was reduced to only six months incarceration, restitution of stolen monies, and paying court costs.[107]

Theft was mentioned in just over thirty of the cases. One of the more serious involved Giuseppe Ugazio, a priest from Galliate, who in 1755 was accused of a string of over twenty thefts dating back to 1746, each worth up to twenty-two lire and some of them from churches. The priest was ordered to make restitution and sentenced to two years in jail and suspension from divine service. His father, Carlo Ugazio, is on record as paying sixty-four lire to one of the churches involved in satisfaction for the debt.[108] A similar case was that of the priest Giuseppe Berta of Belgirate, who was accused in 1759 of various thefts and of fathering a child by a woman named Maria Bellani. Berta's father pledged to make restitution for the things that the priest had stolen.[109]

Over the years the tribunal also heard several cases involving the mental and physical competence of elderly and sickly priests. Thus, in August 1759 Giacomo Francesco Mugetti, archpriest of Lesa and rural vicar, testified that his colleague, Giuseppe Antonio de' Innocenti, archpriest of Belgirate, then in his mid-forties, was mentally ill or disturbed to the point that he could not serve his people as confessor, preacher, or catechist. The people could no longer tolerate his sermons because he rambled on about going to the Father and to heaven. An oblate of San Gaudenzio and San Carlo and thus one of the priests especially dedicated to the service of the diocese, Innocenti accepted various orders given by the rural vicar, including that he cease teaching grammar to boys without proper licence and that he remove certain vagabonds whom he had allowed into his home.[110] He was still serving as curate when Balbis Bertone visited Belgirate in July 1761, with a vice-curate in place to preach and teach catechism while Innocenti served as schoolmaster. His health problems were duly noted.[111]

Accusations of negligence in the care of souls by curates occurred less frequently in the eighteenth century than in the post-Tridentine period, with only twenty-two curates and one vice-curate blamed for this failing. The majority of these cases involved allegations of neglect in caring for the sick and dying. Only four curates and one vice-curate were accused of being absent from their parishes for appreciable periods. One extreme case concerned Carlo Francesco Lodi, archpriest of Barengo in the plains vicariate of Caltignaca, who on 13 December 1753 was accused of a variety of offences, including frequent absences from his parish without permission from his superiors, being remiss in preaching on feast days, not holding catechism lessons in Lent, and failing to minister to the sick. He was also accused of drunkenness, frequently spending the night with women, singing obscene songs, and causing scandal by keeping a young girl in his house as his servant. He was said to be quick to mistreat others including his coadjutor and a chaplain, whom he abused verbally. Barengo was a parish of approximately 900 souls in which the community enjoyed the right to choose its parish priest, and Lodi was said to have obtained his parish by soliciting votes during a community election, extorting them from the debtors of his brother. If these things were not enough, the archpriest was accused of belittling the bishop, the vicar general, the king of Sardinia and the entire Piedmontese nation. The majority of his parishioners were said to view him as usurious and 'with little fear of God' (*poco timorato di Dio*). The reaction of the curia to the accusations was to initiate a further inquiry up to a sentence if need be.[112] Although the sentence is unknown, in 1756 Lodi was replaced as archpriest by Gaudenzio Barberi of Novara.[113]

Another interesting case is that of Giovanni Battista Maffei, curate of Pallanzeno in the Antrona valley, who between 1757 and 1761 was investigated on a series of charges, most of them coming from the widow Maria Chiarabana. The priest, described as being full of bile, was accused of chastising his parishioners even when he was dressed in his sacred vestments in church and of using the confessional to attack his opponents, especially the widow Chiarabana. He was accused of being overly zealous in soliciting offerings, going from house to house berating people if they had not made the normal offering to the Christ Child, the only sustenance for the parish church of the town. 'Like a wolf,' he demanded sole control over funeral masses and tried to increase the fees for these. At least one witness was called upon to describe a series of confrontations between Maffei and the widow, and in February 1762 Maffei was deprived of the parish for failing to preach the gospel and teach catechism and for not appearing when summoned by the curia.[114] It is not known whether Maffei appealed.

On occasion the charges against parish priests seem to have been relatively minor. Thus, in 1754, various 'zealous persons' of the parish of Soriso complained that their curate, Stefano Barletti, an oblate of San Gaudenzio and San Carlo who had studied philosophy at Milan and theology and cases of conscience at the seminaries of Novara and Borgomanero, often failed to preach and teach catechism, celebrated Mass at irregular hours, failed to consecrate sufficient hosts for communion, and was negligent in visiting the sick under pretext of being afraid to travel, especially at night. He was also accused of meddling in the work of the treasurers of the church, making grandiose and superfluous expenditures at Milan, and leaving the parish without permission and without naming a substitute. His abilities as a preacher were also disparaged: it was said that his sermons were too long and 'in such manner that for the most part either little or nothing could be understood.' Although the names of a number of priests were given to provide testimony against Barletti, a detailed investigation led to the charges being dropped by a decree of 5 July 1754. He was still serving as curate of Soriso during the visit of 1761, fulfilling the principle duties required of the position but admonished to be more diligent when preaching on feast days and when called on to take the sacraments to the sick.[115]

More serious were the charges against Giovanni Filippo Loretto, the parish priest and penitentiary of Vanzone in the Anzasca valley and a doctor of theology. On 6 March 1763 Gian Battista Molgatino, procurator general of the parish and community, and Gian Battista Govino, councillor of the community, denounced Loretto, who had served Vanzone since 1756, for failures in the administration of the care of souls and for failing to give a good example to his people. He was accused of negligence in visiting the sick and dying, of delaying baptisms and funerals needlessly, of turning to his own issues when preaching and teaching catechism, and of failing to keep the parish books of baptisms and deaths up to date. His morals were also called into question as he was accused of maintaining friendships with a number of women and visiting them at all hours of day and night – he had even been seen leaving one of their houses at dawn with his face hidden – and on several occasions attempting to strike parishioners with a staff in his hands. He was litigious and menacing to the point that parishioners feared to go to the rectory for their spiritual needs. There followed a lengthy investigation of Loretto's conduct, including ten interrogations of the priest himself. He responded with denials and claims that some of his statements had been misunderstood. In the summer of 1764 Loretto prepared his defence, and in May 1765 the vicar general passed sentence, ordering Loretto to add missing names to the books of baptisms and deaths within two months and to pay the costs of the process. Other than that, Loretto was released from further prosecution and admonished to tend to his parish properly in the future.[116]

Like parish priests, chaplains often came under scrutiny for failing to fulfil their obligations. Several dozen chaplains and priests were accused of failure to celebrate the masses required of them.[117] Such accusations appear to have increased with the passage of time. On occasion, the fault clearly lay with the priest. In December 1784, for example, Pietro Prato of Alagna in the vicariate of Varallo Sesia was accused of frequenting taverns and drinking to excess. His alcoholism was said to be in such an advanced state that he was running up debts, dressing in a manner unbecoming to the clerical estate, and from time to time neglecting to say the masses required by his benefice.[118] On other occasions, priests responded that their Mass obligations were excessive given the lack of money provided by benefices or legacies, an understandable claim as the value of many perpetual chaplaincies established in the seventeenth and early eighteenth centuries had been eroded by inflation and the deterioration of properties. From time to time, the curia responded by reducing the obligations of chaplaincies.

Over a dozen cases involved accusations that priests were involved in secular occupations. For example, in September 1773 Giovanni Battista Bucciolini, a chaplain at Santa Maria Maggiore was ordered to cease selling and serving wine in his house, whence scandals arose because of the raucous games and laughter.[119] In another case, in 1796 a priest of the city named Carlo Ravelli was accused of running a store where he personally sold clothing and second-hand goods. He was also accused of violating earlier injunctions, dating back to 1789, to end this practice. He was suspended from celebrating Mass and declared subject to penalties as required by the sacred canons because he had ignored previous commands to appear before the court. Once again, the vicar general released Ravelli when the latter promised to abandon his store. Ravelli was also to pay court costs.[120] Another case was that of Giuseppe Lottari, a priest from the southern region of Vespolate, who in 1782 was accused of acting as a grain merchant. As well, he was said to be proud and harsh, miserly in his dealings with the poor, and litigatious to the point that he frequently appeared before the lay courts. He rarely celebrated Mass and did not assist with catechism lessons nor other church functions as he was required to do. Information was taken which supported the accusations, but the end of this case is not known.[121]

One of the concerns expressed by Bishop Balbis Bertone in the synod of 1778 was the infiltration and spread of heresy in the diocese, in particular the ideas of the Enlightenment. The records of the tribunal confirm that these ideas were beginning to spread, as at least seven members of the clergy were investigated for heretical beliefs. All of these cases occurred after the late 1770s, and no curate was among the accused. One concerned Bartolomeo Vallana of Maggiora, a priest who in July 1777 confessed to teaching boys, who were his students, that masturbation was not a sin and, under the influence of wine, to forging a memorandum from the vicar general in order to have faculty to hear confessions. He denied a related charge that he had taught his students that fornication was not a sin. Vallana was suspended from sacred functions and sentenced to six months fasting on bread and water.[122]

More serious was a lengthy inquiry conducted in 1784–5 into the beliefs of Gregorio Gnemma, a thirty-one-year-old chaplain of Varallo who was accused, among other things, of praising the works of French authors, of publicly questioning divine providence, the existence of heaven, hell, and purgatory, and of denying the virgin birth, the divinity of Christ, and the immortality of the soul. He had served as an assistant for a parish at Locarno, where he was commonly called '*Calvino*' and '*Cagnazo*,' or a beast having neither law nor faith. His accusers included the parish priests of Civiasco and Locarno, and testimony was taken from several curates, chaplains, and clerics from the Sesia valley and syndics from the city of Locarno. On 19 July 1785 Gnemma presented his defence, or rather confession, in which he begged for clemency and explained that his erroneous opinions were never firmly held. He also claimed that when celebrating Mass and administering other sacraments, he had never once altered the rite or the words. After Gnemma's confession and abjuration, the vicar general sentenced him to be deprived of all ecclesiastical prerogatives, stripped of a benefice he held in the diocese of Locarno, and detained for ten years on the island of San Giulio in the Riviera d'Orta. Vincenzo Colombani, inquisitor of Novara, was consulted and approved the sentence. Gnemma did not serve his entire sentence, for in 1787 he appealed to the archdiocese of Milan. It is not known whether or not his appeal succeeded, but in 1794 the provost of Varallo reported rumours that Gnemma had left Italy for the north, married, and spent time as a proofreader for a press in Paris and then as a teacher or preacher at Basel.[123]

In 1792 similar charges were laid against cleric Gian Pietro Minoli, who possessed a canonical prebend at Domodossola but worked as a weaver. Minoli was denounced by the rural vicar of his region for frequenting dances and the company of women of ill repute and also for expressing heretical opinions. He was alleged to have said that fornication and adultery were not sins, that the Blessed Virgin was not pregnant by the Holy Spirit, that the sacrament of penance was a fraud, that the papacy ended with Peter, that there was no hell, and that the scriptures were falsehoods and inventions. He was cited to appear before Don Gioanni Agostino Zucchi, the vicar general, and on 27 February 1792 agreed to set aside the clerical habit, renounce his benefice, and abjure his heretical statements in return for a suspension of the process against him. The sentence was passed without consulting the inquisitor of Novara. After being ordered to pay court costs of sixty-one lire, Minoli was not detained further but released with the admonition of the vicar general to seek the proper remedies for his transgressions in the 'internal court' (*foro interno*) of his conscience.[124]

Although the period 1745–99 lacks a book of sentences, a considerable amount of information is available about the punishments or remedies imposed by the ecclesiastical tribunal in the eighteenth century. The most common remedy was to order a priest or cleric to undertake spiritual exercises, which were usually administered over a number of weeks at the College of Santa Cristina at Borgomanero, at the oblate house at Novara, or at the house of one of the religious orders. The intent was to secure the amendment of the wayward priest rather than react in a punitive fashion. This penance was imposed on thirty-five priests, only one of them a parish priest. In roughly half of the cases, this was the result of an inquiry, but in the other half, the order to undertake spiritual exercises was part of the initial summons. Undergoing spiritual exercises, done in privacy, probably did not carry a stigma for the accused, for by the eighteenth century the practice was widely recommended for all those in the sacrament of orders and was especially prescribed for those about to undergo ordination.[125] In 1768 the practice of spiritual exercises or retreats of a week's duration was even opened to laymen in the Lenten and Easter seasons.[126]

The use of spiritual exercises points to a more remedial approach on the part of the episcopal curia in the eighteenth century. However, the eighteenth-century tribunal could also be surprisingly rigorous in imposing punishments, going beyond the small fines imposed in the days of Bascapè to so little effect. Approximately ten ecclesiastics, including two curates, were given time in prison and fifteen, including five curates, were confined for lengthy periods in monasteries of the religious orders. Although fines were not as common in the eighteenth century as they had been in the sixteenth and early seventeenth, appearing in approximately ten of the files, thirty-two priests were required to pay court costs, and several were ordered to make restitution for thefts. At times fines, detention, and spiritual exercises were prescribed for a single individual. For example, in 1757 the priest Francesco Antonio Franzi of Pallanza confessed to gambling and dancing in masquerade. He was imprisoned for seven days, fined five scudi, and ordered to undergo spiritual exercises.[127]

One of the more extreme punishments was the loss of benefice. Ten of the cases are known to have resulted in priests being stripped of or resigning their benefices. Six of these were curates, one a chaplain, one a canon, and two clerics. Another fourteen, most of them chaplains and simple priests, suffered the penalty of temporary suspension from the celebration of Mass, which imposed a severe financial strain on them. The removal of curates and the suspension of chaplains were indicative of the greater ability of the Novarese church to replace priests in parishes and churches where the existing priests had caused rumours, dissatisfaction, and scandal.

As in the post-Tridentine period, a number of priests appealed the decision to strip them of a benefice to tribunals outside the diocese. Thus, in the mid-1780s Girolamo Bertoglio, curate of Cervatto in the area of Varallo Sesia, was tried for fathering a child by an unmarried woman and for violating numerous formal admonitions not to deal with her. By a sentence of 6 February 1788, he was deprived of his parish. Bertoglio was also ordered to pay the cost of the process as well as the salary of a vice-curate until a new parish priest could be found.[128] At the same time the rural vicar of the Mastallone valley was ordered to confiscate his property, which he reported doing in February 1788.[129] The case did not end there, however, for in by June, 1788, Bertoglio decided to appeal the sentence to the archdiocese of Milan, even though Novara was no longer in Milanese territory. Aware of the potential difficulties, the curia weighed the possibility of giving Bertoglio a pension of two hundred lire a year, to be paid from the meagre revenues of the parish.[130] It is not known what action was taken.

Exile was used as a punishment in approximately ten cases and tended to be of two sorts. When a priest or cleric was from outside the diocese, exile meant expulsion from the diocese. Thus, in February 1755 the curia expelled the priest Stefano Coradi of Piacenza after he was accused of theft by a Novarese merchant. Coradi had been ordained to his patrimony at Piacenza but had been suspended from sacred functions because of a lengthy criminal record. He had been prosecuted for theft at Piacenza as early as 1731 and sentenced to exile from that city. Subsequent travels had taken him to Rome, Brescia, Genoa, Livorno, Vercelli, Turin, and now Novara.[131] In 1771 the priest Giuseppe Faino, resident at Fontanetto, was prosecuted for impregnating a young woman, ignoring the orders of the curia, bearing arms, and engaging in secular occupations. Although the vicar general found him not guilty of the charge of sexual relations with the young woman and of weapons violations, because he was not a native of the diocese and possessed no benefice he was ordered to leave the city within two weeks or face imprisonment.[132]

Other cases involved exile from specific villages or communities within the diocese. Thus, in 1767 the regents of the village of Casalino accused their vice-curate, Michele Borsotto, of abusing his power by publicly scolding them for spending freely from communal funds when it was in their interests but refusing to hire a sacristan or provide for the needs of the church. Borsotto was exiled from the Casalino, fined 20 scudi, and ordered to pay court costs of 122 lire and 2 soldi.[133]

In the case of clerics who had not yet been ordained to one of the minor orders, there was another remedy not available to those who had been ordained. This was to set aside clerical habit and leave the clerical estate. Such was the case of Gian Pietro Minoli, as well as six others over the decades. For example, in February 1773 two clerics of Galliate, Carlo Giuseppe Monti and Carlo Domenico Brusati, agreed to set aside the clerical habit in order to avoid prosecution after their landlord accused them of excessive familiarity with his daughter and of creating a disturbance when he attempted to evict them.[134]

Not all of the priests who were cited by the tribunal were found guilty of the charges levelled against them. In seven known cases in the eighteenth century, the accused were either found innocent or otherwise exonerated. A case in point is the trial of Valentino Giovanetti who was acquitted of wounding Pietro Feria of Tornaco in the leg because he was acting in self-defence. This was followed by an act of reconciliation between the parties.[135] A more notorious case occurred in 1787 when Giuseppe Capra, the curate of Buglio in the vicariate of Omegna, was accused of a series of rapes and attempted rapes, as well as groping and making lascivious comments towards women of the town who served as his cooks and laundresses. Because of the cost of preparing a defence, Capra resigned the parish, only to request that the case be reopened in 1791 when he had the opportunity to obtain a canonical prebend at the nearby town of Gozzano. New testimony discredited his accusors and revealed that a group of the leading men of Buglio had hoped to force him out as curate in order to obtain a new pastor. On 4 July 1791 Capra was absolved from all the charges.[136]

Earlier in this chapter, I argued that the episcopal tribunal played a lesser role in the disciplining of the clergy in the eighteenth century than it had in the post-Tridentine era and that the ratio of accused clergy as a portion of the total numbers of clergy declined significantly between the two eras. A number of explanations can be offered for this phenomenon, explanations which should be regarded as complementary rather than mutually exclusive. One possibility is that the calibre of priests serving in the diocese – especially of those involved in the care of souls – had improved since the early seventeenth century. Over the decades, measures such as the development of the seminary system and the Cannobian School, the establishment of rural vicars to provide reliable communication between Novara and the countryside, the implementation of monthly congregations for the priests of each vicariate, the foundation of the oblates of San Gaudenzio and San Carlo, and the vigilance of the bishop's tribunal, despite its limitations, had borne fruit in the diocese with the emergence of an educated, professional elite of parish priests.[137]

A good number of priests accepted the ideals of their bishops and vicars general, making the ideals their own. Parish priests and rural vicars often admonished and corrected their fellow priests and clerics before making denunciations. This speaks not only to less formal, more personal ways of solving problems, but also a spirit of pride in the clerical estate.[138] For example, in November 1775 Giuseppe Maria de Giorgi, rector of Cominago and rural vicar in the region of Borgomanero, reported the priest Giovanni Scapardino to the curia for his drunkenness and for excessive familiarity with two women. He also accused the priest of striking the cook of the College of Santa Cristina as well as his own father and his uncle. The rector added that he had earlier tried to reason with Scapardino, but to no avail. The curia ordered Scapardino to prepare his response or defence, but the end of the process is not known.[139]

Another case came to light in February 1771, when Francesco Antonio Zerlia, the parish priest of Gattico, reported that he had tried in vain to persuade Pietro Bertona, chaplain of the community, to end a friendship with Margarita Pontavola of the same town, speaking to him on several occasions, the last in the company of one of his fellow parish priests. He also tried to change the ways of Margarita, whom he described as approximately thirty-six years of age but unwilling to consider marriage after earlier courtships had ended with the imprisonment of one suitor, her betrothed, and the death of a second. Zerlia had hopes of convincing Margarita to return to her mother's house, but found her to be unruly and 'petulant.' On one occasion she had threatened him in the parish church when he admonished her for refusing to cover her head with the proper white veil. Finally, on hearing that Bertona had on two occasions spent time with Margarita behind closed doors late at night, he reported the chaplain to the curia. Bertona was cited to appear by Balbis Bertone himself, and was so mortified when he heard news of this that Zerlia hoped he might finally correct his behaviour.[140] Unfortunately, that was not to be. In November 1776, after Zerlia had died or at least departed from Gattico, Bertona and his new parish priest, Giorgio Bozzetta, were investigated by the tribunal for interfering in the internal affairs of parish confraternities, refusing to make themselves available to the sick, frequenting dances, and being indifferent to ecclesiastical functions and the care of souls. It is not known how this last case ended, but it is evident they had departed from the high standard set by Zerlia.[141]

Although a strong case can be made that the Novarese clergy had developed into a reformed and dedicated body of men, there are limitations to this argument. The clergy continued to be closely tied to the villages and regions from which they came, and the system of benefices in which a parish was regarded as virtually a piece of property remained in place. The many chaplaincies and legacies that had been established since the sixteenth century were tied to the interests of families, confraternities, and communities that sought to control their administration and the appointment of priests. They were a key factor in the expansion in the number of priests who were not involved in the care of souls and, as noted above, their numbers were increasingly regarded as problematic by the eighteenth-century states. Even some members of the hierarchy saw the high number of young men seeking to enter the church as a problem. Carlo Luigi Buronzo Del Signore, who served as bishop of Novara from 1791 until his transfer to Turin in 1797, noted this when he wrote a pastoral letter asking fathers to cease pressuring their sons to enter the ecclesiastical life.[142]

Other explanations can be offered for the declining incidence of prosecutions of members of the clergy. First, as noted above, it is probable that the lay courts were beginning to handle the more serious cases of clerical violence, especially homicides. However, given the low number of homicides in the period 1745 to 1765, it seems doubtful that interventions by the secular courts would have made a great impact on the total numbers. Second, and more important, in the eighteenth century the Novarese bishops and their officials appear to have been less aggressive than the post-Tridentine hierarchy in their use of judicial procedures to discipline the clergy. This should not be attributed to lethargy on their part because the eighteenth-century bishops, Balbis Bertone in particular, had a strong record of residing in the diocese, conducting pastoral visitations, improving seminaries, and promoting the good customs and deportment of the clergy, as expressed in the synod of 1778. The approach taken by the episcopal curia seems to have changed. The old tendency to rush to prosecution, so evident in the early years of Bascapè, seems to have been replaced by a less formal and more remedial approach. Those accused of offences were admonished and corrected by their fellow priests, usually parish priests and rural vicars, and if this failed, they were summoned before the vicar general or the bishop. This would result in confessions, penances, and hopefully personal correction before matters reached the more formal judicial phase. The summary process was more secretive in its execution, avoiding the necessity of interrogating witnesses and reducing the possibility of rumours and scandal. Secrecy was a priority for the episcopal curia, intent on maintaining the dignity of the clerical estate. The heavy recourse of the tribunal to spiritual exercises as the response to improper behaviour underscored a more remedial, pastoral approach, as did the number of cases that appear to have stopped at the stages of admonition and warning. The eighteenth-century episcopate was less willing and eager than their post-Tridentine counterparts to make an example of wayward priests, or to use the court as an instrument of intimidation. As well, the elevated numbers of the clergy in the diocese gave the bishops a luxury that Carlo Bascapè did not enjoy in the post-Tridentine period: they could be more selective in choosing priests for the care of souls and could more easily remove or reassign those who failed in this capacity. Thus the falling ratio of accusations and processes to total clergy in the diocese may have been due to both improvements in the education and sense of professionalism of the clergy and to a change in the methods and approach employed by the curia.

Conclusion: Two Phases of Tribunal Activity

In 1615, the last year of his life, Carlo Bascapè published *Commentarii canonici*, a short work that highlighted points of canon law that had been at the heart of jurisdictional conflicts during his episcopacy and that he held to be crucial to the maintenance of ecclesiastical authority. Front and centre of these was a section on the powers and independence of the bishop's tribunal, which Bascapè placed in the general context of the medieval claim that the ecclesiastical power was superior to the secular and that it was the right of the ecclesiastical authority, the bishops, to command the secular and not the contrary. Bishops, he asserted, had free power (*libera potestas*) in their cities and dioceses to investigate, judge, and punish adulterers and other evil doers. This power included the right to investigate, imprison, and torture the accused. If the secular authority impeded the spiritual, the penalty was excommunication. What was more, the ecclesiastical court could call on the assistance of the secular arm to apprehend the accused, but this was never to be prejudicial to its power and freedom of action. That is, the secular authority could never claim to review such cases before giving its support.[1] In his commentary Bascapè also summarized the ecclesiastical positions on other flashpoints in the recent battles between church and state: the prohibition of dances and theatre performances on Sundays and feast days, the right of the bishop's agents (*famiglia armata*) to bear arms, and the exclusion of the laity from the chancel during ecclesiastical ceremonies.[2] His arguments underscored the importance that the post-Tridentine hierarchy attached to its judicial powers for imposing new standards of morality on society.

The claims which Bascapè made for episcopal jurisdiction would seem to confirm a number of common places in the historiography of the Italian church, both old and new. On the one hand, supporters of the church might see his claims as confirming the vigilance and power of the church as it embarked on the great reforms of the post-Tridentine era. For those who view the church less favourably, Bascapè's commentary might serve as confirmation of the hard line and repressive tactics employed by the church in the early modern era as it imposed its will on both the elites and the masses of Italian society. Both friend and foe might see the commentary as confirmation of the theories of confessionalization and social control, with the church and state supporting each other as they imposed a new religious and moral order on society.

However, in contrast to the sweeping claims made by Bascapè in his commentary, this study has demonstrated that the bishop's tribunal of Novara was limited in its impact on both the clergy and the laity of the diocese, and that with the passage of time its importance diminished rather than increased. The tribunal exercised a modest influence over the lives of laypersons, even when its activity was at a height in the post-Tridentine period. In many ways its power was more threat than reality. Initial interventions in cases of concubinage and adultery declined after 1600, perhaps because of instability created by a new round of conflict with the government of Milan, but more likely because the tribunal simply lacked the resources, human and financial, to do more and felt it better to leave these matters to the internal tribunal of the confessional. It is possible that there was a revived interest in cases of concubinage in the early seventeenth century, paralleling what occurred at Naples and Siena, but the records to put this to the test are lacking, and efforts at Naples were hardly complete successes.

There were few cases involving usury, despite the importance which the church attached to this abuse, and even the accusations of failure to perform the Easter duty, regarded by the hierarchy as the litmus test of being a good Catholic, were relatively rare. The bishop's tribunal continued to be active in dealing with lay assaults on members of the clergy. The attention paid to assaults was in part driven by the complaints of offended ecclesiastics, and in part a response to the belief that such offences could not be overlooked because they undermined the dignity of the clerical estate and resulted in the excommunication of the culprit. However, the majority of the lay cases of assault heard by the bishop's tribunal were relatively minor in nature and it was the secular tribunals that responded to serious attacks on the clergy by laymen, especially homicides.

In the post-Tridentine era the bishop's tribunal played an active role in matters of faith such as blasphemy, heresy, illicit magic, and witchcraft. After initial confrontations between Bascapè and the Dominican Domenico Buelli, the inquisitor of Novara, a degree of cooperation was attained. The inquisitor and the episcopal vicars general held common sessions when the accused were interrogated under torture and when sentence was passed. The degree of activity of the inquisitor of Novara during Bascapè's episcopate remains unknown. Buelli had been extremely active when hunting witches in the northern valleys of the diocese in the 1570s and 1580s, but his death in 1603 and replacement by a new inquisitor may have slowed down activity by his office. The deaths of a number of alleged witches of old age and disease in the episcopal jail in 1610–11 were the blackest mark on the history of the tribunal of Novara, but other than that the tribunal does not appear to have been excessively harsh in its treatment of lay offenders in matters of faith. The travel of northern merchants to Protestant areas was a matter of great concern to the bishops and resulted in a noteworthy trial of merchants from the Antigorio valley in the early 1600s. However, even Bascapè was forced to compromise when the northern merchants complained that his requirements for travel to Switzerland threatened their livelihood. The merchants and labourers of the north remained more open in their dealings with Swiss Protestants than the bishops of Novara would have liked.

In the early eighteenth century Novara passed from the duchy of Milan to the kingdom of Piedmont-Sardinia. By then the bishop's tribunal appears to have dropped any pretence of dealing with lay 'crimes.' Few questions touching on matrimony and only a dozen minor assaults on the clergy are to be found in the files of this period, perhaps because the episcopal curia was wary of confrontation with the kingdom which was assertive of its own jurisdictional power, even though the crown promised to let Novara, as a newly acquired territory, follow the old customs and procedures of the duchy of Milan. The eighteenth-century bishops continued to issue edicts against magic, witchcraft, and relations with Protestants, and added new strictures against reading and disseminating the new views of the Enlightenment. However, this had little impact on the work of the tribunal, and the most serious cases involved not laypersons but a handful of ecclesiastics. Although the Savoyard court had permitted Rome to name new inquisitors for Novara, the limitations which the secular authorities placed on the work of the Inquisition in Piedmont probably warned both inquisitors and episcopal vicars general to tread softly when dealing with matters of faith. The attacks levelled at the Inquisition in neighbouring states, most notably in the duchy of Milan under the Austrian Habsburgs, might have been a further warning to the Novarese bishops and vicars general to avoid more aggressive action as the eighteenth century drew to a close.

In the two periods of this study, the bishop's tribunal devoted most of its attention to the crimes, sins, and deportment of the priests and clerics who were to be the leaders of the new society. The goals set down in diocesan synods and episcopal decrees, which closely followed the Council of Trent and the provincial councils of Milan, amounted to the creation of a professionalized clergy, set apart from the people of the diocese by training, clothing, manners, and sense of spiritual mission. The parish clergy were to be the heart and soul of the penitential system of the diocese. The study of cases of conscience was the core element in the seminary curriculum. Competitions for the award of parishes and examinations for the ability to serve as confessor were based in large part on testing in cases of conscience, and priests of the city and countryside were required to assemble in monthly congregations to study the finer points of the sacrament of confession.

The bishop's tribunal was the final instrument for the reform of the clergy, and in the post-Tridentine period the vicars general and their assistants pursued wayward priests, especially parish priests, with unprecedented vigour. By aggressively demonstrating their command over this area of ecclesiastical jurisdiction, the Novarese bishops and vicars general perhaps hoped to prove the vitality of the ecclesiastical system of law, while at the same time deflecting the criticism of anyone who might question the principle that clerics were immune from prosecution by the secular courts.

At first glance the record of the bishop's tribunal was impressive. An amazing one-fifth of the diocesan clergy were arraigned by the tribunal on one or more occasions during the twenty-three-year episcopate of Bascapè. In the first five years of the episcopate (1593–7) the tribunal arraigned an average of twenty-four priests and clerics a year. Prosecution by the bishop's tribunal could be a significant deterrent to clerical crimes, as a number of key cases demonstrated. To be summoned to Novara, endure time in the episcopal jail, undergo interrogations and possibly torture, and pay for the expenses of a legal defence and a substitute in the care of souls could be major hardships for the accused and were for the most part worse than the sentences which the vicars general imposed on those found guilty. But on closer inspection the tribunal had many weaknesses, even in the days of Tridentine reform. After the first five years of Bascapè's episcopate, arraignments of ecclesiastics fell to slightly fewer than ten a year. The reasons for the decline are not clear, but might have had to do with the distractions created for the bishop and his curia by jurisdictional struggles with the secular government of Milan. More likely, after the initial rush to prosecute priests and clerics, the tribunal ran out of energy. The tribunal depended heavily on the personal initiative, zeal, and ability of the vicars general, who were also occupied with administrative and pastoral duties. Judicial processes were time consuming, the system of benefices made it difficult to remove incumbents, and there was always the possibility of appeal to courts in neighbouring dioceses and at Rome.

An even more fundamental obstacle for the curia was the degree to which the diocesan clergy were embedded in the life of their communities. The great majority were born and raised in the diocese and shared in the desires and attitudes of their parishioners. The tribunal was sorely tested when it confronted what the hierarchy regarded not just as clerical sins, but crimes against the order of God and of the church. Many secular priests simply did not have the sense of religious zeal and commitment demanded of them by their superiors. There were contradictions in what the church expected of the priests. They were to stand apart from the people in everything from spiritual life and morals to clothing and deportment, but their role as mediators between the hierarchy and the people drew them back into their communities. They were allowed to possess property, which they watched over while also administering property of the church. As confessors they were exposed to the most intimate thoughts of males and females alike. Negligence in the care of souls was not a major problem at Novara. Most curates performed their basic duties and the accusations of negligence heard by the tribunal were usually confined to failure to celebrate weekday masses, to teach catechism, and to take the sacraments to the sick. Prolonged absences from parishes and gross neglect of duties were rare. The Novarese tribunal paid considerable attention to suppressing sexual activity on the part of the clergy, a problem which appeared in approximately half of the cases and covered a wide range of activity. Most of the cases concerned dealings with women in more or less lasting relationships or concubinage. It has been argued that parishioners had a high tolerance of clerical concubinage in the early modern era, and that accusations against parish priests would only be made if other serious problems appeared including neglect of the care of souls, incidents of physical violence or verbal abuse, and new attempts at sexual seduction. While there is ample evidence of this at Novara, with many cases involving myriad accusations including concubinage, there were also a dozen occasions when sexual misbehaviour was the only accusation brought against a priest. Was it possible that there was less toleration for sexual offences at Novara than in other dioceses? The fact that a number of women remained in long-term relationships with curates and chaplains suggests that there was a degree of community acceptance of their conduct, or at least a reluctance to make an accusation and incur the displeasure of a parish priest.

Sexual cases, however, were only one part of a broad spectrum of charges which occupied the time and energy of the bishop's tribunal. Charges of assault, up to and including homicides, were almost as common as accusations of sexual misconduct. The fact they were dealt with by the tribunal suggests that the principle of clerical immunity from prosecution by the secular courts was upheld in the diocese of Novara and underscores the independence and initiative enjoyed by the hierarchy in areas that for laypersons would have been the concern of the secular courts. Allegations of theft, gambling, drunkenness, and unruly behaviour appeared with limited frequency, as did involvement in illicit magic.

In that the bishop's tribunal was deemed necessary to keep some members of the clergy on a straight path, it appears to have played a role in the attempt to mould the Novarese clergy into the professionalized body envisaged by the reforming hierarchy. However, many cases did not result in a sentence but ended with the priest or cleric privately confessing his guilt and receiving absolution and a penance. When sentences were passed, the punishments were remarkably light, with absolutions, injunctions to avoid occasions of sin, and modest fines predominating. It has been argued that in the early modern church there was a tendency for the Roman Inquisition to overlap with and intrude in the work of the confessor by trying to make the confessor a front-line agent in the war against heresy.[3] In the case of the bishop's tribunal of Novara, it more often seemed that the spirit of the confessor penetrated into and mitigated the judicial process, or in other words, that the tribunal could be regarded as an extension of the penitential process, to be used when admonition and paternal correction by the rural vicars, the vicar general, and the bishop did not work. Because of the poverty of many parishes and a shortage of capable priests, the bishops of post-Tridentine Novara were forced to temper their use of the tribunal with clemency, permitting the fallen to recover and to continue in the care of souls in spite of their repeat offences.

In the second half of the eighteenth century, the bishop's tribunal of Novara experienced a notable decline in the number of cases, especially in proportion to the rise in the number of priests, which had tripled in the interval since the early seventeenth century. Denunciations of ecclesiastics had fallen to eight or nine a year, and each year only five of these resulted in formal investigations or judicial inquiries. The episcopal curia proceeded with many cases summarily rather than with formal investigations and the full judicial process. Trials were replaced with summons to appear before the bishop or his vicar general for admonition, orders to undertake spiritual exercises, and injunctions to end inappropriate behaviour, especially contacts with specific women. In the eighteenth century, less of the tribunal's time was taken up by parish priests and more of its time by the lower ranks of priests, chaplains, and clerics. A number of explanations can be given for the decline in tribunal activity. It is possible that the years of episcopal residence, the development of the Novarese seminaries, and other measures for reform had improved the behaviour of the clergy of the diocese. The bishops of Novara now enjoyed a larger pool of candidates for the care of souls and examinations and other procedures were in place to help select candidates who were spiritually and intellectually suited to the task. There are limitations to this interpretation, however, because the old ties of priest to the community and the traditional system of benefices continued into the eighteenth century. As well, it also seems possible that if reform efforts had not corrected the behaviour of the clergy, they may at least have caused them to be more adept in hiding their offences and especially their indiscretions with women. A second reason for the decline in tribunal activity might have been that the lay courts were beginning to handle the more serious cases of clerical violence, especially homicides. This would, of course, have been a departure from the principle of clerical immunity or *privilegium fori*, but in line with the trend of state encroachment on ecclesiastical jurisdiction in other regions of Italy and in other parts of Piedmont-Sardinia in that century. However, given the low number of homicides in the period 1745 to 1765, it seems doubtful that interventions by the secular courts would have made a great impact on the total numbers of cases in the years 1765 to 1799.

Perhaps the most plausible explanation for the decline in numbers of inquiries is that the Novarese bishops of the eighteenth century and their officials had changed their tactics in dealing with offences by ecclesiastics. The eighteenth-century tribunal could be stern in punishing wayward priests, as a number were deprived of benefices, suspended from the celebration of Mass, imprisoned, and fined. However, the old tendency to rush to prosecution, so evident in the early years of Bascapè's episcopate, seems to have been replaced by a more informal and remedial approach, with those accused of offences receiving admonition or correction in the first instance from their fellow priests and, if this failed, being summoned to Novara. It was hoped this would result in confessions, penances, and personal correction before matters reached the more formal judicial phase. The heavy recourse of the curia to spiritual exercises as a form of correction underscores the more remedial approach. The eighteenth-century episcopate seems to have been more intent on reforming their prodigal sons through the more penitential regimen of spiritual exercises than through fines and other punishments. They were less willing and eager than their post-Tridentine counterparts to make an example of wayward priests, or to use the external court as an instrument of intimidation.

The history of the bishop's tribunal of Novara gives cause to question modern theories of confessionalization and social control. The tribunal was neither as efficient nor as rigorous as its defenders, and its opponents for that matter, liked to believe. In the post-Tridentine period the tribunal hardly touched the lives of the laity, and cooperation between church and state was severely limited by the state's desire to maintain its judicial powers in the face of what was often regarded as excessive zeal on the part of the reformers. The bishop's tribunal, without a great deal of involvement by the state, focused most of its attention on the clergy, but even here its activity was restricted by shortage of personnel and by lack of suitable candidates for the care of souls. A number of scholars have suggested that the Roman Inquisition stepped into the vacuum left by the weakness of bishops and of their tribunals.[4] It is known that the inquisitor of Novara had his own jail and his own network of rural vicars. But unless his resources were greater than those enjoyed by the episcopal tribunal, and there is no cause to believe that they were, he was probably no more effective in forcing a new moral order on the diocese than the bishop was. Recent studies of the working of the Inquisition in northern Italy have suggested that states in the sixteenth and early seventeenth centuries were unwilling to surrender too much control to the inquisitors, especially when members of the upper ranks of society might be among the accused, or when the activities of the Inquisition jeopardized good relations and trade with Protestant neighbours.[5] By the eighteenth century the prospect of confessionalization had clearly ended as the state came to dominate the church and slowly but surely extended its powers over ecclesiastical courts. Ironically there was probably greater cooperation between the bishops and the Piedmontese state than there had ever existed in the post-Tridentine period. The episcopal tribunal backed away from dealing with laypersons almost completely, and even in its handling of the clergy it adopted a milder, more cautious policy which sought to deal with ecclesiastics more informally and, as it developed, more secretively.

Appendices

Appendix 1: Diocese of Novara, 1616–18

Vicariates	Parishes	Curates and Vice-curates	Other Priests	Population
Lombard Plain				
City of Novara	17	14	47	7,342
Caltignaca	9	9	3	3,151
Cameriano	12	12	2	4,259
Carpignano	8	9	5	3,942
Mosezzo	7	7	1	2,050
Trecate	7	10	18	12,835
Vespolate	11	11	5	6,441
Subtotal	71	72	81	40,020
Centre				
Borgomanero	8	11	5	5,503
Invorio	9	9	0	3,884
Oleggio	7	9	14	7,768
Romagnano Sesia	9	9	9	7,683
Suno	9	9	3	4,872
Varallo Pombia	9	10	5	5,009
Subtotal	51	57	36	34,719
Lakes				
Baveno/Pallanza	6	8	4	3,131
Gozzano	8	8	9	4,095
Intra	11	16	6	8,856
Lesa	9	10	0	3,649
Omegna	12	14	3	8,296
Riviera West	8	8	1	3,272
Riviera East	10	11	20	5,789
Subtotal	64	75	43	37,088
Mountains				
Antigorio	6	8	4	5,980
Borgosesia I	7	10	0	3,637
Borgosesia II	7	9	0	6,760
Domodossola	12	12	3	10,105
Pieve Vergonte	15	16	2	10,380
Scopa	11	11	1	10,304
Vall'Anzasca	12	11	1	11,850
Valle Vigezzo	12	11	0	5,219
Varallo Sesia I	8	11	6	5,960
Varallo Sesia II	6	5	0	4,222
Subtotal	96	104	17	74,417
Total	282	308	177	186,244

Appendix 2: Population of Novara

Vicariates	1616–18	1758–63	% Change
Lombard Plain			
City of Novara	7,342	9,309	26.79
Caltignaca	3,151	3,594	14.06
Cameriano	4,259	5,913	38.84
Carpignano	3,942	6,060	53.73
Mosezzo	2,050	2,212	7.90
Trecate	12,835	17,036	32.73
Vespolate	6,441	8,692	34.95
Subtotal	40,020	52,816	31.97
Centre			
Borgomanero	5,503	7,949	44.45
Invorio	3,884	6,202	59.68
Oleggio	7,768	9,463	21.82
Romagnano Sesia	7,683	10,368	34.95
Suno	4,872	7,829	60.69
Varallo Pombia	5,009	8,594	71.57
Subtotal	34,719	50,405	45.18
Lakes			
Baveno/Pallanza	3,131	4,311	37.69
Gozzano	4,095	5,001	22.12
Intra	8,856	14,952	68.83
Lesa	3,649	4,868	33.41
Omegna	8,296	9,890	19.21
Riviera West	3,272	3,227	–1.38
Riviera East	5,789	6,796	17.40
Subtotal	37,088	49,045	32.24
Mountains			
Antigorio	5,980	4,273	–28.55
Borgosesia I	3,637	5,687	56.37
Borgosesia II	6,760	6,195	–8.36
Domodossola	10,105	10,225	1.19
Pieve Vergonte	10,380	11,849	14.15
Scopa	10,304	10,651	3.37
Vall'Anzasca	11,850	11,549	–2.54
Valle Vigezzo	5,219	4,907	–5.98
Varallo Sesia I	5,960	7,243	21.53
Varallo Sesia II	4,222	5,667	34.23
Subtotal	74,417	78,246	5.15
Total	186,244	230,512	23.77

Appendix 3: Growing Numbers of Clergy from the Early Seventeenth Century to the Mid-Eighteenth Century

Vicariates	Parish Priests		Other Priests		Total Priests		% Increase
	1616–18	1758–63	1616–18	1758–63	1616–18	1758–63	
Lombard Plain							
City of Novara	14	13	47	140	61	153	150.8
Caltignaca	9	10	3	6	12	16	33.3
Cameriano	12	14	2	13	14	27	92.9
Carpignano	9	10	5	21	14	31	121.4
Mosezzo	7	7	1	4	8	11	37.5
Trecate	10	13	18	83	28	96	242.9
Vespolate	11	14	5	31	16	45	181.3
Subtotal	72	81	81	298	153	379	147.7
Centre							
Borgomanero	11	10	5	48	16	58	262.5
Invorio	9	10	0	19	9	29	222.2
Oleggio	9	11	14	84	23	95	313.0
Romagnano Sesia	9	10	9	52	18	62	244.4
Suno	9	10	3	22	12	32	166.7
Varallo Pombia	10	11	5	26	15	37	146.7
Subtotal	57	62	36	251	93	313	236.6

Lakes							
Baveno/Pallanza	8	11	4	30	12	41	241.7
Gozzano	8	10	9	29	17	39	129.4
Intra	16	22	6	45	22	67	204.5
Lesa	10	13	0	12	10	25	150.0
Omegna	14	16	3	32	17	48	182.4
Riviera West	8	10	1	18	9	28	211.1
Riviera East	11	14	20	64	31	78	151.6
Subtotal	75	96	43	230	118	326	176.3
Mountains							
Antigorio	8	10	4	19	12	29	141.7
Borgosesia I	10	14	0	34	10	48	380.0
Borgosesia II	9	14	0	33	9	47	422.2
Domodossola	12	19	3	34	15	53	253.3
Pieve Vergonte	16	21	2	31	18	52	188.9
Scopa	11	20	1	23	12	43	258.3
Vall'Anzasca	11	17	1	34	12	51	325.0
Valle Vigezzo	11	16	0	21	11	37	236.4
Varallo Sesia II	11	13	6	48	17	61	258.8
Varallo Sesia II	5	6	0	15	5	21	320.0
Subtotal	104	150	17	292	121	442	265.3
Total	308	389	177	1071	485	1460	201.0

Notes

Abbreviations

AEM	Milan Archdiocese, *Acta Ecclesiae Mediolanensis a Carlo Cardinali s. Praxedis condita, Federici Card. Borromaei Archiepiscopi Mediolani iussu collecta et edita*. Milan, 1599
APB	Archivio provinciale dei Barnabiti, church of San Barnaba, Milan
ASBR	Archivio Storico dei Padri Barnabiti di Roma
ASDN	Archivio Storico Diocesano di Novara
ASN	Archivio di Stato, Novara
AST	Archivio di Stato, Torino
ASV	Archivio Segreto Vaticano
BA	Biblioteca Ambrosiana, Milan
DBI	*Dizionario biografico degli Italiani*. Alberto Ghisalberti, ed. Rome: Istituto della Enciclopedia italiana, 1960–
DS	*Dictionnaire de spiritualité ascétique et mystique, doctrine et histoire*. Marcel Vallier, F. Cavallera, and J. de Guibert eds. Paris: Beauchesne, 1932–95

Note on Currency

1 ASDN XII, 2, 5, *1596–1603*, fol. 150v.
2 For exchange rates on scudi, ducatoni, and ducats, see Hanlon, *Early Modern Italy*, x. For Bascapè's comment, see ASBR, Bascapè, *Registri di lettere*, 3, letter 18, to Orazio Besozzo, 19 July 1594.
3 ASDN III, 5, 1, Report of Antonio Tornielli to Cardinal Ferdinando Taverna (1616).
4 Deutscher, 'Growth of the Secular Clergy,' 388–90.

Introduction

1 ASDN XII, 2, 11, *1591–8*, fols. 28v–29r; ASDN XII, 2, 6, *1576–83, 1593*, fols. 176r–182v.

2 ASDN XII, 2, 8, *1596–8*, fols. 97r–v, 101r–102r.

3 ASDN XII, 2, 9, *1601–2*, fols. 59r–64v; ASDN XII, 2, 9, *1605–6*, fols. 29r–32v. The quote is found in *1605–6*, fol. 30v: 'dando non poco da maravigliare a laici et scandalo con queste sua angustia del lavoro non per esercitio, o giusto aquisto di tempo ne lavoranti, ma per troppa ansietà e avarizia.'

4 ASBR, Bascapè, *Registri di lettere*, 22, letter 140, to the curate of Premosello, vice-vicar, 4 August 1608.

5 On the parish priest as intermediary, see the now classic article by Allegra, 'Il parocco.'

6 Bascapè, *Commentarii canonici*, 165–77.

7 On the question of the boundaries between sin and crime, see Schilling, '"History of Crime" or "History of Sin"?' Basing his arguments on select Calvinist communities in Germany and the Netherlands, Schilling argues for a strict separation of the concepts of sin and crime. For an alternate view, that the work of the secular and ecclesiastical courts was too closely intertwined to separate the two concepts, see Ingram, 'History of Sin or History of Crime?' Both authors, however, seem to be in agreement that the Catholic tribunals did not draw such a line between sin and crime. Schilling (294) writes that the medieval ecclesiastical courts provided a 'mix of religious-spiritual discipline and purely secular jurisdiction,' which was abolished in principle within the Protestant countries, while Ingram (94) points out that the Catholic ecclesiastical courts 'doubled as formal legal tribunals and the forum for the exercise of a more pastorally oriented discipline' both before and after the Reformation era. For an Italian perspective on the issue of morality and the law, see Prodi, *Una storia della giustizia*. Prodi argues that the traditional, pluralistic legal systems of the West were founded on Christian concepts of morality, but that modern secular law has become monolithic and broken away from its moral underpinnings. Also important is Lavenia's *L'infamia e il perdono*. Lavenia examines the writings of moral theologians, natural philosophers, and jurists, from the Middle Ages to the early seventeenth century, on such questions as the distinction between sin and crime and whether the seal of confession could be broken in the case of heresy and serious crimes.

8 Botero, *Reason of State*, book 2, chapter 16, 66.

9 The term 'confessionalization' was first proposed by the German historian Ernst Walter Zeeden in the late 1950s. For the growing literature on the age of confessionalization, see Schilling, 'Confessionalization in the Empire.' Reinhard's

argument is presented in 'Reformation, Counter-Reformation, and the Early Modern State.'

10 Reinhard, 'Reformation, Counter-Reformation, and the Early Modern State.' See also Myers, *'Poor Sinning Folk'*, 116–23, for a discussion of steps taken by church and state to ensure religious conformity in sixteenth- and seventeenth-century Bavaria and Austria, including the use of force to ensure that parishes and parishioners observed the rule of annual confession and communion.

11 Di Simplicio, *Peccato, penitenza, perdono*, 59–60, and *Inquisizione, stregoneria, medicina*, 17.

12 Prosperi, *Tribunali della coscienza*, 270–1.

13 De Boer, *Conquest of the Soul*, 79–83.

14 De Boer, *Conquest of the Soul*, 70–3.

15 De Boer, *Conquest of the Soul*, 58–9.

16 For a comment on the theme of confessionalization in the Catholic context, see Mary Laven's contribution in MacCulloch et al., 'Recent Trends in the Study of Christianity in Sixteenth-Century Europe,' 706–20.

17 De Boer, *Conquest of the Soul*, 328–30.

18 Forster, *Catholic Revival in the Age of the Baroque*, 14–16.

19 Romeo, *Esorcisti, confessori, e sessualità femminile*, 155–6.

20 Zardin, 'La "Perfettione" nel proprio "stato",' 116, and 'Relaunching Confraternities in the Tridentine Era.'

21 De Boer, *Conquest of the Soul*, 245–55.

22 Borromeo, ed., *L'inquisizione*; Del Col, *L'Inquisizione in Italia*. Studies of the Roman Inquisition have likewise been impeded by the dispersed and fragmentary condition of its files and the lack of access to historians. Many Inquisitorial records were destroyed in the late eighteenth century to protect the accused and their families, while others were lost when Napoleon ordered their transfer to Paris. For the destruction of the records of the Roman Inquisition at Milan in 1788, see Fumi, *L'Inquisizione romana e lo stato di Milano*, 12–13.

23 On the disordered state of Italian diocesan archives, see Donati, 'Curie, tribunali, cancellerie episcopali in Italia.'

24 De Boer, 'Calvin and Borromeo.'

25 Zardin, *Riforma cattolica*, 94–106.

26 Prosperi, *Tribunali della coscienza*, 340–1, suggests that even if episcopal tribunals initially attempted to be involved in matters pertaining to the Inquisition – with which they shared common objectives, territory, and even personnel – in the long run their principal occupation consisted in controlling, at times protecting, an undisciplined clergy who often lived in concubinage and were culturally unprepared for the care of souls. As for the interactions of the tribunals with the laity, intricate matrimonial questions were enough to occupy any residual energy.

Prodi, while conceding the need for further studies, goes as far as saying that after an initial flurry of activity, the episcopal officials and prisons little by little became 'for the most part pathetic' (*quasi patetiche*) institutions. When the state was weak and there was a void to fill, it was the Roman Inquisition that moved in to occupy the space. *Una storia della giustizia*, 294–5.

27 Donati lists five types of cases attended to by the episcopal court of the diocese of Trent in 1764, and for that reason subject to court fees: civil cases, cases concerning benefices, matrimonial cases, criminal cases, and matters of 'arbitration and grace,' such as the erection of a confraternity or the decision to allow a burial in a church. 'Curie, tribunali, cancellerie episcopali in Italia,' 213–29.

28 For example, the vicariate of Trecate was visited in 1590, 1594, 1617, 1625, 1657, 1665 (Galliate), 1678, 1690, 1709, 1762, and 1785–6. See ASDN *Acta visitationis.*

29 See appendices 1–3.

30 ASBR, Bascapè, *Registri di lettere.*

1. The Diocese of Novara and Its Bishops

1 The figure 7300 is based on reports from the parishes of Novara during the visitations of 1617–18. Deutscher, 'Growth of the Secular Clergy.' In 1590 Bishop Speciano, in his visit to Rome, gave a higher estimate of the city's population: ten thousand. ASV, *Congregazione Concilio*, fol. 69r.

2 Cognasso, *Storia di Novara*, 400–5 and 425–6.

3 See appendix 1.

4 AEM, 1273.

5 Bascapè, *Novara, seu de ecclesia novariensis*, 3. Novara was bordered by the dioceses of Milan on the east, Pavia and Vigevano on the south, Vercelli on the west, Como on the northeast, and Sion on the northwest.

6 *Dictionnaire historique et biographique de la Suisse* 6:515–16 and 7:18. For maps, see Ammann and Schik, *Historischer Atlas der Schweiz*, esp. maps 13, 33, 34, 52, 53, and 65.

7 Bascapè listed seventeen urban parishes in *Scritti publicati*, 578.

8 ASDN *Acta visitationis* 67.

9 ASDN *Acta visitationis* 80.

10 ASV, *Congregazione Vescovi e Regolari, Positiones, 1594* (M–N). Other parishes named were Morando, Foresto, Breia, Carafanzo, and Ara in the Sesia valley, and Montossolano, Nibbio, Anzola, Castillio, and Cimamulera in the Ossola valley.

11 *Dictionnaire historique et biographique de la Suisse* 7:18.

12 Bendiscioli, 'Politica, amministrazione e religione nell'età dei Borromei,' 10:130.

13 ASBR, Bascapè, *Registri di lettere*, 2, letter 440, to Orazio Besozzo, agent at Rome, 24 May 1594.

14 In 1615 Bascapè reported that pensions had declined to only three hundred ducats. He used his new income to fund seminary construction at Novara, extensive repairs to the episcopal residence at Gozzano, chapels at the Sacro Monte of Varallo, renovations at the Barnabite church of San Marco, and relief for the poor. ASBR, Bascapè, *Registri di lettere*, 26, letter 245, to Sig. Abbate Aiazza at Santa Maria dell'Abbondanza, 31 August 1615.
15 Longo, 'Problemi di vita religiosa,' 1:328ff. The religious houses were of the Canons Regular of St Augustine, the Hermits of St Augustine (two), the Franciscan Conventuals and Observants, the Dominicans, the Carmelites, the Hieronymites, and the Capuchins.
16 ASV, *Congregazione Vescovi e Regolari, Positiones, 1601* (I–O).
17 Deutscher, 'Carlo Bascapè e la riforma delle monache di Novara.'
18 For the Milanese convents, see AEM, 1273; for those of Cremona, see Marcocchi, *La Riforma dei monasteri femminili a Cremona*, xx.
19 ASBR, Bascapè, *Registri di lettere*, 2, letter 313, to Orazio Besozzo, 5 April 1594.
20 For recent studies of the Spanish presence in sixteenth-century Italy, see Hanlon, *Early Modern Italy*, 62–75; and Dandelet, 'Politics and the State System.'
21 Chabod, *Per la storia religiosa dello stato di Milano.*
22 Such was the case at Cerrano, Galliate, Pernate, and Cameri. ASDN *Acta visitationis* 2, fols. 22r, 98v, 102r–103v, 100r–101v.
23 'Malam vitam ducendo more meretricio.' ASDN XII, 2, 1, *1563–4*, fol. 7r–v.
24 Measures taken to curb the infiltration of heretical books through the town of Domodossola are discussed by Chabod, *Per la storia religiosa*, 309–10.
25 For the challenges posed by the presence of foreign mercenary soldiers in the state of Milan and the problems created when the Inquisition of Milan chose to prosecute a handful of Protestant soldiers from Basel, see de Boer, 'Soldati in terra straniera.'
26 Tavuzzi, *Renaissance Inquisitors*. For the post-Tridentine period, see Deutscher, 'Role of the Episcopal Tribunal of Novara in the Suppression of Heresy and Witchcraft'; and Beccaria, 'Inquisizione episcopale.'
27 The texts of the reform decrees are found in Stoppa, 'Quattro decreti generali novaresi simultanei ai Concilio Lateranese V finora sconosciuti e inediti'; and in Longo, 'Problemi di vita religiosa,' 1:79–97 and 1:151–6.
28 For example, in the Antigorio valley new parishes were established at San Rocco in 1556, Cravegna in 1564, and Motio in 1578. See ASDN *Acta visitationis* 6, fols. 203r and 205v–207v.
29 Chabod, *Per la storia religiosa*, 47–65.
30 For brief notes on each of the post-Tridentine bishops, see Bascapè, *Novaria*, 577–93. The two other bishops to hold the see in the years 1563 to 1593 were Geronimo Ragazonio, who was transferred to Bergamo almost immediately after

his appointment in 1576, and Pomponio Cotta, who governed from February 1577 to his death in September 1579. For more recent studies, see Longo, 'Appunti su Cesare Speciano, Vescovo di Novara'; Stoppa and Longo, 'Sinodi e congregazioni del Vescovo Francesco Bossi'; Stoppa, 'Quattro decreti generali novaresi'; and Longo, 'Problemi di vita religiosa.'

31 See Novara Diocese, *Synodus novarien … Serbellonum … MDLXVIII*; *Decreta edita et promulgata … 1576 … Archinto*; *Synodus dioecesana … Speciano … MDXC*. No decrees survive from Bossi's synods.

32 ASDN *Acta visitationis* 11, fol. 11r, and *Acta visitationis* 19, fols. 24r–26r.

33 Longo, 'Appunti su Cesare Speciano.'

34 For the origins of rural vicars and prefects in the diocese of Novara, see Longo, 'Problemi di vita religiosa,' 1:215–44. Also of value is Speciano's report *ad limina apostolorum* of 1591 in ASV, *Congregazione Concilio*, 71r.

35 The remote Antigorio valley, for example, was visited by the vicar general of Serbelloni in 1571, by Bishop Archinto between 1574 and 1576, and by visitors general of Bossi and Ponzone in 1582 and 1592. Acts of visitation survive for all but Archinto's visit: ASDN *Acta visitationis* 3, fols. 75r–82r; *Acta visitationis* 6, fols. 191r–212v; *Acta visitationis* 18.

36 Bascapè, 'Facultas vicarii generalis,' in *Scritti publicati*, 759–60.

37 ASBR, Bascapè, *Registri di lettere*, 1, letter 217, to Card. Cusano, 19 May 1593.

38 Bascapè, 'Facultas cancellarii episcopali,' in *Scritti publicati*, 767.

39 Bascapè, *Commentarii canonici*, 165–71.

40 Bascapè, 'Facultas visitatoris' and 'Facultas visitatoris generalis,' in *Scritti publicati*, 760.

41 ASBR, Bascapè, *Registri di lettere*, 23, letter 415, to Canon Dolci, vicar for nuns, 24 April 1610.

42 Borromeo, with an archdiocese of over 750 parishes, developed an extensive organization which included, in addition to the vicar general and vicars for civil and criminal cases, six visitors for the diocese and sixty rural vicars (*vicarii foranei*). See Bendiscioli, 'Politica, amministrazione e religione nell'età dei Borromei,' 10:141–3. For a general overview of episcopal administration in Italy, see Donati, 'Curie, tribunali, cancellerie episcopali in Italia.' Donati (216) adds that the curia of Milan employed a host of chancellors, notaries, and actuaries, many of whom were laypersons and lived outside the episcopal palace. More recently, Danilo Zardin has studied the curia of Milan as it extended into the seventeenth century. See 'La curia arcivescovile al tempo del Cardinal Federico,' which provides an updated list of the officials of the curia. Zardin argues that the Milanese curia attained an almost iconic status in the early seventeenth century, viewed by the adherents of the church as a well-oiled machine that from an administrative point of view was a second Rome in Italy's north. However,

he questions whether the archdiocese could have maintained its pace after the waning of the spiritual impulse of the Borromeos and in the face of the centralizing tendencies of Rome and of the Roman Inquisition in the middle decades of the seventeenth century. Also of interest is Elena Brambilla's 'La polizia dei tribunali ecclesiastici e le riforme della giustizia penale,' which takes a broad view of ecclesiastical powers of enforcement, including not just episcopal tribunals and the Roman Inquisition but also parish priests and reserved cases as factors in the enforcement of a legal system based on Christian morals.

43 Bascapè, 'Facultas vicarii foranei,' in *Scritti publicati*, 763–5.

44 ASBR, Bascapè, *Registri di lettere*, 1, letter 612, to the vicar of Baveno, 15 October 1593. Gian Giacomo Ottolino, the curate of Montrigiasco, was arraigned on 17 November 1593 to respond to charges concerning drunkenness and shortcomings in the care of souls. See ASDN XII, 2, 7, *1593–4*, fols. 32r–36v. The curate of Fosseno was not prosecuted.

45 Bascapè, 'Facultas vicarii foranei,' in *Scritti publicati*, 763–5.

46 A document defending the right of canons to receive the fruits of their benefices while on pastoral visitations is found in the APB, *Fondo miscellaneo*, gruppo 4, 6.

47 ASBR, Bascapè, *Registri di lettere*, 1, letter 344, to Cardinal Cusano, 2 August 1593.

48 ASBR, Bascapè, *Registri di lettere*, 7, letter 77, to the vicar of Omegna, 25 July 1598. For a decree of the first provincial council on the appointment of rural vicars, see AEM, 22–3.

49 ASBR, Bascapè, *Registri di lettere*, 24, letter 394, to Padre don Andrea Balbo, the provost of San Marco, 15 January 1613.

50 ASBR, Bascapè, *Registri di lettere*, 1, letter 332, to Cardinal Cusano, 19 July 1593.

51 Among the non-Milanese collaborators of Carlo Borromeo were Niccolò Ormaneto of Verona, his first vicar general, Cesare Speciano of Cremona, his agent in Rome, and Silvio Antoniano, one of his secretaries. See Bendiscioli, 'Politica, amministrazione e religione nell'età dei Borromei,' 10:159–63.

52 Between 1593 and 1594 Bascapè was assisted by Padre Don Giacomo, a Barnabite from Pavia. ASBR, Bascapè, *Registri di lettere*, 1, letter 291, to Orazio Besozzo, 25 July 1595.

53 Deutscher, 'Growth of the Secular Clergy.'

54 For Bascapè's edicts, see *Scritti publicati*.

55 For example, in 1604 Bascapè recommended Niccolò Leonardi, a cleric of good morals, doctor of laws, and member of a leading Novarese family, for a prebend of the cathedral in the gift of Rome. ASBR, Bascapè, *Registri di lettere*, 18, letter 358, to Mons. the Datary of His Holiness at Rome, 9 November 1604.

56 'Et all'avvenire ragguagliarà prima che le spedisca, et non doppo.' ASBR, Bascapè, *Registri di lettere*, 2, letter 297, to the vicar general, 23 March, 1594.

57 ASBR, Bascapè, *Registri di lettere*, 19, letter 34, to P. Don Aurelio, cleric regular, Bologna, 14 June 1605.

58 BA, *Ms. Trotti*, 38, 78r.

59 ASBR, Bascapè, *Registri di lettere*, 19, letter 335, to Signor Croce, 19 October 1605.

60 ASBR, Bascapè, *Registri di lettere*, 21, letter 539, to the cardinal of Monreale, 18 March 1608.

61 ASBR, Bascapè, *Registri di lettere*, 24, letter 245, to Signor Croce, 25 November 1611.

62 ASBR, Bascapè, *Registri di lettere*, 2, letter 122, to the Father Procurator General of San Biagio, 3 January 1594.

63 ASBR, Bascapè, *Registri di lettere*, 2, letter 187, to Mons. Boido, vicar general, 26 February 1594.

64 ASBR, Bascapè, *Registri di lettere*, 24, letter 409, to Cardinal Bellarmine, 9 February 1613.

2. Episcopal Jurisdiction Put to the Test: Rival Ecclesiastical Courts and Confrontation with the State of Milan, 1563–1615

1 The advent of Tridentine reform in the second half of the sixteenth century and the activity of reforming bishops such as Carlo Borromeo led to efforts to reassert the powers of the episcopal tribunals in the face of encroachments not only from the state but also from the papacy itself. John Tomaro speaks of Rome's efforts to harness episcopal authority to its own purposes in 'San Carlo Borromeo and the Implementation of the Council of Trent.'

2 ASBR, Carlo Bascapè, *Registri di lettere*, 4, letter 437, to Mons. Seneca, vicar general, Milan, 24 July 1595. The interrogation of Beniolo is found in ASDN XII, 2, 7, *1593–4*, fols. 187r–189v, dated on 10 June 1594. Beniolo was also accused of being ordained before the canonical age without dispensation. On 12 September 1594, he was fined one hundred scudi and excommunicated for violating an injunction not to leave the city of Novara. ASDN XII, 2, 11, *1591–8*, fols. 45v–46r. He had probably fled to Milan to make his appeal to the archdiocese.

3 For the trials of Aloysio, see ASDN XII, 2, 9, *1601–2*, fols. 98r–101v, 118r–157r; and XII, 2, 9, *1603–4*, fols. 100r–114v. His *status personalis* appears in Bascapè's visitation of 1594, at which time he was described as being 'of bad reputation, although nothing could be proved against him.' ('Male audit; sed nihil eius delictum probatum est.') ASDN *Acta visitationis* 23, fols. 139v–140r. He had been absolved of assault charges in 1591. ASDN XII, 2, 11, *1591–8*, fols. 5r–6r. For Bascapè's account of his escape and capture, see ASBR, Bascapè, *Registri di lettere*, 17, letter 66, to P. Antonio Marchesi, rector of the College of Jesus in Turin, 11 June 1604.

4 ASV, *Congregazione Vescovi e Regolari. Positiones, 1612* (L–N).

5 For another example of an appeal to a neighbouring diocese, see the case of Serafino Comiti, canon of the cathedral of Novara, who in 1603 attempted to have his case transferred to the tribunal of Pavia, alleging that the court of Novara was proceeding too slowly. ASBR, Bascapè, *Registri di lettere*, 14, letter 174, to the cardinal of San Giorgio. Comiti, of noble birth and a doctor in both civil and canon law, was accused of neglecting the care of souls of the parish of San Pietro that was attached to his benefice so that he could conduct a case before the tribunal of Milan. Additional charges were living in the same house as a young woman, allegedly a servant, and adultery. He had replied defiantly that he had hired a vice-curate to tend to the parish, and that he had nothing to do with the young woman who had long been a servant of his family, in whose house he lived. ASDN XII, 2, 9, *1601–2*, fols. 104r–114v.

6 ASBR, Bascapè, *Registri di lettere*, 1, letter 586, to Orazio Besozzo, Rome, 2 October 1593.

7 The names and brief biographies of inquisitors who served at Novara are found in an eighteenth-century manuscript published by Luigi Madaro, 'Gli inquisitori a Novara dal 1351 al 1732.' For the fifteenth- and early sixteenth-century activity of the Inquisition in northern Italy, see Tavuzzi, *Renaissance Inquisitors*, 149–208. For records of the Inquisition now held at University College, Dublin, and a reference to a Novarese trial of 1580, see Monter and Tedeschi, 'Toward a Statistical Profile of the Italian Inquisitions,' esp. 140.

8 Del Col, *L'Inquisizione in Italia*, 200–1.

9 For more information on the structure and organization of the Roman Inquisition, see Del Col, 'Le strutture territoriali e l'attività dell'inquisizione Romana,' and *L'Inquisizione in Italia*, 284–301, 510–27. For the role of rural vicars in the work of the Inquisition in the archdiocese of Milan, see Turchini, 'Vicari foranei, Parroci, Inquisizione a Milano.' Also useful is Prosperi, *Tribunali della coscienza*, 327–8. On the confraternity of the Crocesignati, see Cremonini, 'La congregazione dei Crocesignati milanesi tra 1644 e 1767.'

10 For an overview of the officials of the local Inquisitions and the sins or crimes that came under their purview, see Brambilla, 'La polizia dei tribunali ecclesiastici.'

11 Beccaria, 'Inquisizione episcopale.'

12 ASBR, Bascapè, *Registri di lettere*, 1, letter 586, to Orazio Besozzo, Rome, 2 October 1593. For a fuller discussion, see Deutscher, 'Role of the Episcopal Tribunal.'

13 ASBR, Bascapè, *Registri di lettere*, 6, letter 83, to the cardinal of Santa Severina, 25 February 1597. For the role of rural vicars in the work of the Inquisition in the archdiocese of Milan, see Turchini, 'Vicari foranei, Parroci, Inquisizione a Milano'; Prosperi, *Tribunali della coscienza*, 327–8; and Del Col, *L'Inquisizione in Italia*, 518–19.

14 On questions concerning the enforcement of the Index, see ASBR, Bascapè, *Registri di lettere*, 6, letter 83, to the cardinal of Santa Severina, 25 February 1597. On the matter of regulating travel to northern lands, see ASBR, Bascapè, *Registri di lettere*, 15, letter 344, to the vicar general of Novara, 1 November 1603.

15 The requirements were set out in the papal constitution *Multorum querela*, which was issued early in the fourteenth century by Clement V. See Borromeo, 'Contributo allo studio dell'inquisizione.'

16 Madaro, 'Gli inquisitori a Novara,' 207–9.

17 For a discussion of the extensive number of familiars of the inquisitor of Cremona and the controversy raised in the 1590s over their right to bear arms, see Peyronel Rambaldi, 'Inquisizione e potere laico.' Cremona, a city of 35,000 people, had undergone a significant crisis in the 1580s when a number of priests and clerics were accused and tried for Calvinist opinions.

18 On the growing pains of the Roman Inquisition in the duchy of Milan, see three studies by Giannini: 'Fra autonomia politica e ortodossia religiosa'; 'Per beneficio della città e religione'; and 'Inquisizione romana e politica asburgica nella Milano di metà Cinquecento.' Also valuable are de Boer's comments on Catholic-Protestant interaction on the borderlands in 'Soldati in terra straniera.'

19 Catalano and Martino, *Potestà civile e autorità spirituale in Italia*, 14.

20 *Catholic Encyclopedia* 7:717–18.

21 In 1568 Pope Pius V reissued the bull with new provisions prohibiting the taxation of ecclesiastical property. For the opposition created in the Spanish dominions and the compromise which resolved the matter for a time, see Giannini, 'Tra politica, fiscalità e religione.'

22 Novara Diocese, 'Libellus casuum reservatorum: Casus excommunicationis reservati in processu Bullae, quae lata est in die coenae Domini,' in *Decreta edita et promulgata ... 1576 ... Archinto*, 54v–56v.

23 ASBR, Bascapè, *Registri di lettere*, 1, letter 541, to the vicar of Ossola, 8 September 1593.

24 'Fifth Lateran Council, Bull against exempt persons, in which are included some points regarding ecclesiastical liberty and episcopal dignity,' in *Decrees of the Ecumenical Councils* 1:630–1.

25 Stoppa, 'Quattro decreti generali novaresi.'

26 Borromeo, 'Archbishop Carlo Borromeo and the Ecclesiastical Policy of Philip II in the State of Milan,' in *San Carlo Borromeo*, 86. Also essential is Tomaro's contribution to the same collection, 'San Carlo Borromeo and the Implementation of the Council of Trent.'

27 Luigi Prosdocimi, *Il Diritto ecclesiastico dello stato di Milano*, 308–9, argues that early efforts by the Council of Trent to draft a decree on the 'reform' of princes met such opposition from the secular rulers that it was replaced in session 25 with

a more generic exhortation to the princes that they favour and protect the church in their territories and a general renewal of councils and canons in defence of ecclesiastical liberty and the immunity of clerical persons.

28 'Council of Trent, Session 25, Decree on General Reform' in *Decrees of the Ecumenical Councils* 2:795–6.

29 Borromeo, 'Archbishop Carlo Borromeo,' 86.

30 The number four hundred is given by Gian Pietro Giussani, one of Borromeo's biographers, and is cited by Bendiscioli, 'Politica, amministrazione e religione,' 142–3.

31 Bendiscioli, 'Politica, amministrazione e religione,' 142. See also Zardin, 'La curia arcivescovile al tempo del Cardinal Federico.'

32 Borromeo, 'Archbishop Carlo Borromeo,' 89–90. Borromeo cites Prosdocimi, *Il Diritto ecclesiastico*, 310–12, on this point.

33 Borromeo, 'Archbishop Carlo Borromeo,' 91–4. A similar attitude seems to have prevailed in the Milanese state's response to heresy and the work of the Roman Inquisition. It was only with difficulty that the officials of the Roman Inquisition were able to function in the state of Milan in the quarter century after its foundation in 1542, and at one point, in 1563, Philip II considered installing the Spanish Inquisition at Milan. Giannini, 'Fra autonomia politica e ortodossia religiosa.'

34 Borromeo, 'Archbishop Carlo Borromeo,' 88–9.

35 Prodi, 'San Carlo Borromeo,' esp. 199.

36 Borromeo, 'Archbishop Carlo Borromeo,' 98–9.

37 Borromeo, 'L'arcivescovo Carlo Borromeo,' 266.

38 Borromeo, 'Archbishop Carlo Borromeo,' 99–100.

39 AEM, 'Editto per la prohibitione di giostre e spectaculi nella Domeniche e Feste,' 7 March 1579, 434–5.

40 Prodi, 'San Carlo Borromeo,' 213–18.

41 In 1579 Bascapè had demonstrated his usefulness and loyalty by penning a diatribe against dancing and other forms of worldly amusement. Although the pamphlet, *De Choreis et spectaculis in festis diebus non exhibendis*, was not published until 1662 because of its volatile subject matter, Borromeo had received it with enthusiasm and had presented it to Gregory XIII. Manzini, *San Carlo e il Ven. Bascapè*, 29.

42 Manzini, *San Carlo e il Ven. Bascapè*, 30–1n2, quotes at length Speciano's letter of 23 April 1580 to Cardinal Borromeo.

43 Bascapè, 'Relazione.'

44 Bascapè, 'Relazione.'

45 Prodi, 'San Carlo Borromeo,' 227–32.

46 See ASV, *Congregazione Concilio*, fol. 134r, for Bascapè's report of December 1606.

47 The best accounts of the controversy are Bendiscioli, 'Politica, amministrazione e religione,' 314–30; and Bascapè's 'I primi diciotto anni dell'arcivescovo di Milano Federico cardinale Borromeo.' Bendiscioli bases much of his analysis on Bascapè's work. Innocenzo Chiesa follows Bascapè's account in *Vita del Bascapè*, 438–50, 535–49. Rivola provides a view more sympathetic to Federico Borromeo in *Vita di Federico Borromeo*, 208–21, 445–51.

48 Bendiscioli, 'Politica, amministrazione e religione,' 327–30. The terms of the concordat are found in volume four of the 1897 edition of the *Acta ecclesiae mediolanensis*, edited by Achille Ratti (who would later become Pope Pius XI), columns 493–506. In *Il Diritto ecclesiastico dello stato di Milano*, 319, Prosdocimi suggests that the state recognized the jurisdictional rights claimed by the church but limited their practical application. For relations between church and state at Milan in the mid-seventeenth century and the troubled episcopate of Alfonso Litta, archbishop of Milan from 1652 to 1679, see Signorotto, *Milano Spagnola*, 236–73.

49 Bascapè, 'I primi diciotto anni,' 54.

50 ASBR, Bascapè, *Registri di lettere*, 5, letter 301, to Padre Ramirez in the convent of the Carmini, Milan, 7 November 1596.

51 Bascapè described the incident in 'I primi diciotto anni,' 60–4. For pertinent correspondence, see ASBR, Bascapè, *Registri di lettere*, 5, letter 391; and 6, letters 57, 73, and 113, to Orazio Besozzo, his agent in Rome, between 6 December 1596 and 18 February 1597.

52 ASV, *Congregazione Concilio*, 295r.

53 On the need for a concordat, see ASBR, Bascapè, *Registri di lettere*, 23, letter 354, to the cardinal of Santa Cecilia, Cremona, 27 February 1610.

54 Bascapè, 'I primi diciotto anni,' 103–5; and Chiesa, *Vita del Bascapè*, 542–9.

55 'In modo che fra pochi anni non havremo altra giurisditione nei laici che di celebrargli la messa, et amministrargli i S.mi Sacramenti essendo la proprietà del male a cui non si porge rimedio di crescere sempre col tempo.' BA, *Ms. G.* 204 *inf.*, 234r–236r, bishop of Casale to Borromeo, 14 November 1609.

56 ASBR, Bascapè, *Registri di lettere*, 23, letter 354, to Paolo Emilio Sfondrati, the cardinal of Santa Cecilia, Cremona, 27 February 1610. See also Bascapè, 'I primi diciotto anni,' 103–5.

57 BA, *Ms. G.* 204 *inf.*, 260, Seneca to Borromeo, 20 February 1610.

58 Bascapè long maintained that he did not know whether Paul V wrote to Spain, but Seneca at least came close to telling him the truth. On 15 May 1610 Seneca wrote to Borromeo that he told Bascapè that he did not believe the Pope had written to Madrid, and that Bascapè too came to this conclusion due to several factors which were clearly evident. BA, *Ms. G.* 203 *inf.*, 170.

59 Bascapè, 'I primi diciotto anni,' 105. Bascapè had this to say of the conduct of Federico Borromeo and Cardinal Paolo Emilio Sfondrati, bishop of Cremona,

in 1610: 'If one can speak entirely freely, I strongly grieve that two Cardinals in the greater province could not do more for Ecclesiastical Jurisdiction, especially in imitation of the Blessed Carlo. I do not know by what judgment of God we might see our rights collapse into a worse condition, and yet we say nothing.' (Omnino si libere dicendum est, duos Cardinales in provincia majora non fecisse pro Ecclesiastica Jurisdictione vehementer doleo, praesertim B. Caroli imitatione. Nescio quo Dei judicio jura nostra in pejus ruere videamus, et tacemus.)

60 Bascapè, 'I primi diciotto anni,' 68: 'In the days of Carlo, the church experienced the same wrongs, but was set free after three months: so much more serious was the Pontiff in insisting, so much more agreeable the King and so much more favourable the Duke, to those things which were seen to be more proper.' (Caroli quidem tempore eadem mala Ecclesia sensit, sed post tres menses liberata est: tum graviter instante Pontifice, tum Rege consentiente, tum duce, ad ea, quae magis pia viderentur, semper propenso.)

61 Bascapè, 'I primi diciotto anni,' 77.

62 A number of historians have argued that Federico Borromeo lacked the sense of perspective that enabled his cousin Carlo Borromeo to subordinate the jurisdictional struggle to pastoral concerns, thus contributing to the decline of the religious life in Milan. See Cattaneo, 'La religione a Milano,' esp. 303–5; Bendiscioli, 'Politica, amministrazione e religione,' 324; and Prodi's biography of Federico Borromeo in *DBI* 13:36–7.

63 Giannini, 'Politica spagnola e giurisdizione ecclesiastica nello Stato di Milano' and 'Con il zelo di sodisfare all'obligo di re e principe.'

64 Bendiscioli, 'Politica, amministrazione e religione,' 323.

3. The Bishop's Tribunal and the Disciplining of the Clergy, 1563–1615

1 'Council of Trent, Session 22, Decree on Reform, Canon 1,' in *Decrees of the Ecumenical Councils* 2:737–8.

2 Di Simplicio, *Peccato, penitenza, perdono*, 23–5, 76–99; Forster, *Counter-Reformation in the Villages*, 5–60; Forster, *Catholic Revival in the Age of the Baroque*, 14–16; and Turchini, 'La nascita del sacerdozio come professione.'

3 Synods were held in 1568, 1576, 1590, 1594, 1598, and 1615.

4 Novara Diocese, 'De vita et honestate clericorum,' chapter 8 of *Synodus Novarien … Serbellonum … MDLXVIII*, 29–32: 'Ut ipsi pre oculis semper habeant, non illam modo vivendi rationem quae in communi fidelium usu & consuetudine posita, sed aliam praestantiorem, et ab ea seiunctam, et nunquam querentes quae sua sunt, sed quae Iesu Christi, cum ipsi sint lux mundi, sal terrae, et tanquam Civitas supra montem posita.' The section on clothing reads: 'clericalem vestem

superiorem talarem quae ad collum clausa sit, inferiorem vero, quae vel ad medium saltem crus descendat, vel quod decentius, usque ad talos sit demissa.'

5 The *Manipulus curatorum* was a basic guidebook for the parish priest written by Guido de Monte Rocherii, a Spanish theologian of the fourteenth century. It contained three sections: on the sacraments, on penance, and on the things necessary for the Christian to know (Apostles' Creed, Our Father, and Ten Commandments). See the article by Pierre Michaud in *DS* 6, cols. 1303–4. For a fuller discussion of summas of cases of conscience and other works required of parish priests, see Deutscher, 'Seminaries and the Education of Novarese Parish Priests' and 'Distribution of Devotional Works among the Novarese Parish Clergy.'

6 Novara Diocese, 'De quibusdam generaliter ecclesiasticam disciplinam concernentibus,' in *Decreta edita et promulgata ... 1576 ... Archinto*, 20v–26v.

7 Bascapè's most important letters on the appeal of the clergy are found in ASBR, Carlo Bascapè, *Registri di lettere*, 9, letters 101 and 153, to the Bishop of Aversa, papal secretary, 15 and 22 February 1600; and letter 155, to Signor Croce, Bascapè's agent in Rome, 22 February 1600. For the appeal itself, see ASV, *Congregazione vescovi e regolari. Positiones, 1600* (M–P).

8 Bascapè, *Commentarii canonici*, 16. In contrast, Carlo Borromeo had called eleven diocesan synods during his episcopate, while his successors Gaspare Visconti and Federico Borromeo had held six and fourteen, respectively.

9 Deutscher, 'Seminaries and the Education of Novarese Parish Priests'; Negruzzo, 'La Diocesi e i suoi seminari in età moderna' and *Collegij a forma di Seminario*, 333–92.

10 Deutscher, 'Seminaries and the Education of Novarese Parish Priests' and 'From Cicero to Tasso.'

11 ASDN III, 5, 1, Report of Canon Antonio Tornielli to Cardinal Ferdinando Taverna (1616) and Report of Cardinal Taverna *ad limina* (1617). In 1616 the College of Santa Cristina housed twenty-one clerics in major and minor orders, under the direction of the oblate Francesco Quagliotti of Galliate, aged thirty-three, with the assistance of another oblate and two others who cared for the building and the material needs of the students. In 1617 the seminaries of the Island of San Giulio and Suna were said to have eighteen clerics each while that of Varallo Sesia, established for poor boys of the mountain regions by the Adda family of Milan, held only three clerics.

12 For a recent overview of the slow development and limitations of Italian seminaries, highlighting the intricacies involved in the canonical erection of seminaries and the problems created by attempts to fund seminaries by the taxation of the beneficed clergy and the incorporation of the revenues of simple benefices, see Fantappiè, 'I problemi giuridici e finanziari dei seminari tridentini.'

For the problems faced by seminaries in Tuscany, see Comerford, 'Chierici e seminari nei primi decenni del periodo post-tridentino,' and more recently, Comerford, *Reforming Priests and Parishes*. In contrast, Xenio Toscani takes the position that seminaries in the ecclesiastical province of Milan developed earlier and on a stronger foundation than those elsewhere in Italy. See 'Seminari e collegi nello Stato di Milano fra Cinque e Seicento.' Toscani includes the development of colleges of the new orders and congregations of Jesuits, Somaschi, and Barnabites as part of an expansion of educational opportunities in Lombardy. For another perspective, see Guasco, 'La formazione del clero.'

13 ASBR, Bascapè, *Registri di lettere*, 3, letter 213, to the vicar general, 13 September 1594; and letter 216, to S. Dottore Hieronimo Gritti, 17 September 1594. Canon Tornielli had been denounced to the tribunal in January 1581 for involvement with the wife of Battista de Forla, frequenting her house and keeping her in his own house for a month. ASDN XII, 2, 6, *1576–83*, fols. 87r–88r.

14 Deutscher, 'Growth of the Secular Clergy,' esp. 388; Toscani, 'Il reclutamento del clero.'

15 ASDN XII, 2, 1.

16 Andena's edicts were published under the title *Aedicta et ordinationes ... Caesaris Andenae Laudensis ... d. Io. Antonii Serbelloni ... Ecclesiae Novariensis perpetui administratoris ac Comites etc. Vicarii* (Novara: 1562). See Longo, 'La Chiesa novarese tra XVI e XVIII secolo,' esp. 218–19.

17 ASDN XII, 2, 1, *1563–4*, fol. 3r–v.

18 'Il vicario non ha da comandare alli frati e più presto che ubedirli voliamo ... renegar la fede.' ASDN XII, 2, 1, *1563–4*, fols. 8v–9r.

19 ASDN XII, 2, 1, *1563–4*, fol. 23r.

20 ASDN XII, 2, 1, *1563–4*, fol. 27r–v.

21 ASBR, Bascapè, *Registri di lettere*, 2, letter 122, to the Father Procurator General of San Biagio, 3 January 1594.

22 See appendix 1 for the numbers of priests in the diocese, 1616–18.

23 Of this group, thirty-seven were prosecuted at least twice, ten of them three times, and two four times.

24 Among chaplains and priests, eleven made two or more appearances before the tribunal.

25 Seven of the canons were prosecuted on more than one occasion: four of them twice, two of them three times, and one four times.

26 See, for example, ASBR, Bascapè, *Registri di lettere*, 1, letter 404, to Sig. Don Pietro Aldobrandini, papal nephew, 10 August 1593; and 2, letter 130, to the archdeacon of Novara, 27 January 1594. In the latter letter, Bascapè lamented the 'great shortage of curates' and instructed the archdeacon to search for clerics of good conduct who could be made suitable for benefices with a little study.

For comments by Bascapè's successors, see ASDN III, 5, 1, Reports *ad limina* of Cardinal Ferdinando Taverna (1617) and Giovanni Pietro Volpi (1625 and 1636).

27 *New Catholic Encyclopedia* 2:305–7. Benefices could be terminated ipso facto when the incumbent married or attempted marriage, when he took solemn vows in a religious order, or when he failed to be ordained in the prescribed time. In other cases, deprivation would require a judicial process.

28 ASDN III, 5, 1, Report of Canon Antonio Tornielli to Cardinal Ferdinando Taverna (1616).

29 For example, on 28 July 1596 Bascapè instructed the rural vicar of Omegna to gather evidence on certain priests of the parish of Intra in the lakes region of the diocese. He was to call on the assistance of the *podestà* (chief magistrate) of Intra and was to have power to imprison the accused in any place of the diocese within reason. ASBR, Bascapè, *Registri di lettere*, 5, letter 30. On 11 November of the same year he instructed Domenico Duelli of Quarona to ask the *podestà* of Varallo to let the rural vicar use his guards, especially since they were paid by the people. He added that this would be a good work and free the conscience of the *podestà* from the danger of impeding ecclesiastical jurisdiction and falling under the penalties of the bull *In Coena Domini*. ASBR, Bascapè, *Registri di lettere*, 5, letter 305.

30 The only case where the strappado was not used involved a layman. In 1602 Cesare de Marco of Isella, an elderly grain merchant accused of blasphemy, was tortured with fire because of his age and because he had a hernia, which did not permit the use of the rope. ASDN XII, 2, 5, *1596–1603*, fol. 181r–187r.

31 ASDN XII, 2, 10, *1609–10*, fols. 33r–37r, 74r–79v.

32 ASDN XII, 2, 3, *1590–1*, fols. 1r–4r.

33 ASDN XII, 2, 11, *1591–8*, fol. 1r–v; ASDN XII, 2, 3, *1590–1*, fols. 1r–48r.

34 ASDN XII, 2, 7, *1594–5*, fols. 35r–38v.

35 ASDN XII, 2, 11, *1591–8*, fols. 46v–47r.

36 Thus, on 1 February 1591 Francesco de Scholari or de Gratiano, one of the curates of Varallo, was suspended from the care of souls for a month because of his negligence, specifically reprimanding a parishioner in confession in a loud voice and neglecting to take the sacraments to a sick person. He was freed of other charges, which included falsifying baptismal records and maligning the bishop's visitor. ASDN XII, 2, 11, *1591–8*, fol. 2r–v; ASDN XII, 2, 3, *1590–1*, fols. 114r–122v. He was still a parish priest at Varallo in 1617. See ASDN *Acta visitationis* 80, 374r, for his *status personalis* and the list of books in his library.

37 This sentence was passed against Maffezone on 23 June 1594. ASDN XII, 2, 11, *1591–8*, fols. 38r–40v. Maffezone was accused of having sex with at least three women as well as pinching and speaking indecently to a household servant named Madalena. His principal accuser was Francesca Raseghina, a married

woman of Novara of bad reputation who testified that the curate had sex with her in his house and in the house of Canon Bozzola of Novara after using his role as confessor to seduce her. She also testified that Domenico Gambara, his co-curate at Galliate, tried to suborn her to commit perjury, to wit by signing a document to the effect that Maffezone was a good man and had not had sex with her, a charge which Gambara denied and Francesca maintained under torture. Testimonies were taken between October and December 1593. ASDN XII, 2, 7, *1593–4*, fols. 9r–21v, 45r–62r. For the visitation of Galliate in 1595, see ASDN *Acta visitationis* 22, fols. 421v–422v.

38 ASDN XII, 2, 1, *1563–4*, fols. 41r–43r.

39 Romeo, *Esorcisti, confessori, e sessualità femminile*, 13, 155–7.

40 Di Simplicio, *Peccato, penitenza, perdono*, 180.

41 One of the more thorough studies of this question is Stephen Haliczer's *Sexuality in the Confessional*, which draws on cases conducted by Inquisitions in Spanish territories from the sixteenth century to the early eighteenth century. Haliczer also argues that new restrictions that reformers placed on sexual expression placed the sacrament of penance under added stress. Attempts to restrict contact between priests and women, the repression of premarital sex, and the limitations placed on the sexual practices of married couples, he argues, could be counterproductive at times. Other contributions on the prosecution of the offence of solicitation in the confessional from an Italian perspective are to be found in Prosperi, *Tribunali della coscienza*, 508–48; and de Boer, 'Ad audiendi non videndi commoditatem.'

42 ASDN XII, 2, 6, *1576–83*, fols. 11r–13v.

43 ASDN *Acta visitationis* 77, fols. 252r–v, 255r–256v. In 1617 there were only 37 families in the parish, including seven farms (*cascina*) and a total of 151 souls. The curate was Alfonso Curtio from Milan, who had been provided with the parish in January 1600 on nomination of the Fisrengo family.

44 ASDN XII, 2, 6, *1576–83*, fol. 120r.

45 ASDN XII, 2, 2, *1585–9*, fols. 120r–121r.

46 See chapter 4, 88.

47 ASDN XII, 2, 11, *1591–8*, fols. 25v–26r.

48 ASDN XII, 2, 9, *1603–4*, fols. 169r–173v; and chapter 3, 72.

49 ASDN XII, 2, 9, *1605–6*, fols. 61r–65r; ASDN XII, 2, 10, *1609–10*, fols. 23r–25v.

50 ASDN *Acta visitationis* 83, visit of Lovario.

51 ASDN XII, 2, 6, *1576–83, 1593*, fols. 184r–204v.

52 ASBR, Bascapè, *Registri di lettere*, 2, letter 8, to the curate of Mezzomerico, 23 December 1593.

53 ASDN XII, 2, 7, *1594–5*, fols. 22r–25v.

54 ASDN *Acta visitationis* 52, fols. 432–3. *Summa Navarri* was the name commonly given to the *Manuale sive Enchiridion confessariorum et poenitentium* written by

Martin de Azpilcueta (1493–1586) who was from the kingdom of Navarre and rose to become apostolic penitentiary. Deutscher, 'Seminaries and the Education of Novarese Parish Priests,' esp. 313.

55 ASDN *Acta visitationis* 89, fols. 307r–308r; ASDN *Acta visitationis* 111, fol. 293r.

56 ASDN XII, 2, 7, *1594–5*, fols. 39r–44v. The words attributed to Tornielli were 'che le donne sonno tuta da bene mentre non stano ricercate a far del male.'

57 Those accused of sexual offences included thirteen canons, seventeen chaplains or simple priests, four clerics, two friars, and four nuns.

58 Di Simplicio, *Peccato, penitenza, perdono*, 111–21, 137–44. Di Simplicio's point on the high level of community tolerance for the concubinage of priests at Siena is given a broader application for Italy by Giovanni Romeo in *Amori proibiti*, 13. See also Lucciano Allegra's now classic study, 'Il parocco,' 914–18.

59 ASDN XII, 2, 11, *1591–8*, fols. 63v–64r.

60 ASDN XII, 2, 7, *1593–4*, fols. 156r–166v.

61 For the *status personalis* of Margheritis, see ASDN *Acta visitationis* 64, fol. 17r–v. His 1617 *status personalis* is found in *Acta visitationis* 87, fol. 302v.

62 ASDN XII, 2, 11, *1591–8*, fols. 62r–63r. Another rare case where prostitution is specifically mentioned was that of Giacomo de Giulio, curate of Prato, questioned in December 1594 and March 1595 on charges of having a prostitute in his home, fathering a child by another woman, possession of a prohibited weapon, public drunkenness on at least one occasion, and various irregularities in the care of souls. De Giulio denied the charges. ASDN XII, 2, 7, *1594–5*, fols. 128r–129v, 167r–170v.

63 ASDN XII, 2, 7, *1594–5*, fols. 121r–123v.

64 ASDN XII, 2, 8, *1596–8*, fols. 107r–109v, 112r–113r; ASDN XII, 2, 10, *1609–10*, fols. 16r–22v.

65 ASDN XII, 2, 7, *1594–5*, fols. 161r–164r. Zuffo's *status personalis* for the visit of 1595 mentions previous attempts to end his relationship with Maria and his allegations that he had many powerful enemies. ASDN *Acta visitationis* 46, fol. 20r–v.

66 ASDN XII, 2, 9, *1601–2*, fols. 45r–48v, 142r–v.

67 ASDN *Acta visitationis* 62, fols. 2v–3r.

68 ASDN XII, 2, 9, *1603–5*, fols. 119r–121v; *1605–6*, fols. 21r–22r.

69 ASDN *Acta visitationis* 68, fols. 45r–46v. For Celera's trial, see ASDN XII, 2, 10, *1611–14*, fols. 146r–148v, 153r–158r.

70 ASDN *Acta visitationis* 68, fols. 20v, 25r–26r, 93r, 105bis.

71 ASDN *Acta visitationis* 46, fols. 16v, 20r.

72 ASDN *Acta visitationis* 62, fols. 10r–12r.

73 ASDN *Acta visitationis* 18, fol. 72v; *Acta visitationis* 46, fol. 20r–v. In the visit of 1596, companies of the Rosary and of the Blessed Sacrament were said to be established.

74 ASDN XII, 2, 11, *1591–8*, fol. 54r.

75 ASDN XII, 2, 9, *1605–6*, fol. 36r–v; ASDN XII, 2, 10, *1609–10*, fols. 80r–83r; ASDN XII, 2, 10, *1611–14*, fols. 28r–33v.

76 ASDN XII, 2, 11, *1591–8*, fol. 51r–v. See ASDN *Acta visitationis* 46, fol. 151r–v, for Lorenzo Palluda's *status personalis*. He was from the village of Baceno, and received first tonsure in 1576. In 1586, after studying the humane letters at Novara and serving as schoolmaster for six years, he was presented to the parish of Baceno by the cathedral chapter of Novara, which enjoyed the right of nomination. In the same year, he received the major orders. As parish priest at Baceno he preached to the people, taught catechism, studied the scriptures and cases of conscience as required, and taught boys the rudiments of grammar, having received permission of the episcopal curia to do so.

77 ASDN XII, 2, 8, *1596–8*, fols. 169r–172v, 176r–182v.

78 ASDN *Acta visitationis* 68, fols. 296*r*, 317r–351v.

79 ASDN XII, 2, 8, *1595–6*, fols. 136r–139v. Ottolino was twenty-five years of age in 1595, living with his family and, according to the visitation of 1595, spending some of his time (*aliquod tempus*) in the study of cases of conscience and assisting with catechism lessons and other parish functions. ASDN *Acta visitationis* 64, fol. 51r–v.

80 ASDN XII, 2, 11, *1591–8*, fols. 54v–55r.

81 ASBR, Bascapè, *Registri di lettere*, 4, letter 203, to Sig. Antonio Curzio Gattico, 31 March 1595.

82 ASDN XII, 2, 9, *1605–6*, fols. 58r–60v, 66r–76r. The *status personalis* of Alberto de Alberti appears in the visitation of Pieve Vergonte in 1597. He was from Anzola, born in 1554, ordained in 1579, and provided to Cuzzago in 1590. He was said to be '*tolerabilis*' in knowledge of cases of conscience and in performing parish duties, and capable of teaching others. ASDN *Acta visitationis* 49, fol. 253r–v. The visit of Cuzzago of 1618 is in *Acta visitationis* 96.

83 ASDN XII, 2, 8, *1596–8*, fols. 173r–175v, 183r; ASDN XII, 2, 9, *1603–4*, fols. 13r–15r. For an injunction from Bascapè that Bertolio have no dealings with Margarita, either directly or indirectly, under penalty of deprivation of benefice, see the 1599 visitation of Rocca, ASDN *Acta visitationis* 50, fol. 169r.

84 ASDN XII, 2, 1, fols. 3r–4v. Toquata's words were: 'finite de ammazzare, se non che domatina lui andava al vicario.'

85 ASDN XII, 2, 2, *1590*, fols. 78r–114v, 142r–167v, 178r–179v, 184r–187v.

86 ASDN XII, 2, 8, *1595–6*, fols. 124r–128v; ASDN XII, 2, 9, *1601–2*, fols. 57r–58v; ASDN XII, 2, 11, *1591–8*, fol. 17r–v.

87 ASBR, Bascapè, *Registri di lettere*, 9, letter 396. The curate of Soriso was Domenico Parucono, who was twenty-five years of age and newly appointed when Bascapè visited the parish in 1594. ASDN *Acta visitationis* 25, 109v. In his

second visit, conducted in 1601, Bascapè noted that Parucono had been deprived of the benefice. ASDN *Acta visitationis* 54, fol. 84r.

88 ASDN XII, 2, 9, *1603–4*, fols. 93r–97v.

89 ASDN XII, 2, 9, *1605–6*, fols. 139r–143v.

90 ASDN *Acta visitationis* 98.

91 ASDN XII, 2, 9, *1601–2*, fols. 12r–14v, 22r–28v.

92 ASDN *Acta visitationis* 87, fol. 112r–v. In the visit of 1595 Pizzolo said that he instructed a number of boys who roomed and boarded with him in a part of the house he shared with his family and brothers. ASDN *Acta visitationis* 34, fol. 374. Pizzolo was arraigned in June 1603, but the charges concerned allegations that he had defrauded his fellow canons of part of their income. ASDN XII, 2, 9, *1603–5*, 20r–24v.

93 ASDN XII, 2, 1, *1563–4*, 7r–v.

94 ASDN XII, 2, 6, *1593*, 3v–8r, with the quote on 8r.

95 Deutscher, 'Carlo Bascapè e la riforma delle monache.'

96 ASDN XII, 2, 7, *1594–5*, fols. 14r–15v.

97 ASDN XII, 2, 8, *1596–8*, fols. 71r–72v.

98 ASDN XII, 2, 2, *1585–9*, fol. 30r–v.

99 ASDN XII, 2, 2, *1585–9*, fols. 84r–119v, 125r–127r. Fara in turn accused Gambara of conspiring to have false testimony presented to the vicar general.

100 ASDN *Acta visitationis* 22, fols. 421v–422r.

101 ASDN *Acta visitationis* 73, fol. 387v.

102 ASDN XII, 2, 7, *1593–4*, fols. 140r–171v; ASDN XII, 2, 7, *1594–5*, fols. 3r–10r.

103 ASDN XII, 2, 9, *1601–2*, fols. 185r–190v; ASDN XII, 2, 9, *1603–4*, fols. 25r–26v. For the 1617 visitation of Caddo, see ASDN *Acta visitationis* 67.

104 ASDN XII, 2, 11, *1591–8*, fols. 64r–65v. Bascapè appears to have been watching Applano for some time, warning him in December 1594 to expel his brothers and their friends from his house. ASBR, Bascapè, *Registri di lettere*, 3, letter 446, to the priest Niccolò Applano, canon of Intra. The interrogation of Applano is found in ASDN XII, 2, 8, *1596–8*, fols. 117r–120v, 132r–133v.

105 ASDN XII, 2, 9, *1603–5*, fols. 129r–134v.

106 ASDN XII, 2, 10, *1611–14*, fols. 23r–25r. The cleric was also accused of receiving money which Gemelli extorted from Giovanni Battista Martello.

107 ASDN XII, 2, 10, *1611–14*, fols. 126r–128v.

108 ASDN XII, 2, 9, *1603–5*, fols. 135r–152r.

109 ASDN XII, 2, 9, *1605–6*, fol. 106r–v.

110 ASDN *Acta visitationis* 264, fol. 42v.

111 ASDN XII, 2, 9, *1603–4*, fols. 169r–173v; ASDN XII, 2, 9, *1605–6*, fols. 2r–6v, 25r–28v, 33r–v, 94r–96v, 181r–183v. Berella was also accused of having sexual relations with a woman, being absent from his parish, neglecting his duties,

and celebrating Mass in the presence of two excommunicated men. Most of the interrogation focused on his role in making peace between the factions and in the conspiracy.

112 ASDN XII, 2, 10, *1609–10*, fols. 52r–55r.

113 ASDN *Acta visitationis* 85, visit of Ara.

114 ASDN XII, 2, 10, *1611–14*, fols. 105r–123v, 159r–164v, 174r–176v.

115 ASV, *Congregazione Vescovi e Regolari. Positiones, 1615* (N–O).

116 ASDN XII, 2, 2, *1590*, fols. 6v–8v, 11r–v.

117 ASDN XII, 2, 8, *1595–6*, fols. 91r–92v.

118 ASDN XII, 2, 8, *1596–8*, fols. 138r–139r.

119 'Mi pare che in simili tempi convenghi ad ogni uno aiutarsi, tanto più per li pericoli di tempesta, e d'altri infortunij.' ASDN XII, 2, 9, *1601–2*, fols. 29r–31r.

120 ASDN XII, 2, 9, *1605–6*, fols. 101r–103r.

121 'Monsignor, io sono homo da bene tanto come voi e guardare bene come mi parlare.' ASDN XII, 2, 2, *1590*, fols. 173r–177v.

122 ASDN XII, 2, 8, *1595–6*, fols. 93r–96r.

123 ASDN XII, 2, 7, *1594–5*, fols. 165r–166v. Viscardi's *status personalis* is found in the visit of 1596, ASDN *Acta visitationis* 46, fol. 216r–v.

124 ASDN XII, 2, 9, *1605–6*, fol. 146r–v. Magnetti's *status personalis* is found in the 1617 visit to Stresa, when he admitted that he rarely preached and rarely taught catechism. He had obtained the parish of Stresa in 1603 when he was in his mid-twenties. ASDN *Acta visitationis* 87, fol. 269v.

125 ASDN *Act visitationis* 73, fols. 71r–72v. Giuliano held a degree in theology from the academy of his order at Piacenza and was authorized to conduct exorcisms in the diocese.

126 ASDN XII, 2, 10, *1609–10*, fols. 117r–129r.

127 For the *status personalis* of Caccia, see the visits of 1617 and 1626–7, ASDN *Acta visitationis* 73, fol. 77r–v, and *Acta visitationis* 100, fol. 298r.

128 ASDN XII, 2, 2, *1590*, fol. 2r–4v, 188r–192v.

129 ASDN XII, 2, 11, *1591–8*, fols. 55v–56r.

130 ASDN XII, 2, 10, *1609–10*, fols. 83r–86v.

131 ASDN *Acta visitationis* 84.

132 ASDN XII, 2, 9, *1603–4*, fols. 6r–12v.

133 ASDN XII, 2, 9, *1603–4*, fols. 78r–80v.

134 ASDN XII, 2, 8, *1596–8*, fols. 138r–139r.

135 ASDN *Acta visitationis* 54, fols. 34r–39r; ASDN *Acta visitationis* 285, fol. 237r.

136 ASDN *Acta visitationis* 71, fols. 228v–229r; ASDN *Acta visitationis* 103, fol. 271r.

137 ASDN XII, 2, 8, *1595–6*, fols. 105r–107v, 115r–118r. Balbo was also accused of being late for Mass and vespers so that he could play cards, of selling some oak trees which belonged to his church, and of having sexual relations with a woman.

138 ASDN *Acta visitationis* 38, fols. 287r–288r.
139 ASDN XII, 2, 9, *1603–5*, fols. 88r–92v.
140 ASDN XII, 2, 11, *1591–8*, fol. 35r–v; ASDN XII, 2, 7, *1593–4*, fols. 116r–122v.
141 In 1596 the parish priests of Crodo were Domenico Zuffo and Domenico Palluda, mentioned above. ASDN *Acta visitationis* 46, fol. 20r–v.
142 ASBR, Bascapè, *Registri di lettere*, 1, letter 628, to Besozzo, agent in Rome, 10 October 1593.
143 ASDN XII, 2, 7, *1594–5*, fols. 74r–87r.
144 See page 65–6 above.
145 ASDN XII, 2, 11, *1591–8*, fols. 49r–50r.
146 See ASDN XII, 2, 11, *1591–8*, fols. 64r–65v, for the sentence given to Niccolò Applano and Bartolomeo Guerrino on 21 July 1598.
147 ASDN XII, 2, 7, *1593–4*, fols. 1r–8v, 41r–42r; ASDN XII, 2, 11, *1591–8*, fols. 18r–19r.
148 ASDN XII, 2, 9, *1601–2*, fols. 168r–184v; ASDN XII, 2, 9, *1603–4*, fols. 37r–38r.
149 ASDN XII, 2, 8, *1595–6*, fols. 58r–65v, 71r–74r, 112r–114v, 121r–122v.
150 ASDN XII, 2, 10, *1609–10*, fols. 111r–112v, 135r–138v.
151 ASDN XII, 2, 5, *1596–1603*, fols. 94v–106v, 116r–117v. For the history of heresy and witchcraft trials at Novara, see Deutscher, 'Role of the Episcopal Tribunal of Novara.'
152 The matter is discussed in detail by Prosperi, *Tribunali della coscienza*, 219–77.

4. The Bishop's Tribunal and the Laity, 1563–1615

1 This chapter is a modified version of the article 'The Bishop's Tribunal and the Laity.' Sections of the chapter are also based on 'The Role of the Episcopal Tribunal of Novara in the Suppression of Heresy and Witchcraft.'
2 Zardin, 'La "Perfettione" nel proprio "stato",' 115–28.
3 In a pastoral letter of 5 April 1572 Borromeo encouraged heads of families to hold evening prayers, meditations, and examination of conscience in their households. AEM, 1003–8. At Novara, Bascapè asked heads of households to lead morning and evening prayers and to read from homilies or spiritual books. Bascapè, *Scritti publicati*, 18.
4 Bascapè, *Lettere di governo episcopale*, 21, 34–5, 37.
5 ASBR, Bascapè, *Registri di lettere*, 25, letter 175, to Canon Ferrino, rural vicar of the Island of San Giulio, 12 February 1614.
6 For one of Bascapè's attacks on dances as 'seminaries of sin,' see his pastoral letter 'De Balli' in *Scritti publicati*, 110–40.
7 Deutscher, 'Seminaries and the Education of Novarese Parish Priests.'

8 See Novara Diocese, 'Avvertenze per chi havera d'amministrar il Sacramento della Penitenza in questa Città e Diocesi di Novara,' in *Decreta edita et promulgata … 1576 … Archinto*, 64r–66r.
9 On the monitoring of annual confession and communion in the archdiocese of Milan, see de Boer, *Conquest of the Soul*, 184–97.
10 De Boer, *Conquest of the Soul*, 215. For a view of reserved cases in the broader context of the ecclesiastical legal system, see Elena Brambilla's 'La polizia dei tribunali ecclesiastici.'
11 Novara Diocese, 'Casus episcopo reservati,' in *Decreta edita et promulgata … 1576 … Archinto*, 62v–63v.
12 ASBR, Bascapè, *Registri di lettere*, 7, letter 274, to all rural vicars, 4 March 1599. In addition to instructions on the administration of reserved cases, the letter included a list of approximately sixty curates and vice-curates with faculty to absolve from reserved cases. On reserved cases in the archdiocese of Milan and similar precautions to ensure secrecy, see Prosperi, *Tribunali della coscienza*, 318–19.
13 For an estimate of the diocesan population and numbers of secular priests based on pastoral visitations see appendices 1 and 2.
14 Emmison, *Elizabethan Life*, 1–2, 231–40. For a detailed description of the working of ecclesiastical courts in England, see Ingram, *Church Courts*, 27–69.
15 Nine of the laypersons questioned under torture were men and six were women. In most cases they were accused of heresy, blasphemy, magic, and witchcraft. However, one man was tortured under the accusation that he had impregnated his sister, and another after being accused of deserting his wife and hiding behind a false name. Two women were tortured because of charges that they had engaged in sexual relations with priests. In all but one case the instrument of torture was the strappado, and only one layperson is known to have changed her testimony as a result of this process. This was Magdalena de Marinero, whose case is discussed in chapter 3, 54.
16 See ASDN XII, 2, 11, *1591–8*, fol. 24r–v, for the sentence of Battista and Giovanni Borando and Francesco de Bonetto, who were twice cited but did not appear to answer assault charges laid by the curate of Garbagna. They were declared contumacious and excommunicated on 26 January 1594.
17 ASBR, Bascapè, *Registri di lettere*, 22, letter 474, to the cardinal of San Giorgio, Grand Penitentiary, 30 June 1609. Bascapè wrote to the Grand Penitentiary in the hopes that his office could find a suitable way of castigating and making an example of those who had raised their hand against members of the priesthood in this way.
18 ASDN XII, 2, 2, *1590*, fols. 72r–78r.

19 ASDN XII, 2, 9, *1601–1602*, fols. 74r–75r.
20 ASDN XII, 2, 7, *1594–1595*, fols. 58r–67r, 92r–113v.
21 ASDN XII, 2, 2, *1585–1589*, fols. 1r–3v.
22 ASDN XII, 2, 9, *1603–1605*, fol. 50r–v.
23 'Council of Trent, Session 24, Canons on the reform of marriage,' in *Decrees of the Ecumenical Councils* 2:755–9. Chapter 8 of the canons on the reform of marriage called for the excommunication of men who refused to leave their concubines after being admonished to do so three times, while women in similar circumstances were to suffer the harsher punishment of exile from city and diocese. For a comment on the diversity of marriage practices before and after Trent, see Seidel Menchi, 'Percorsi variegate, percorsi obbligati.'
24 For a study of the complex interactions of the episcopal tribunal and the community in cases of adultery and concubinage in the Sicilian diocese of Monreale, see Pizzolato, 'Ordinarie trasgressioni.'
25 For recent studies of the diocesan archives on matrimonial cases, see three volumes edited by Seidel Menchi and Quaglioni: *Coniugi nemici*; *Matrimoni in dubbio*; and T*rasgressioni, seduzione, concubinato, adulterio, bigamia*. Also valuable are Ferrante, 'Il matrimonio disciplinato'; and Ferraro, *Marriage Wars in Late Renaissance Venice*.
26 Di Simplicio, *Peccato, penitenza, perdono*, 177–209, esp. 181–2. Also see Romeo, *Esorcisti, confessori, e sessualità femminile*, 13–14, 155–60.
27 Di Simplicio, *Peccato, penitenza, perdono*, 187–91.
28 Romeo, *Amori proibiti*, 34–40, 150–69, 213–6.
29 Emmison, *Elizabethan Life*, 1–2. On the moral thrust of English ecclesiastical courts, see as well Ingram, *Church Courts, Sex and Marriage in England*, 68–9.
30 ASDN XII, 2, 9, *1605–6*, fols. 166v–179r.
31 Emmison, *Elizabethan Life*, 2–6. For the list of reserved sins under Romulo Archinto, see Novara Diocese, *Decreta edita et promulgata ... 1576 ... Archinto*, fols. 62v–63v.
32 ASDN XII, 2, 1, *1563–4*, fol. 58r.
33 ASDN XII, 2, 6, *1576–1583*, fols. 171r–v, 176r–178r.
34 ASDN XII, 2, 2, *1590*, fols. 9r–11v.
35 ASBR, Bascapè, *Registri di lettere*, 4, letter 55, to the curate of Orta, 6 March 1595. Martelli's sentence is found in ASDN XII, 2, 11, *1591–8*, fol. 37r–v. The sum of one hundred scudi was twice the annual income of most parish priests.
36 ASBR, Bascapè, *Registri di lettere*, 4, letter 105 to the curate of Orta, 20 March 1595.
37 ASDN XII, 2, 8, *1596–8*, fols. 73r–76r.
38 ASDN XII, 2, 6, *1576–83*, fol. 39r–v.
39 See the articles 'Incest' by I.G. Miller in *New Catholic Encyclopedia* 7:377–8 and 'Affinity' by C. Henry in *New Catholic Encyclopedia* 1:150–2.

40 ASDN XII, 2, 6, *1576–83*, fols. 18r, 34r–35v.
41 ASDN XII, 2, 7, *1594–5*, fols. 185r–187r.
42 ASDN XII, 2, 5, *1596–1603*, fols. 47r–59r.
43 ASDN XII, 2, 1, *1563–4*, fols. 28r–36v.
44 ASDN XII, 2, 9, *1601–2*, fols. 32r–37v, 44r–v.
45 ASDN XII, 2, 9, *1605–6*, fols. 118v–123r.
46 ASDN XII, 2, 10, *1609–10*, fols. 90r–95r.
47 For example, Bascapè referred to the jurisdictional controversies of the day as impeding his efforts to combat concubinaries and usurers in his report *ad limina apostolorum* in 1597. ASV *Congregazione Concilio*, fol. 134r–v.
48 ASDN III, 5, 1, Report of Antonio Tornielli to Cardinal Ferdinando Taverna (1616).
49 The requirements were set out in the papal constitution *Multorum querela*, issued early in the fourteenth century by Clement V (r. 1305–14). See Borromeo, 'Contributo allo studio dell'inquisizione,' 225–7.
50 See chapter 2, 29–30.
51 ASDN XII, 2, 11, *1591–8*, fols. 7v–8v.
52 ASDN XII, 2, 9, *1603–5*, fols. 44r–45v.
53 ASBR, Bascapè, *Registri di lettere*, 19, letter 125, Postscript to a letter to Agostino Croce, Rome, 31 July 1605.
54 ASDN XII, 2, 11, *1591–8*, fols. 24v–25r.
55 ASDN XII, 2, 5, *1609–14*, fols. 193r–195v.
56 Grendler, *Roman Inquisition and the Venetian Press*, 57–8.
57 Del Col, 'Le strutture territoriali e l'attività dell'inquisizione Romana,' esp. 371–2.
58 *Dictionnaire historique et biographique de la Suisse* 7:18. Dependent territories of the Swiss cantons, the modern day Canton Ticino, lay to Novara's northeast. These were firmly Catholic by the late sixteenth century. *Dictionnaire historique et biographique de la Suisse* 6:515–16.
59 Bascapè, *Scritti publicati*, 467–9, 472–3. Bascapè's edicts were based on decrees of the third and sixth provincial councils. AEM, 89, 299. For an account of the treatment of northern Protestants in Italy, see Schmidt, 'L'Inquisizione e gli stranieri.' As well, de Boer discusses the complications involved in a trial of four Swiss and German soldiers prosecuted in Milan in 1619 in 'Soldati in terra straniera.' For more information on non-Italian soldiers on the frontiers of northern Italy and the appearance of a number of them before the Inquisition at Crema in Venetian territory, often to renounce Protestantism and embrace Catholicism, see Peyronel, 'Frontiere religiose e soldati in antico regime.'
60 ASBR, Bascapè, *Registri di lettere*, 9, letter 374, to the deputy vicar of Domodossola, 26 May 1600.
61 For the trial of Pignolo and his associates, see ASDN XII, 2, 5, *1596–1603*, fols. 121r–164v.

62 ASBR, Bascapè, *Registri di lettere*, 22, letter 74, to Lorenzo Palluda, 16 July 1608.
63 ASDN *Acta Visitationis* 68, fols. 353r–354r, 365r–v.
64 'Quando io stavo di quà delle monti et in Suitto, mi piaceva più il vivere di qui, et di Suitto, et quando stavo in Aslea mi piaceva più quello vivere di là, et hora che sono quà, mi piace più questo.' ASDN XII, 2, 5, *1596–1603*, fol. 161r.
65 Monter and Tedeschi, 'Toward a Statistical Profile of the Italian Inquisitions.'
66 Novara Dicoese, 'Edictum ... de superstitionibus evitandis,' in *Synodus dioecesana ... Speciano ... MDXC*, 154–9.
67 Bascapè described the practices of witches in *De vita e rebus gestis Caroli card*, 582–5.
68 Cesare Cantu attributes a report on the execution of the witches of the Mesolcina valley in the early 1580s to Bascapè. See Cantu, *Gli eretici d'Italia* 2:387–8.
69 Bascapè, *Scritti publicati*, 332. The decrees were of the first and fourth provincial councils of 1565 and 1576. AEM, 5, 119.
70 ASDN XII, 2, 1, *1563–4*, fol. 9v.
71 ASDN XII, 2, 11, *1591–8*, fols. 61v–62r; ASDN XII, 2, 5, *1596–1603*, fols. 1r–11r.
72 ASDN XII, 2, 5, *1596–1603*, fols. 16r–25v, 36v–46r.
73 ASDN XII, 2, 5, *1596–1603*, fols. 167r–179r.
74 ASDN XII, 2, 8, *1595–6*, fols. 13r–19v, 79r–84v, 173r–178v.
75 ASDN XII, 2, 5, *1609–14*, fols. 59r–63v.
76 ASDN XII, 2, 5, *1609–14*, fols. 34v–35v.
77 ASDN XII, 2, 5, *1609–14*, fols. 30v–32v.
78 Tedeschi, 'Roman Inquisition and Witchcraft,' esp. 176. The Trinity College, Dublin, reference is MS 1225, fol. 282. See also Abbott, *Catalogue*, 250.
79 ASDN XII, 2, 5, *1609–14*, fols. 19r–58r, 70r–97r, 114r–155v, 159r–167v.
80 ASDN XII, 2, 5, *1609–14*, fols. 112r–113v.
81 Monter and Tedeschi, 'Toward a Statistical Profile of the Italian Inquisitions,' 141–2.
82 ASDN XII, 2, 5, *1609–14*, fols. 58v, 95v, 96r, 154v, 155r, 167v.
83 ASBR, Bascapè, *Registri di lettere*, 24, letter 138, to Giovanni Battista Gera, 24 August 1611.
84 The observation is made by Andrea Del Col when speaking of the role of the papacy and of the Inquisition in 'Le strutture territoriali e l'attività dell'inquisizione Romana,' 345–79.

5. Shifting Patterns of Activity: The Bishop's Tribunal, 1745–1799

1 The cases for 1618–19 are found in ASDN XII, 2, 10, *1618–19*.
2 ASDN IV, 4. The miscellaneous collections of documents include such things as requests for permission to wear ecclesiastical clothing or to receive tonsure, testimonials of good behaviour by clerics prior to ordination, calls for potential

candidates for a vacant parish to appear for examination, documents pertaining to disputes over property, requests for permission to establish new legacies, chaplaincies, and altars, and statements that individuals were free to marry. From time to time, a document with relevance for the work of the episcopal tribunal appears. For example, the collection of licences for 1650 contains a request from Pietro Farinetti of Alagna, former curate of Formazza, to return to his home town to earn a living by celebrating masses in fulfilment of legacies. Farinetti had confessed to being involved with a woman for over four years and having three children by her, for which he suffered imprisonment and the loss of his parish. ASDN IV, 4, *1650*.

3 Donati, 'Vescovi e diocesi d'Italia.'

4 Silvestrini, *Politica della religione*, 313. For the encroachment of the Inquisition on the episcopal sphere, see Prosperi, *Tribunali della coscienza*, 330–5.

5 Di Simplicio, *Peccato, penitenza, perdono*, 187–91; Romeo, *Amori proibiti*, 112–82.

6 Donati, 'Vescovi e diocesi d'Italia,' 362–72.

7 For example, in his report *ad limina* of 1636 Bishop Giovanni Pietro Volpi (r. 1622–6) mentioned the suffering caused by military invasion: Vespolate, Gozzano, Auzati, Soriso, Bugnato, Pogno, and Bolsano had been sacked and in some cases burned. ASDN III, 5, 1.

8 Longo, 'La Chiesa novarese.'

9 The cultural formation of the Novarese parish clergy of the seventeenth century is put in relief by the lists of personal books possessed by the parish clergy. In the post-Tridentine era, Novarese bishops, like those of Milan and other dioceses, required parish priests to obtain books that would assist them in the administration of the care of souls. For example, Carlo Bascapè instructed parish priests to obtain copies of specific books, such as the Bible, the Roman catechism, the decrees of the Council of Trent and of the provincial councils of Milan, and other works falling into four categories: summas of cases of conscience, collections of sermons, commentaries or paraphrases of the gospels and psalms, and devotional treatises. See Bascapè, *Lettere di governo episcopale*, 63. The Acts of Visitation of the period 1615 to 1665 contain over three hundred lists submitted by priests, the majority of them curates, to demonstrate their compliance with this regulation. The book lists varied in length from ten to over two hundred titles, with an average length in the range of forty books. In an age when books were expensive items for persons who were not in the upper ranks of society, the holdings of the Novarese libraries were impressive, especially since they were the possessions of individual priests. Between 60 and 70 per cent of them had received at least part of their training at one of the Novarese seminaries or at the Cannobian School, maintained by the Jesuits. For further information, see Deutscher, 'From Cicero to Tasso' and 'Distribution of Devotional Works.'

10 Negruzzo, 'La Diocesi e i suoi seminari.' The seminary of Varallo, under patronage of the Adda family, continued to function with a low number of students.

11 From the 1760s to the 1780s the vicar general of Novara was Carlo Enrico, doctor in civil and canon law, canon of the cathedral, and protonotary apostolic. In November 1786, due to advanced age and failing health, he was replaced by Paolo Lamberto D'Allegre, who was also doctor in both laws, a canon of the cathedral, and protonotary apostolic. ASDN V, 1, 28/3, *1780–9*.

12 The diocese's westernmost valley, the Sesia valley, had passed to Savoy in 1707. Silvestrini, *Politica della religione*, 37.

13 Silvestrini, *Politica della religione*, 301, states that the papacy continued to nominate the bishops of Novara, Tortona, and Gobbio because the concordat of 1742 was not valid in the newly acquired Lombard areas. It was only in 1791 that Pope Pius VI (r. 1775–99) extended the royal right of nomination to these regions. However, the nominations of the first Savoyard bishops, including Bernardino Ignazio Rovèro, Ignazio Rovèro Sanseverino, and Marco Aurelio Balbis Bertone came after consultations and with the approval of the crown. See Guenzi, 'Pastorale dei vescovi novaresi,' 266–7.

14 See Symcox, *Victor Amadeus II*, 211–17. As well, see Pastor, *History of the Popes* 34:146–54, on negotiations for the concordat of 1727.

15 Silvestrini, *Politica della religione*, 337.

16 Silvestrini, *Politica della religione*, 14–15, 371–3.

17 For a discussion of how negotiations developed on questions pertaining to the award of benefices, especially those subject to lay patronage, see Silvestrini, *Politica della religione*, 185–98. For a more general statement of the position of the bishops in the state and their collaboration with the government in jurisdictional matters, see 373–5.

18 Silvestrini, *Politica della religione*, 9–26.

19 For example, in 1702 a document called 'Manifesto senatorio concernente la giurisdizione ecclesiastica' was issued, which ordered local officials (prefects) and judges to inform the senate at Turin before granting use of the secular arm to the ecclesiastical courts in cases against laypersons. They were permitted to act on their own initiative in cases involving ecclesiastics. This had implications for the ability of the ecclesiastical tribunals to gather evidence, to arrest the accused, and to execute sentences. In one of many statements on the issue, the first president of the senate, St Mellarede, noted that since bishops did not possess territory or a military arm of their own, they could not exercise jurisdiction unless the sovereign gave them assistance, the force of the secular arm. This, he said, required the secular and ecclesiastical authorities to work together so that crimes would not go unpunished. Permission to use the secular arm was, however, to be carefully guarded by the authorities of the state. AST, *Inventario*, 79–1. For more

on this and on negotiations to restrict the right of members of the clergy to bear arms, which resulted in a series of compromises, see Silvestrini, *Politica della religione*, 82–4.

20 Meyer, 'Religiosi fuorilegge.'

21 Tortona was added to the Savoyard state in 1736 at the same time as Novara, while Vigevano and Bobbio were acquired in 1748. Silvestrini, *Politica della religione*, 37–8.

22 Guenzi, 'Pastorale dei vescovi novaresi.'

23 Silvestrini, *Politica della religione*, 305.

24 For the pastoral visitations of Bishop Balbis Bertone, see ASDN *Acta visitationis* 290–361. His concern for the life and customs of the clergy is evident in Novara Diocese, *Synodus dioecesana novariensis ... Balbis Bertone ... MDCCLXXVIII*, esp. 117–22 (*De Sacris Ordinationibus*) and 133–9 (*De vita et honestate clericorum*).

25 Toscani, 'Il reclutamento del clero.'

26 For the population of Novara, see appendix 2.

27 Musgrave, 'Small Towns of Northern Italy.'

28 See appendix 3.

29 Rosa, *Clero cattolico*, 72–3; Toscani, 'Il reclutamento del clero.'

30 For information on clerical studies in the diocese of Novara, see Deutscher, 'Seminaries and the Education of Novarese Parish Priests,' and 'Growth of the Secular Clergy.'

31 Oscar Di Simplicio, noting the increasing number of secular priests at Siena in the seventeenth century, suggests that the reforms of the Council of Trent led to a spirit of anxiety in Italy which resulted in the endowment of masses for the dead which created more spaces for priests. *Inquisizione, stregoneria, medicina*, 81. See also Toscani, 'Il reclutamento del clero.'

32 See appendix 3. Of the 1460 priests found in the visitations of 1758–63, only 389 were directly involved in the care of souls as parish priests, coadjutors, and vice-curates, an increase of 26 per cent from the 308 parish priests of 1616–18.

33 Greco, 'I giuspatronati laicali nell'età moderna,' esp. 538–9.

34 Deutscher 'Growth of the Secular Clergy,' 392–3. The norm was for priests to sign contracts with communities or confraternities to serve as chaplain-schoolmasters. For example, see the case of Michele de Baldessario of Varallo Sesia who, in February 1774, signed a three-year agreement with the councillors and regents of Soriso to teach reading, arithmetic, and Latin to the boys of the town. The school was to be held in the house of the community in the plaza of Soriso, which was also to be the chaplain's home. Other duties involved saying the dawn Mass on feast days, playing the organ for all major celebrations at the parish church, and when called upon, administering the sacraments to the sick and dying. His pay

was to be 200 lire annually for teaching the boys and 175 lire annually for playing the organ. ASDN V, 1, 28/2, *1770–9.*

35 Sangalli, 'Maestri, preti-maestri, e scuole.' At Venice, priests and clerics were often to be found in the ranks of private tutors. For a more general account of the wide variety of educational opportunities available in Bergamo and other cities of the Veneto, see Carlsmith, *A Renaissance Education.*

36 ASDN V, 1, 28/2, *1770–9.* The proclamation stated that clerics would enjoy full exemption from lay tribunals and could not be arrested or imprisoned by the secular authorities. However, to protect royal rights, when there was a question of contraband goods being held in a church or pious place, the bishops and their vicars were to give access to the authorities when it was requested. In Lombardy, the Emperor Joseph II (r. 1780–90) took more drastic steps by attempting to restrict ordinations of new priests to the number of candidates required for the care of souls. As well, in a further step to pare clerical numbers, the educational standards of the secular clergy were to be improved, most notably by abolishing local seminaries and creating more comprehensive establishments such as the Grand Seminary of Pavia in the Lombard state. See Toscani, 'Il reclutamento del clero.'

37 ASDN XII, 1/1, 25. The men were given forty days to fulfil the Easter duty under penalty of interdict, and should they die in this state they were to be denied Christian burial.

38 ASDN XII, 1/1, 25.

39 ASDN XII, 1/1, 30.

40 ASDN XII, 1/1, 15, *1766–8.*

41 In May 1762 investigations were conducted into two cases of violation of sanctuary, one involving a fugitive taken from the parish church of Invorio, the second involving a man taken from the parish church of Alagna in the vicariate of Varallo Sesia. In the later case the authorities returned the fugitive to the church. ASDN XII, 1/1, 11, *1762.*

42 ASDN V, 1, 28/2, *1760–9.* The letter was published as well in the appendix of Balbis Bertone's synod of 1778. Novara Diocese, *Synodus dioecesana novariensis ... Balbis Bertone ... MDCCLXXVIII*, 292–301.

43 See chapter 4, 88.

44 ASDN XII, 1/1, 16, *1768–70.*

45 ASDN XII, 1/1, 6, *1759–60.*

46 ASDN XII, 1/1, 10, *1762.*

47 ASDN XII, 1/1, 25.

48 ASDN XII, 1/1, 24, *1793–4.*

49 An edict of Bishop Giovanni Battista Visconti on the Inquisition of the city and diocese of Novara, published with the synod of 1707, called on the faithful to

denounce those invoking the demon, those employing superstitious means or signs, and those abusing sacred objects or the sacraments. The edict also forbade the printing and sale of heretical or lascivious books and required those going to places suspect of heresy to obtain episcopal license, which could be obtained from curates if absences were frequent. Novara Diocese, *Synodus Dioecesana novariensis ... Vicecomite*, 12–16.

50 Silvestrini, *Politica della religione*, 238, 268–70, 284. See also Del Col, *L'Inquisizione in Italia*, 707–11.

51 ASDN XII, 1/1, 22, *1788–9*.

52 See Novara Diocese, *Synodus dioecesana novariensis ... Balbis Bertone ... MDCCLXXVIII*, 21, chapter 2, 'De impedimentis fidei avertendis,' x.

53 Novara Diocese, *Synodus dioecesana novariensis ... Balbis Bertone ... MDCCLXXVIII*, 20–1, chapter 2, 'De impedimentis fidei avertendis,' i–iv.

54 Fumi, *L'Inquisizione romana e lo stato di Milano*, 255–99, discusses the steady campaign of Count Kaunitz to weaken and finally destroy the Roman Inquisition by gradualist means. Beginning in the 1760s, the government curtailed the ability of the Inquisition to incarcerate the accused, removed censorship from its hands, abolished the Confraternity of the Crocesignati, its support group, and refused to recognize new inquisitors when old ones were transferred or died. Although Joseph II declared religious toleration in 1781, the remaining inquisitors continued in office until the time of the Cisalpine Republic, established by Napoleon. One of the last was Pietro Placido Novelli, who was prosecuted in 1797 when he was seventy-two years of age. At his trial, Novelli claimed that he had conducted no trials in ten and a half years as an inquisitor, but only absolved those who appeared 'voluntarily.' He was freed after promising not to practice as an inquisitor.

55 Silvestrini, *Politica della religione*, 233–91. Silvestrini points out that the Roman Inquisition continued to function in the territory of Piedmont until it was suppressed by the French provisional government in 1799. See also Del Col, *L'Inquisizione in Italia*, 699–710, and the brief comments by Romeo in *L'Inquisizione nell'Italia moderna*, 114–16.

56 Silvestrini, *Politica della religione*, 291. Del Col, who questions Silvestrini's numbers, has argued that at Modena, Siena, and other centres, there was an increase in inquisitorial activity in the eighteenth century. See *L'Inquisizione in Italia*, 700–10. Elena Brambilla suggests that the majority of cases dealt with at Modena were of a 'summary' type, inflicting light punishments and rarely conducted in public so that the accused would not be humiliated. See *La giustizia intollerante*, 228.

57 Silvestrini, *Politica della religione*, 268–70.

58 Silvestrini, *Politica della religione*, 273.

59 Silvestrini, *Politica della religione*, 246–7.

60 See Madaro's 'Gli inquisitori a Novara,' which lists the inquisitors at Novara up until 1732.

61 ASDN XII, 1/1, 2, *1753–4*. Mazola went on to describe the cleric as lazy and known to frequent taverns and dances, to keep bad company, and to have scandalous relationships with women. He also went about in lay clothing.

62 Brambilla, *La giustizia intollerante*, 228, notes that many of the cases in the eighteenth-century Modena were spontaneous appearances made on the insistence of confessors.

63 ASDN XII, 1/1, 25.

64 ASDN XII, 1/1, 25.

65 ASDN XII, 1/1, 22, *1788–9*.

66 Prodi, *Il Cardinale Gabriele Paleotti* 1:71–5.

67 ASDN XII, 1/1, 26.

68 ASDN XII, 1/1, 25.

69 ASDN XII, 1/1, 24, *1793–4*.

70 'La fraterna correzione in spirito di unità non solamente riuscirebbe con uso iniutile, ma perniciosa, se non in mano forte.' ASDN XII, 1/1, 20, *1779–87*. In 1779 Viola had undergone spiritual exercises with the oblates of Novara to attone for his relationship with Clara Giovanna di Buglio. He had begged for the clemency of the bishop rather than prepare a formal defence. As early as 1763 he had been accused of making threats against people at Crusinallo. ASDN XII, 1/1, 28.

71 ASDN V, 1, 27; ASDN V, 1, 28/1, *1756–65*; ASDN V, 1, 28/2, *1770–9*; ASDN V, 1, 28/3, *1780–9*.

72 A similar ratio holds true if only the 230 cases known to have resulted in a formal inquiry are considered: of the 230, slightly over 50 priests were directly involved in the care of souls.

73 ASDN XII, 1/1, 5, *1757–9*.

74 ASDN *Acta visitationis* 298, vicariate of Bullio (Omegna), parish of Crusinallo; ASDN XII, 1/1, 20, *1779–87*; ASDN XII, 1/1, 23, *1789–93*; ASDN XII, 1/1, 27; ASDN XII, 1/1, 28.

75 The ratio would fall to one in fifteen if the numbers of cases resulting in inquiries (54 of 778) were used.

76 For a comment on the history of Italian diocesan archives and their disordered state, see Donati, 'Curie, tribunali, cancellerie episcopali.'

77 Giannini, 'Tra politica, fiscalità e religione,' esp. 84.

78 ASDN XII, 1/1, 3, *1754*.

79 ASDN XII, 1/1, 8, *1762*. The Sacred Congregation of the Council eventually granted Mauletti a dispensation from the excommunication incurred through his act of homicide. ASDN V, 1, 28/1, *1756–65*.

80 ASDN XII, 1/1, 11, *1762.*

81 ASDN *Acta visitationis* 358, fols. 20r–21r.

82 ASDN V, 1, 28/2, *1760–9.*

83 ASDN XII, 1/1, 13, *1763–4.*

84 ASDN XII, 1/1, 13, *1763–4.* The *status personalis* of Maraschi, who was a chaplain with the obligation to teach boys in his house for fifty lire a year, appears in Balbis Bertone's visit of Granozzo in the vicariate of Casalvolone (Camariano) in 1760. ASDN *Acta visitationis* 305.

85 ASDN XII, 1/1, 13, *1763–4.*

86 ASDN XII, 1/1, 5, *1757–9.*

87 ASDN XII, 1/1, 3, *1754.* De Marchis appears to have been exonerated or at least he escaped serious punishment. In the visit of 1760, Giacomo Antonio de Marchis appears as a fifty-five-year-old chaplain who had studied moral theology and possessed the faculty to hear confessions. ASDN *Acta visitationis* 315, visit of Mollia.

88 ASDN XII, 1/1, 11, *1762.* Bovio's *status personalis* is found in ASDN *Acta visitationis* 290–3, fol. 1104. He was twenty-six years of age in 1758, ordained to his patrimony and a lifelong chaplaincy for the confraternity of the rosary.

89 ASDN XII, 1/1, 16, *1768–70.*

90 ASDN XII, 1/1, 20, *1779–87.*

91 ASDN XII, 1/1, 20, *1779–87.*

92 ASDN XII, 1/1, 30.

93 ASN, *Editti e manifesti, 1789–94*, fol. 379v. The precise location of Brazzo is not known.

94 ASDN XII, 1/1, 15, *1766–8.*

95 In Lombardy steps were taken by the Emperor Joseph II of Austria (r. 1780–90) to have the clergy subjected to the civil courts while the ecclesiastical tribunals were to deal with 'spiritual' matters only. Annoni, 'Giurisdizionalismo ed episcopalismo.'

96 Di Simplicio, *Peccato, penitenza, perdono*, 111–21.

97 ASDN XII, 1/1, 22, *1788–9*; ASDN XII, 1/1, 26; ASDN XII, 1/1, 30.

98 ASDN XII, 1/1, 21, *1787.*

99 ASDN XII, 1/1, 6, *1759–60*; ASDN XII, 1/1, 7, *1760–2.* Lorenzino's *status personalis* appears in the visit of 1759, at which time it was noted that he had been prosecuted two or three times, to that point without resolution. He was then forty years of age. ASDN *Acta visitationis* 301, visit of Beura.

100 ASDN XII, 1/1, 18, *1771–3.*

101 ASDN XII, 1/1, 23, *1789–93.*

102 ASDN XII, 1/1, 19, *1773–7.*

103 ASDN XII, 1/1, 30, for the process, and ASDN XII, 1/1, 24, *1793–4*, for the 1799 sentence. See also ASDN XII, 1/1, 22, *1788–9*, for Olgina's petition for clemency in 1785–8.

104 ASDN XII, 1/1, 28.

105 ASDN XII, 1/1, 26.

106 ASDN XII, 1/1, 8, *1762.*

107 ASDN XII, 1/1, 21, *1787.*

108 ASDN XII, 1/1, 4, *1755–6.*

109 ASDN XII, 1/1, 5, *1757–9.*

110 ASDN XII, 1/1, 5, *1757–9.*

111 ASDN *Acta visitationis* 326, Belgirate.

112 ASDN XII, 1/1, 2, *1753–4.*

113 ASDN *Acta visitationis* 320, parish of Barengo.

114 ASDN XII, 1/1, 7, *1760–2.* In the visit of Pallanzeno of 1759, it was noted that Maffei was forty years old and had studied speculative theology at Milan. ASDN *Acta visitationis* 302–3, parish of Pallanzeno.

115 'In modo che per lo più o poco o nulla vien inteso.' ASDN XII, 1/1, 3, *1754.* Barletti was still serving as curate of Soriso during the visit of 1761. It was noted that he had been criticized because of his preaching and on occasion detained (*delatus*). ASDN *Acta visitationis* 327.

116 ASDN XII, 1/1, 12, *1763.* Loretto's *status personalis* is found in Balbis Bertone's visit of 1759, ASDN *Acta visitationis* 300–2.

117 See ASDN XII, 1/1, 28, for inquiries in the early 1780s into over twenty priests who had failed to celebrate the masses required of them.

118 ASDN XII, 1/1, 25.

119 ASDN XII, 1/1, 28. A similar charge had been levelled against the parish priest of Morghengo, Francesco Xaviero Ragno, in 1762. Ragno was also accused of evading the tax on wine. ASDN XII, 1/1, 10, *1762.*

120 ASDN XII, 1/1, 23, *1789–93.*

121 ASDN XII, 1/1, 25.

122 ASDN XII, 1/1, 25.

123 See ASDN XII, 1/1, 20, *1779–87*, for the accusations and testimony against Gnemma, his statement of defence, the sentence of 1785, and the letter of 17 June 1794 from the provost of Varallo, Innocenzo Imbrico.

124 ASDN XII, 1/1, 23, *1789–93.*

125 In the diocesan synod of 1707 Bishop Giovanni Battista Visconti ordered all candidates to undergo spiritual exercises in the month before ordination, citing Pope Innocent XI's pastoral letter of 9 October 1682. Novara Diocese, *Synodus Dioecesana novariensis … Vicecomite*, 47. In 1778 Balbis Bertone encouraged all priests with the care of souls and with power to hear confession to undergo spiritual exercises yearly or at least every three years to revitalize their spiritual life. Novara Diocese, *Synodus dioecesana novariensis … Balbis Bertone … MDCCLXXVIII*, 135.

126 ASDN V, 1, 28/2, *1760–9*.
127 ASDN XII, 1/1, 5, *1757–9*.
128 ASDN XII, 1/1, 22, *1788–9*, gives the sentence.
129 ASDN XII, 1/1, 23, *1789–93*.
130 ASDN V, 1, 28/3, *1780–9*.
131 ASDN XII, 1/1, 4, *1755–6*.
132 ASDN XII, 1/1, 18, *1771–3*.
133 ASDN XII, 1/1, 15, *1766–8*.
134 ASDN XII, 1/1, 18, *1771–3*.
135 ASDN XII, 1/1, 13, 1763–4.
136 See ASDN XII, 1/1, 28, for the process of 1787; and ASDN XII, 1/1 29, for Capra's exoneration.
137 Forster, *Counter-Reformation in the Villages*, 185–213; Di Simplicio, *Peccato, penitenza, perdono*, 23–5, 76–99; Turchini, 'La nascita del sacerdozio come professione.'
138 For an overview of the cultural life of the Novarese clergy, with an emphasis on activity in the areas of preaching and catechesis, see Guenzi, 'La cultura e la pastorale ecclesiale del settecento Novarese.'
139 ASDN XII, 1/1, 15, *1771–3*.
140 ASDN V, 1, 28/2, *1770–9*.
141 ASDN XII, 1/1, 10, *1773–7*.
142 Guenzi, 'La Pastorale dei vescovi novaresi.'

Conclusion: Two Phases of Tribunal Activity

1 Bascapè, *Commentarii canonici*, 165–77.
2 Bascapè, *Commentarii canonici*, 137–62, 197–8.
3 The matter is discussed in detail by Prosperi, *Tribunali della coscienza*, 219–77.
4 Prosperi, *Tribunali della coscienza*, 316–42; Donati, 'Vescovi e diocese d'Italia dall'età post-tridentina.'
5 See the articles by Giannini: 'Fra autonomia politica e ortodossia religiosa'; 'Per beneficio della città e religione'; and 'Inquisizione romana e politica asburgica.' Also essential is de Boer's 'Soldati in terra straniera.'

Bibliography

Manuscript Sources

Archivio di Stato, Novara (ASN)

Editti e manifesti, 1789–94. 'Nota dei banditi ... che il Senato di Piemonte ha fatto descrivere nel primo e secondo catalogo rispettivamente nell'anno 1791, in data 31 gennajo 1792' and 'Nota dei banditi ... che il Senato di Piemonte ha fatto descrivere nel primo e secondo catalogo rispettivamente nell'anno 1792, in data 31 marzo 1793.'

Archivio di Stato, Torino (AST)

Inventario 79–1. *Materie Ecclesistiche* 7 Categoria, Mazzo 1. Braccio secolare, no. 10.

Paesi Nuovo Acquisto. Novarese. Città di Novara. Mazzo 1.

Archivio provinciale dei Barnabiti, church of San Barnaba, Milan (APB)

Fondo miscellaneo, gruppo 4.

Archivio Segreto Vaticano (ASV)

Congregazione Vescovi e Regolari, Positiones. Indice 1104.

Congregazione Vescovi e Regolari, Positiones.

Congregazione Concilio. Relationes Dioecesium. Novarien. Indice 1104.

Archivio Storico dei Padri Barnabiti di Roma (ASBR)

Carlo Bascapè. *Registri di lettere del tempo del suo vescovado dal 1593 al 1615.* 26 vols.

Archivio Storico Diocesano di Novara (ASDN)

III, 5, 1, *Inventari Relazioni. Relationes ad limina.*

IV, 4, *Acta Curia. Licentiarum.*

V, 1, 27. *Vescovi. Balbis Bertone.*

V, 1, 28/1, *Vescovi. M.A. Balbis Bertone. Lettere varie senza data, 1756–65.*

V, 1, 28/2, *Vescovi. M.A. Balbis Bertone. Lettere varie e Appunti, 1760–9.*

V, 1, 28/2, *Vescovi. M.A. Balbis Bertone. Lettere 1770–9.*

V, 1, 28/3, *Vescovi fino al 1817. M.A. Balbis Bertone, 1780–9.*

XII, 1/1, 1–24, *Foro. Atti Processuali, Cause 1745–94*. 24 files.

XII, 1/1, 25–6, *Foro. Atti Processuali, Precetti, Lettere, Notificazioni di M. Balbis Bertone*. 2 files.

XII, 1/1, 27, *Foro. Atti Processuali, Precetti, Lettere, Notificazioni di Burongo Delsignore Melano da Portula.*

XII, 1/1, 28–30, *Foro. Atti Processuali. Miscellanea sec XVIII*. 3 files.

XII, 2, 1, *Foro ecclesiastico. Libro di verbali di denuncie (1563–4) fatto dal Vicario Generale Cesare Andena, Vicario del Card. Gian Antonio Serbelloni.*

XII, 2, 2, *Foro ecclesiastico. Libri e registri. Libri Informationum, 1585–90.*

XII, 2, 3, *Foro ecclesiastico. Libri e registri. Libri informationum, 1590–1.*

XII, 2, 5, *Foro ecclesiastico. Libri e registri. Libri constitutorum in causis fidei, 1596–1614.*

XII, 2, 6, *Foro ecclesiastico. Libri e registri. Criminalia, 1576–83, 1593.*

XII, 2, 7, *Foro ecclesiastico. Libri e registri. Constitutorum, 1593–5.*

XII, 2, 8, *Foro ecclesiastico. Libri e registri. Constitutorum, 1595–8.*

XII, 2, 9, *Foro ecclesiastico. Libri e registri. Constitutorum, 1601–6.*

XII, 2, 10, *Foro ecclesiastico. Libri e registri. Constitutorum, 1609–14, 1618–19.*

XII, 2, 11, *Foro ecclesiastico. Libri e registri. Libri sententiarum, 1591–8.*

Acta Visitationis. 361 vols.

Biblioteca Ambrosiana, Milan (BA)

Ms. G. 204 *inf.*

Ms.Trotti 38.

Printed Sources

Abbott, T.K. *Catalogue of the Manuscripts in the Library of Trinity College, Dublin*. Dublin: 1900. Reprint, Hildesheim: Olms, 1980.

Allegra, Luciano. 'Il parocco: Un mediatore fra alta e bassa cultura.' In *Storia d'Italia. Annali 4: Intelletuali e potere*, ed. Corrado Vivanti, 895–947. Turin: Giulio Einaudi editore, 1981.

Ammann, Hektor, and Karl Schik, eds. *Historischer Atlas der Schweiz*. Aarau: H.R. Sauerländer, 1958.

Annoni, Ada. 'Giurisdizionalismo ed episcopalismo.' In *Chiesa e società: Appunti per una storia delle diocesi lombarde*, ed. A. Caprioli, A. Rimoldi, and L. Vaccaro, 140–77. Brescia: Editrice la Scuola, 1986.

Bascapè, Carlo. *Commentarii canonici*. Novara, 1615.

– *De vita e rebus gestis Caroli card. S. Praxedis Archiepiscopi Mediolani*. Modern ed. with Italian translation. Milan: Veneranda Fabbrica del Duomo, 1965.

– 'I primi diciotto anni dell'arcivescovo di Milano Federico cardinale Borromeo.' In *Documenti spettanti alla storia della S. Chiesa Milanese la prima volta pubblicati ed offerti in omaggio a Sua Eminenza il Cardinale Arcivescovo pel fausto suo arrive alla pieve di Canturio*, ed. Carlo Annoni, 43–111. Como: C.P. Ostinelli, 1839.

– *Lettere di governo episcopale*. Novara, 1613.

– *Novaria, seu de ecclesia novariensi, libri duo. Primus de locis, alter de episcopis*. Novara, 1612.

– 'Relazione delle cause trattate in Spagna per ordine di San Carlo dal Padre Don Carlo Bescapè Barnabita, che fu poi Vescovo di Novara.' In *Documenti circa la vita e le geste di S. Carlo Borromeo* 1, ed. Aristide Sala, 70–80. Milan, 1865.

– *Scritti publicati … nel governo del suo vescovato dall'anno 1593 fino al 1609*. Novara, 1609.

Beccaria, Battista. 'Inquisizione episcopale e inquisizione romano-domenicana di fronte alla stregoneria nella Novara post-tridentina (1570–1615): I processi del Buelli (1580) conservati al Trinity College di Dublino.' *Novarien* 34 (2005): 165–221.

Bendiscioli, Mario. 'Politica, amministrazione e religione nell'età dei Borromei.' In *Storia di Milano* 10:1–350.

Bertolino, Rinaldo. *Ricerche sul Giuramento dei vescovi: Contributo allo studio del diritto ecclesiastico subalpino*. 2 vols. Turin: G. Giappichelli editore, 1971–6.

Bireley, Robert. *The Refashioning of Catholicism, 1450–1700: A Reassessment of the Counter Reformation*. Washington, DC: Catholic University of America Press, 1999.

Borromeo, Agostino. 'Archbishop Carlo Borromeo and the Ecclesiastical Policy of Philip II in the State of Milan.' In Headley and Tomaro, *San Carlo Borromeo*, 85–111.

– 'L'arcivescovo Carlo Borromeo, la Corona spagnola e le controversie giurisdizionali a Milano.' In Buzzi and Zardin, *Carlo Borromeo*, 257–71.

– 'Contributo allo studio dell'inquisizione e dei suoi rapporti con il potere episcopale nell'Italia spagnola del cinquecento.' *Annuario dell'Istituto Storico Italiano per l'età moderna e contemporanea* 29–30 (1977–8): 219–76.

– ed. *L'inquisizione: Atti del Simposio internazionale. Città del Vaticano, 29–31 ottobre 1998*. Comitato del Grande Giubileo dell'anno 2000, Commissione Theologico-storica. Città del Vaticano: Biblioteca Apostolica Vaticana, 2003.

Botero, Giovanni. *The Reason of State*. Translated by P.J. and D.P. Waley, with an introduction by D.P. Waley. New Haven: Yale University Press, 1956.

Brambilla, Elena. *La giustizia intollerante: Inquisizione e tribunali confessionali in Europa (secoli IV–XVIII)*. Rome: Carocci editore, 2007.

– 'La polizia dei tribunali ecclesiastici e le riforme della giustizia penale.' In *Corpi armati e ordine pubblico in Italia (XVI–XIX sec.)*, ed. Livio Antonielli and Claudio Donati, 73–110. Soveria Mannelli: Rubbettino, 2003.

Buzzi, Franco, and Danilo Zardin, eds. *Carlo Borromeo e l'opera della 'Grande Riforma': Cultura, religione e arti del governo nella Milano del pieno Cinquecento*. Milan: Silvana editoriale, 1997.

Cantu, Cesare. *Gli eretici d'Italia: Discorsi storici*. 3 vols. Turin: Unione tipografico-editrice, 1865–6.

Carlsmith, Christopher. *A Renaissance Education: Schooling in Bergamo and the Venetian Republic, 1500–1650*. Toronto: University of Toronto Press, 2010.

Catalano, Gaetano, and Fredrico Martino, eds. *Potestà civile e autorità spirituale in Italia nei secoli della riforma e controriforma*. Milan: Giuffrè editore, 1984.

The Catholic Encyclopedia: An International Work of Reference on the Constitution, Doctrine, Discipline and History of the Catholic Church. Edited by Charles G. Herbermann, Edward A. Pace, Condé P. Pallen, Thomas J. Shahan, and John J. Wynne. New York: Appleton, 1907–1912.

Cattaneo, Enrico. 'La religione a Milano nell'età della controriforma.' In *Storia di Milano* 11:283–331.

Cavigioli, G. 'La posizione di Mons. Marco Aurelio Balbis Bertone, Vescovo di Novara (1757–1789) nelle polemiche ecclesiastiche dell'età sua.' *Bolletino Storico per la Provincia di Novara* 32 (1938): 101–7.

Chabod, Federico. *Per la storia religiosa dello stato di Milano durante il dominio di Carlo V. Note e documenti*. 2nd ed. Edited by Ernesto Sestan. Rome: Istituto storico italiano per l'età moderna e contemporanea, 1962.

Chiesa, Innocenzo. *Vita del Bascapè*. Edited by Sergio Pagano. Florence: Leo S. Olschki, 1993.

Cognasso, Francesco. *Storia di Novara*. Novara: Libreria Lazzarelli, 1971.

Comerford, Kathleen M. 'Chierici e seminari nei primi decenni del periodo post-tridentino.' In Sangalli, *Per il cinquecento religioso italiano*, 363–72.

– *Reforming Priests and Parishes: Tuscan Dioceses in the First Century of Seminary Education*. Leiden-Boston: Brill, 2006.

Cremonini, Cinzia. 'La congregazione dei Crocesignati milanesi tra 1644 e 1767. Alcune considerazioni.' *Studia Borromaica: Saggi e documenti di storia religiosa e civile della prima età moderna* 23 (2009): 489–519.

Dandelet, Thomas J. 'Politics and the State System after the Habsburg-Valois Wars.' In *Early Modern Italy, 1550–1796*, ed. John A. Marino, 11–29. Oxford: Oxford University Press, 2002.

De Boer, Wietse. '"Ad audiendi non videndi commoditatem," Note sull'introduzione del confessionale soprattutto in Italia.' *Quaderni storici* 77 (1991): 543–72.

– 'Calvin and Borromeo: A Comparative Approach to Social Discipline.' In *Early Modern Catholicism: Essays in Honour of John W. O'Malley, S.J.*, ed. Kathleen Comerford and Hilmar M. Pabel, 84–96. Toronto: University of Toronto Press, 2001.

– *The Conquest of the Soul: Confession, Discipline, and Public Order in Counter-Reformation Milan*. Studies in Medieval and Reformation Thought 84. Leiden: Brill, 2001.

– 'Soldati in terra straniera: La fede tra inquisizione e ragion di stato.' *Studia Borromaica: Saggi e documenti di storia religiosa e civile della prima età moderna* 23 (2009): 403–27.

Decrees of the Ecumenical Councils. 2 vols. Edited by Norman P. Tanner. Washington: Sheed & Ward and Georgetown University Press, 1990.

Del Col, Andrea. *L'Inquisizione in Italia, dal XII al XXI secolo*. Milan: Oscar Mondadori, 2006.

– 'Le strutture territoriali e l'attività dell'inquisizione Romana.' In Borromeo, *L'inquisizione*, 345–79.

Deutscher, Thomas. 'The Bishop's Tribunal and the Laity: The Diocese of Novara, 1563 to 1614.' In *The Renaissance in the Streets, Schools, and Studies: Essays in Honour of Paul F. Grendler*, ed. Konrad Eisenbishler and Nicholas Terpstra, 183–209. Toronto: Centre for Renaissance and Reformation Studies, 2008.

– 'Carlo Bascapè e la riforma delle monache di Novara.' In *Da Carlo Borromeo a Carlo Bascapè: La Pastorale di Carlo Borromeo e il Sacro Monte di Arona, Atti della Giornata Culturale, Arona 12 settembre 1984*, 299–315. Novara: Associazione di Storia della Chiesa Novarese, 1984.

– 'The Distribution of Devotional Works among the Novarese Parish Clergy (1616–1663).' *Rivista di storia e letteratura religiosa* 39 (2003): 109–39.

– 'From Cicero to Tasso: Humanism and the Education of the Novarese Parish Clergy (1565–1663).' *Renaissance Quarterly* 55 (2002): 1005–27.

– 'The Growth of the Secular Clergy and the Development of Educational Institutions in the Diocese of Novara (1563–1772).' *The Journal of Ecclesiastical History* 40 (1989): 381–97.

– 'The Role of the Episcopal Tribunal of Novara in the Suppression of Heresy and Witchcraft, 1563–1615.' *The Catholic Historical Review* 77 (1991): 403–21.

– 'Seminaries and the Education of Novarese Parish Priests, 1563–1627.' *The Journal of Ecclesiastical History* 32 (1981): 303–19.

Dictionnaire de spiritualité ascétique et mystique, doctrine et histoire. Edited by Marcel Vallier, F. Cavallera, and J. de Guibert. Paris: Beauchesne, 1932–95.

Dictionnaire historique et biographique de la Suisse. 7 vols. Neuchâtel: Administration du Dictionnaire historique et biographique de la Suisse, 1921–33.

Di Simplicio, Oscar. *Inquisizione, stregoneria, medicina: Siena e il suo stato (1580–1721)*. Siena: Edizioni il Leccio, 2000.

– *Peccato, penitenza, perdono: Siena 1575–1800: La formazione della coscienza nell'Italia moderna*. Milan: FrancoAngeli Storia, 1994.

Dizionario biografico degli Italiani. Edited by Alberto Ghisalberti. Rome: Istituto della Enciclopedia italiana, 1960–.

Donati, Claudio, 'Curie, tribunali, cancellerie episcopali in Italia durante i secoli dell'età moderna: percorsi di ricerca.' In *Fonti ecclesiastiche per la storia sociale e religiosa d'Europa: XV–XVIII secolo*, ed. Cecilia Nubola and Angelo Turchini, 213–29. Bologna: Il Mulino, 1999.

– 'Vescovi e diocesi d'Italia dall'età post-tridentina alla caduta dell'antico regime.' In Rosa, *Clero e società nell'Italia moderna*, 321–89.

Emmison, F.G. *Elizabethan Life: Morals & The Church Courts. Mainly from Essex Archidiaconal Records*. Chelmsford: Essex County Council, 1973.

Fantappiè, Carlo. 'I problemi giuridici e finanziari dei seminari tridentini.' In *Chiesa, Chierici, Sacerdoti: Clero e seminari in Italia tra XVI e XX secolo. Siena, Archivio di Stato, Seminario arcivescovile, 21 maggio 1999*, ed. Maurizio Sangalli, 86–109. Rome: Herder editrice e libreria, 2000.

Ferrante, Lucia. 'Il matrimonio disciplinato: processi matrimoniali a Bologna nel Cinquecento.' In Prodi, *Disciplina dell'anima*, 901–27.

Ferraro, Joanne M. *Marriage Wars in Late Renaissance Venice*. Oxford: Oxford University Press, 2001.

Forster, Marc R. *Catholic Revival in the Age of the Baroque: Religious Identity in Southwest Germany, 1550–1750*. Cambridge: Cambridge University Press, 2001.

– *The Counter-Reformation in the Villages: Religion and Reform in the Bishopric of Speyer, 1560–1720*. Ithaca: Cornell University Press, 1992.

Fumi, Luigi. *L'Inquisizione romana e lo stato di Milano: Saggio di ricerche nell'Archivio di Stato*. Milan: Tipografia editrice L.F. Cogliati, 1910. Published as an extract from *Archivio Storico Lombardo* 13:5–124, 285–414, and 14:145–220.

Giannini, Massimo Carlo. '"Con il zelo di sodisfare all'obligo di re e principe." Monarchia cattolica e stato di Milano nella Visita General di don Felipe de Haro (1606–1612).' *Archivio storico lombardo* 120 (1994): 165–207.

– 'Fra autonomia politica e ortodossia religiosa: Il tentativo d'introdurre l'inquisizione "al modo di Spagna" nello stato di Milano (1558–1566).' *Società e storia* 91, no. 23 (2001): 79–134.

– 'Inquisizione romana e politica asburgica nella Milano di metà Cinquecento: I due processi ad Ascanio Marso, agente presso i cantoni elvetici.' *Studia Borromaica: Saggi e documenti di storia religiosa e civile della prima età moderna* 23 (2009): 369–402.

– 'Per beneficio della città e religione. Governo politico e inquisizione nello stato di Milano a metà cinquecento.' In *L'Italia di Carlo V: Guerra, religione e politica nel primo cinquecento*, ed. Francesca Cantù and Maria A. Visceglia, 303–36. Rome: I Libri di Viella, 2003.

– 'Politica spagnola e giurisdizione ecclesiastica nello Stato di Milano: Il conflitto tra il cardinale Federico Borromeo e il visitador regio don Felipe de Haro (1606–7). *Studia Borromaica: Saggi e documenti di storia religiosa e civile della prima età moderna* 6 (1992): 195–226.

– 'Tra politica, fiscalità e religione: Filippo II di Spagna e la pubblicazione della bolla "In Coena Domini" (1567–1570),' *Annali dell'Istituto storico italo-germanico in Trento* 23 (1997): 83–152.

Greco, Gaetano. 'I giuspatronati laicali nell'età moderna.' In *Storia d'Italia. Annali 9: La Chiesa e il potere politico dal medioevo all'età contemporanea*, ed. Giorgio Chittolini and Giovanni Miccoli, 531–72. Turin: Giulio Einaudi editore, 1986.

Grendler, Paul. *The Roman Inquisition and the Venetian Press, 1540–1605*. Princeton: Princeton University Press, 1977.

Guasco, Maurilio. 'La formazione del clero: I seminari.' In *Storia d'Italia. Annali 9: La Chiesa e il potere politico dal medioevo all'età contemporanea*, ed. Giorgio Chittolini and Giovanni Miccoli, 631–715. Turin: Giulio Einaudi editore, 1986.

Guenzi, Pier Davide. 'La cultura e la pastorale ecclesiale del settecento Novarese.' In Vaccaro and Tuniz, *Diocesi di Novara*, 559–78.

– 'La Pastorale dei vescovi novaresi nell'età dei lumi.' In Vaccaro and Tuniz, *Diocesi di Novara*, 265–92.

Haliczer, Stephen. *Sexuality in the Confessional: A Sacrament Profaned*. New York: Oxford University Press, 1996.

Hanlon, Gregory. *Early Modern Italy, 1550–1800: Three Seasons in European History*. New York: St Martin's Press, 2000.

Headley, John M., and John B. Tomaro, eds. *San Carlo Borromeo: Catholic Reform and Ecclesiastical Politics in the Second Half of the Sixteenth Century*. Washington: Folger, 1988.

Ingram, Martin. *Church Courts, Sex and Marriage in England, 1570–1640*. Cambridge: Cambridge University Press, 1987.

– 'History of Sin or History of Crime? The Regulation of Morality in England, 1450–1750.' In *Institutionen, Instrumente und Akteure: Sozialer Kontrolle und Disziplinierung im Frühneuzeitlichen Europa*, ed. Heinz Schilling and Lara Behrisch, 87–103. Frankfurt and Main: Klostermann, 1999.

Lavenia, Vincenzo. *L'infamia e il perdono: Tributi, pene e confessione nella teologia morale della prima età moderna*. Bologna: Il Mulino, 2004.

Longo, Pier Giorgio. 'Appunti su Cesare Speciano, Vescovo di Novara.' *Novarien* 2 (1968): 128–54.

– 'La Chiesa novarese tra XVI e XVIII secolo.' In Vaccaro and Tuniz, *Diocesi di Novara*, 209–64.

– 'Problemi di vita religiosa nella diocesi di Novara prima del episcopato di Carlo Bascapè (1593) e con particolare riferimento al periodo 1580–1590.' 2 vols. Tesi di laurea, Facoltà de Lettere e Filosofia, Università degli Studi di Torino, 1969–70.

MacCulloch, Diarmaid, Mary Laven, and Eamon Duffy. 'Recent Trends in the Study of Christianity in Sixteenth-Century Europe.' *Renaissance Quarterly* 59 (2006): 697–731.

Madaro, Luigi. 'Gli inquisitori a Novara dal 1351 al 1732 (da un manoscritto della Biblioteca Civica di Alessandria).' *Novara* 6 (1925): 205–12.

Manzini, P.L. *San Carlo e il Ven. Bascapè*. Monza: 1910.

Marcocchi, Massimo. *La Riforma dei monasteri femminili a Cremona: Gli atti ineditti della visita del Vescovo Cesare Speciano (1599–1606)*. Annali della Biblioteca governativa e Libreria civica di Cremona 7. Cremona: 1966.

Meyer, Frédéric. 'Religiosi fuorilegge: I regolari di fronte alla giustizia in Savoia nel secolo XVIII.' *Quaderni storici* 119 (2005): 519–53.

Milan Archdiocese. *Acta Ecclesiae Mediolanensis a Carlo Cardinali s. Praxedis condita, Federici Card. Borromaei Archiepiscopi Mediolani iussu collecta et edita*. Milan, 1599.

– *Acta Ecclesiae Mediolanensis ab eius initiis usque ad nostram aetatem*. 4 vols. Edited by Achille Ratti. Milan, 1890–97.

Monter, E. William, and John Tedeschi. 'Toward a Statistical Profile of the Italian Inquisitions, Sixteenth to Eighteenth Centuries.' In *The Inquisition in Early Modern Europe: Studies on Sources and Methods*, ed. Gustav Henningsen and John Tedesch, in association with Charles Amiel, 130–57. DeKalb, IL: Northern Illinois University Press, 1986.

Musgrave, Peter. 'The Small Towns of Northern Italy in the Seventeenth and Eighteenth Centuries: An Overview.' In *Small Towns in Early Modern Europe*, ed. Peter Clark, 250–70. Cambridge: Cambridge University Press, 1995.

Myers, W. David. *'Poor Sinning Folk': Confession and Conscience in Counter-Reformation Germany*. Ithaca: Cornell University Press, 1996.

Negruzzo, Simona. *Collegij a forma di Seminario: Il sistema di formazione teologica nello Stato di Milano in epoca spagnola*. Brescia: Editrice La Scuola, 2001.

– 'La Diocesi e i suoi seminari in età moderna.' In Vaccaro and Tuniz, *Diocesi di Novara*, 529–40.

New Catholic Encyclopedia. 2nd ed. New York: McGraw-Hill, 1967–74; Detroit: Gale in association with the Catholic University of America, 2003.

Novara Diocese. *Decreta edita et promulgata in synodo dioecesana novariensi habita anno 1576. die. 28 februarii, sub Reverendiss. D. Romulo Archinto Episcopo Novariensi, & Comite & c.* Novara, 1576.

– *Synodus dioecesana novariensis ab excell.mo et rev.mo D.D. Marco Aurelio Balbis Bertone, Episcopo Novariae, habita diebus I, II, & III Julii Anno MDCCLXXVIII*. Novara, 1779.

– *Synodus Dioecesana novariensis ab illustrissimo, et reverendissimo Domino D. Ioanne Baptista Vicecomite … celebrata in basilica cathedrali diebus VI, VII, VIII iunij anni MDCCVII*. Novara, n.d.

– *Synodus dioecesana sub Reverendiss. Domino D. Cesare Speciano … primo habita anno Domini MDXC*. Novara, 1591.

– *Synodus novarien. Per Illustriss. Et Reverendiss. D.D. Io. Antonio Serbellonum … celebrata die ix maii, MDLXVIII*. Novara, 1571.

Pastor, Ludwig von. *The History of the Popes: From the Close of the Middle Ages*. London: K. Paul, Trench, Trubner, 1938–57.

Peyronel Rambaldi, Susanna. 'Frontiere religiose e soldati in antico regime: il caso di Crema nel Seicento.' In *Alle Frontiere della Lombardia: Politica, guerra e religione nella età moderna*, ed. Claudio Donati, 19–39. Milan: FrancoAngeli, 2006.

– 'Inquisizione e potere laico: Il caso di Cremona.' In *Lombardia Borromaica Lombardia Spagnola, 1554–1659*, ed. Paolo Pissavino and Gianvittorio Signorotto, 2:579–617. Rome: Bulzoni Editore, 1995.

Pizzolato, Nicola. 'Ordinarie trasgressioni: Adulterio e concubinato dal vicinato al tribunale (diocesi di Monreale, 1590–1680).' *Quaderni storici* 124 (2007): 231–60.

Prodi, Paolo, ed., with the collaboration of Carlo Penuti. *Disciplina dell'anima, disciplina del corpo e disciplina della società tra medioevo ed età moderna*. Annali dell'Istituto storico italo-germanico, Quaderno 40. Bologna: Società editrice il Mulino, 1994.

– *Il Cardinale Gabriele Paleotti (1522–1597)*. 2 vols. Rome: Edizioni di storia e letteratura, 1959–67.

– 'San Carlo Borromeo e le trattative tra Gregorio XIII e Filippo II.' *Rivista di storia della chiesa in Italia* 11 (1957): 195–240.

– *Una storia della giustizia: Dal pluralismo dei fori al moderno dualismo tra conscienza e diritto*. Bologna: Società editrice il Mulino, 2000.

Prosdocimi, Luigi. *Il Diritto ecclesiastico dello stato di Milano: Dall'inizio della signoria viscontea al periodo tridentino (sec. XIII–XVI)*. Milan: Edizioni de 'L'arte,' 1941. Reprint, 1973.

Prosperi, Adriano. *Tribunali della coscienza: Inquisitori, confessori, missionari*. Turin: Giulio Einaudi, 1996.

Reinhard, Wolfgang. 'Reformation, Counter-Reformation, and the Early Modern State: A Reassessment.' *The Catholic Historical Review* 75 (1989): 383–404.

Rivola, Francesco. *Vita di Federico Borromeo cardinale del titolo di Santa Maria degli Angeli, ed archivescovo di Milano*. Milan, 1656.

Romeo, Giovanni. *Amori proibiti: I concubini tra Chiesa e Inquisizione: Napoli, 1563–1656*. Rome and Bari: Editori Laterza, 2008.

– *Esorcisti, confessori, e sessualità femminile nell'Italia della controriforma: A proposito di due casi modenesi del primo Seicento*. Florence: Casa editrice le Lettere, 1998.

– *L'Inquisizione nell'Italia moderna*. Rome: Laterza, 2002.

Rosa, Mario. *Clero cattolico e società europea nell'età moderna*. Rome-Bari: Editori Laterza, 2006.

– ed. *Clero e società nell'Italia moderna*. Rome, Bari: Editori Laterza, 1992.

Rossi, Santino. 'Marc'Aurelio Balbis Bertone, Vescovo di Novara e i Problemi del suo Tempo (1725–1789).' Tesi di laurea, Facoltà di Magisterio, Università Cattolica del Sacro Cuore, Milan, 1967–8.

Sangalli, Maurizio. 'Maestri, preti-maestri, e scuole a Siena e a Venezia nel secondo cinquecento.' In Sangalli, *Per il Cinquecento religioso Italiano*, 373–403.

– ed. *Per il cinquecento religioso italiano: Clero, cultura, società. Atti del Convegno internazionale di studi, Siena, 27–30 giugno 2001*. Rome: Edizioni dell'Ateneo, 2003.

Schilling, Heinz. 'Confessionalization in the Empire: Religious and Societal Change in Germany between 1555 and 1620.' In *Religion, Political Culture,and the Emergence of Early Modern Society: Essays in German and Dutch History*, ed. Schilling, 205–45. Leiden: E.J. Brill, 1992.

– '"History of Crime" or "History of Sin"? Some Reflections on the Social History of Early Modern Church Discipline.' In *Politics and Society in Reformation Europe: Essays for Sir Geoffrey Elton on his Sixty-Fifth Birthday*, ed. E.I. Kouri and Tom Scott, 289–310. London: Macmillan Press, 1987.

Schmidt, Peter. 'L'Inquisizione e gli stranieri.' In *L'Inquisizione e gli storici: Un cantiere aperto. Tavola rotonda nell'ambito della conferenza annuale della ricerca (Roma, 24–25 giugno 1999)*. Rome: Accademia Nazionale dei Lincei, 2000: 365–72.

Seidel Menchi, Silvana. 'Percorsi variegate, percorsi obbligati. Elogio del matrimonio pre-tridentino.' In Seidel Menchi and Quaglioni, *Matrimoni in dubbio*, 17–60.

Seidel Menchi, Silvana, and Diego Quaglioni, eds. *Coniugi nemici: La separazione in Italia dal XII al XVIII secolo*. I processi matrimoniali degli archivi ecclesiastici italiani. Bologna: Società editrice il Mulino, 2000.

– eds. *Matrimoni in dubbio: Unioni controverse e nozze clandestine in Italia dal XIV al XVIII secolo*. I processi matrimoniali degli archivi ecclesiastici italiani. Bologna: Società editrice il Mulino, 2001.

– eds. *Trasgressioni, seduzione, concubinato, adulterio, bigamia (XIV-XVIII secolo)*. I processi matrimoniali degli archivi ecclesiastici italiani. Bologna: Società editrice il Mulino, 2004.

Signorotto, Gianvittorio. *Milano Spagnola*. Milan: Sansoni Editore, 1996.

Silvestrini, Maria Teresa. *La Politica della religione: Il governo ecclesiastico nello stato sabaudo del XVIII secolo*. Florence: Leo S. Olschki editore, 1997.

Stoppa, Angelo. 'Quattro decreti generali novaresi simultanei ai Concilio Lateranese V finora sconosciuti e inediti.' *Novarien* 2 (1968): 48–104.

Stoppa, Angelo, and Pier Giorgio Longo. 'Sinodi e congregazioni del Vescovo Francesco Bossi (1579–1584).' *Novarien* 4 (1970): 32–92.

Storia di Milano. 16 vols. Milan: Fondazione Treccani degli Alfiere per la Storia di Milano, 1953–.

Symcox, Geoffrey. *Victor Amadeus II: Absolutism in the Savoyard State 1675–1730*. Berkeley: University of California Press, 1983.

Tavuzzi, Michael. *Renaissance Inquisitors: Dominican Inquisitors and Inquisitorial Districts in Northern Italy, 1474–1527*. Leiden: Brill, 2007.

Tedeschi, John. 'The Roman Inquisition and Witchcraft: An Early Seventeenth-Century "Instruction" on Correct Trial Procedure.' *Revue de l'Histoire des Religions* 2 (1983): 163–87.

Tomaro, John. 'San Carlo Borromeo and the Implementation of the Council of Trent.' In Headley and Tomaro, *San Carlo Borromeo*, 67–84.

Torre, Angelo, 'Politics Cloaked in Worship: State, Church and Local Power in Piedmont 1570–1770.' *Past and Present* 134 (1992): 42–92.

Toscani, Xenio. *Il clero Lombardo dall'ancien regime alla restaurazione*. Bologna: Il Mulino, 1979.

– 'Il reclutamento del clero (secoli XVI–XIX).' In *Storia d'Italia. Annali 9: La Chiesa e il potere politico dal medioevo all'età contemporanea*, ed. Giorgio Chittolini and Giovanni Miccoli, 573–682. Turin: Giulio Einaudi editore, 1986.

– 'Seminari e collegi nello Stato di Milano fra Cinque e Seicento.' In Sangalli, *Per il cinquecento religioso italiano*, 313–61.

Turchini, Angelo. 'La nascita del sacerdozio come professione.' In Prodi, *Disciplina dell'anima*, 225–56.

– 'Vicari foranei, Parroci, Inquisizione a Milano: Appunti per una ricerca *In Fieri*.' *Studia Borromaica: Saggi e documenti di storia religiosa e civile della prima età moderna* 23 (2009): 429–65.

Vaccaro, L. and D. Tuniz, eds. *Diocesi di Novara*. Storia religiosa della Lombardia. Brescia: Editrice La Scuola, 2007.

Zardin, Danilo. 'La curia arcivescovile al tempo del Cardinal Federico.' *Studia Borromaica: saggi e documenti di storia religiosa e civile della prima età moderna* 17 (2003): 31–56.

– 'La "Perfettione" nel proprio "stato": Strategie per la riforma generale del costume nel modello borromaico di governo.' In Buzzi and Zardin, *Carlo Borromeo*, 115–28.

– 'Relaunching Confraternities in the Tridentine Era: Shaping Conscience and Christianizing Society in Milan and Lombardy.' In *The Politics of Ritual Kinship: Confraternities and Social Order in Early Modern Italy*, ed. Nicholas Terpstra, 190–209. Cambridge: Cambridge University Press, 2000.

– *Riforma cattolica e resistenze nobiliari nella diocesi di Carlo Borromeo*. Milan: Jaca Book, 1983.

Index

www.ingramcontent.com/pod-product-compliance
Lightning Source LLC
LaVergne TN
LVHW041114090826
844660LV00062B/897/J
* 9 7 8 1 4 4 2 6 4 4 4 2 7 *